FANCY GOLDFISH CULTURE

FANCY GOLDFISH CULTURE

by

FRANK W. ORME

Published by **SPUR PUBLICATIONS**
SAIGA   PUBLISHING CO., LTD
1 ROYAL PARADE, HINDHEAD GU26 6TD
SURREY, ENGLAND

Typesetting by Inforum Ltd. Printed and bound in Great Britain at The Pitman Press, Bath

Published by SAIGA PUBLISHING CO. LTD HINDHEAD, SURREY, ENGLAND

Contents

Monochrome Illustrations

Colour Illustrations

Acknowledgments

My grateful thanks are due to those many friends who persuaded me to write this book; Messrs George F. Hervey and Jack Hems, together with their publishers, Messrs Faber & Faber Limited, for permission to quote from their book *The Goldfish*. Above all I must thank my family — who have tolerated my fishy interests for so many years — and, in particular, my wife, Iris, who spent many hours typing and re-typing the manuscript with each revision that I made.

F.W.O.

Introduction

As a child I knew a favourite place where only the song of a bird or the distant bark of a dog would disturb my enraptured contemplation of the mysterious world in and around a magical water. I recall the pleasure of finding my way across a marshy area, jumping from one piece of firm ground to the next. My destination was a small clear stream that burbled over a stony bed in which drifts of underwater plants grew. Amidst the vegetation could be seen minnows and sticklebacks, quietly swimming against the gentle water-flow to maintain their position until, suddenly, turning and vanishing from view into the greenery. Undisturbed by the presence of admonishing adults, I would enter a world of childish dreams as I lay on a low grassy bank and gazed with fascination at the life below the water surface — or the darting flight of a gaudy dragonfly.

How pleasant it was to remove socks and shoes and step into the cool tumbling waters. Carefully I would move upstream, against the current, hunting those glittering elusive fish, and oh the thrill when one was captured!

Nostalgia recalls my first real aquarium constructed so many years ago by my father. With growing excitement I watched as strips of brass were bent, lengthways, into angles, cut and mitred, and then soldered to form the frame. I remember my impatience as several coats of aluminium paint were applied. But, at long last, the final coat of green enamel was dry and the glass glazed into the frame — the 'real' aquarium was completed and ready for use. Although not any great size, to a small boy it seemed tremendously large — surely no one else had anything so splendid.

Such fish as sticklebacks, and the like, were hardly suitable residents for so magnificent a home — so decreed my father. We travelled into the city; touring pet-stores in search of fish regal enough to be granted a home in 'the aquarium'. In those days pet stores carried stocks of native and foreign coldwater fishes, many including goldfish. My father and I visited a number of establishments and eventually found one that had just what we sought — Royalty! A pair of bright golden-hued fantail goldfish haughtily eyed us from their glass bowl. We knew instantly that they were the only fish worthy to grace the magnificence of the waiting aquarium. Money and fish exchanged hands and, with almost unbearable excitement, they were carried home. From their new residence they coolly accepted many hours of awed admiration.

Those two fish lived for many years and were a constant source of pleasure. It was during those halycon days that my interest in fish was first formed.

With time my interest waned, also the Second World War required that I should don a uniform. However, the time arrived when I could leave the army and return to civilian life, a young wife and baby son — and a renewed interest in the goldfish. That interest has provided a lasting and constant pleasure.

My first two aquariums measured 24″ x 12″ x 12″ (610mm x 305mm x 305mm), the bases were covered with a depth of fine gravel in which various plants were set. My earlier experience had taught me the advantages of allowing a week or two for the plants to take root, before introducing any fish. During this settling down period a search was made for a source of fancy goldfish; many of the pre-war pet shops no longer existed. Eventually an amateur goldfish breeder was located who lived some distance away and, following a letter, the gentleman confirmed that he could offer me some fancy goldfish. I duly arrived at his home.

Until that time I had only imagined a few indoor aquariums; I was therefore fascinated to be conducted to a greenhouse in which there were a number of large tanks containing different varieties of fancy goldfish — both young and adult. Unfortunately this elderly man, who died some years ago, refused to offer advice or discuss any aspect of keeping goldfish. I was bluntly informed that he had no intention of revealing his 'secrets'. Subsequently I found this attitude to be quite common amongst the goldfish breeding fraternity of those days. (I have often pondered whether this reluctance by the 'old-timers' to impart information is the reason that so few good books about goldfish are available).

Long ago I resolved to answer any questions that a novice might ask me, and have always endeavoured to do so, for there are no secret methods involved in the successful keeping, management and breeding of the goldfish. It is certainly true that, with the exception of those mentioned in chapter 13, there are few, if any, comprehensive modern books about the goldfish. Some years ago there were one or two excellent works available, but they are no longer in print — and would be very out-dated if they were.

By early 1949 I was the proud owner of my own fish-house, in which the fish thrived and I spent the greater part of my non-working hours.

Inevitably, within a very few years, I acquired a larger greenhouse into which I placed large tanks; incorporated a water exchange system; and spent all of my spare time. Due to the water exchange system less time and effort was required to maintain the larger tanks than had been necessary in the previous fish-house. And so the hobby became even more enjoyable.

Having arranged my labour saving fish-house, I decided that the time had come to specialise. For a long time I had hoped to obtain fish of the Lionhead variety; therefore, when the opportunity came to purchase two Chinese-bred fish I did not hesitate. Fortunately they proved to be a true pair; the quality, however, left a lot to be desired.

Having taken the plunge I resolved to set about improving the various features and create my own line of Lionhead goldfish. It was my intention to develop a strain of fish that would become recognised for its ability to withstand the temperatures of a normal British winter, and also do well on the show bench. To achieve these aims has taken many years of selective breeding — there have been disappointments — but, I believe, I have had reasonable success. However, I continue to strive to improve the strain in the hope that one day I shall produce 'the perfect fish'.

From time to time the assertion is made that the goldfish is merely a variety of the Crucian carp — from which, it is claimed, the goldfish has originated. Such statements are, I believe, erroneous.

The Goldfish, the Common carp, and the Crucian carp (see the frontispiece) are all similar in one respect or another. It is also a well known fact that the three species can show variations in their body shapes — they will readily interbreed with each other. If it is said that the Goldfish has certain features found only in the Crucian carp, it should also be stated that it has features found only in the Common carp. No matter how similar the outward appearances may be, it is possible to decide accurately the true species. A count of the scales and fin rays, plus the form of the pharyngeal teeth, will determine whether a fish is a true species or only a variation.

The identification features of these three species of carp are:

Common Carp *(Cyprinus carpio)*. Originated from the Black Sea area and eastwards to Turkestan. It can grow to 40 inches (102 cm) or more.
Strongly forked caudal fin.
17 to 22 branched rays in the dorsal fin. The third spine, and that of the anal fin, is strong and serrated. Concave edge to the dorsal fin.
2 barbels to each side of the mouth.
Pharyngeal teeth arranged in three rows, on each side in the order $1 - 1 - 3. 3 - 1 - 1$.
Scale count from front of dorsal fin to lateral line = 6½ scales, along the lateral line there are 34 — 40.
Goldfish *(Carassius auratus)*. Asiatic origin, it can reach a length of around 24 inches (61 cm).
Moderately forked caudal fin.
Straight or concave edge to dorsal fin, which has 17 to 22 rays and a strong, coarsely serrated spine.
No barbels.
Pharyngeal teeth arranged in a single row, on each side, in the order $4 - 4$.
Scale count from front of dorsal fin to lateral line = 5 — 6½, along the lateral line are 25 to 30 scales.
Crucian Carp *(Carassius carassius)*. Asian origin. Seldom grows very large, but has been known to reach 15 inches (38 cm).
Shallow fork to caudal fin.
Edge of dorsal fin convex, 14 to 21 rays. The dorsal fin spine is weak and finely serrated.
No barbels.
Pharyngeal teeth arranged $4 - 4$ in a single row on each side.
Scale count from start of dorsal fin to lateral line = 6½ to 9, and along the lateral line 28 to 35 scales.

Thus it can be seen that the Goldfish is no mere variation of the

Crucian carp.

Little could I have dreamed, in those far off days of my childhood, that time would eventually lead me into the fascinating hobby of breeding fancy goldfish. Many are the lessons which I have been taught during the intervening years and, no doubt, there is still much to learn.

Nor did I realise, when bowing to the gentle pressure from many quarters to put my limited knowledge on record, the many months of work that would go into the writing of the following pages. There was much more that could have been included but a line had to be drawn somewhere. It is almost certain that some readers will not agree with my methods and beliefs. To those I would say, "If you have evolved a satisfactory system which is successful, do not change it — for there are many roads to success." To others I merely say that if within these pages you are assisted to derive greater pleasure in keeping goldfish, I shall be well pleased — I shall have succeeded in my objective.

Frank W. Orme

Rubery, Birmingham.
1979

I would not have it thought hereby
The dolphin swim I mean to teach,
    Nor yet the falcon learn to fly;
I row not so far beyond my reach.

(Anon. 1577.)

CHAPTER 1

The Ornamental Pond

PRIMARY CONSIDERATIONS

In the cool of the evening, after a hot summer day, it is pleasant to sit beside a pond enjoying the quiet contentment of contemplating the clear placid water. Insects dancing in air scented by the sweet fragrance of Water Hawthorn. The waxen blossoms of the water lily nodding to a gentle breeze, while below the shading rounded leaves the colourful forms of goldfish can be seen. With graceful ease the fish glide through their watery world, occasionally rising to snatch a morsel of food from the surface. Such an idyllic setting is indeed a place to relax and dream the cares of the day away. Fortunate are those who possess a natural pond — for the rest of us must create our own.

The desire for an ornamental pond will manifest itself in nearly all lovers of coldwater fish sooner or later, and there are few gardens that would not benefit from such an asset. A pond, however, must attract and charm the eye — it becomes a focal point — and to do so it requires careful consideration. It is not enough merely to dig a hole, line it with some waterproof material, and fill it with water. To be a success a pond must be planned with care. The right position must be chosen, the size and shape thought out, the method of construction decided and carefully executed. A pond by its very nature is a permanent feature — and permanent features invariably prove difficult to alter or move without a great deal of hard work.

A thoughtfully planned, well designed pond can be a joy, but a badly sited shoddily made pond will forever be a nuisance — an offence to man and Nature!

CHOOSING THE SITE

Just as aquarium plants demand light so do plants in a pond. It is often impossible to bring light to a pond that has been built in a situation that is permanently in shade; it is, on the other hand, always possible to devise a means of shading a pond that receives too much light.

The roots of trees will reach for the cool moisture of such as the concrete constructed pond and will, eventually, cause it to fracture and leak. Leaves will fall into the water and decompose and, if allowed to accumulate excessively, will heavily pollute the water to the danger of the fish. The leaves of laburnum, laurel, holly and rhododendrons are toxic to fish; in particular the seeds which follow the yellow flowers of the laburnum are very dangerous — they contain the alkaloid cytisine, soluble in water and poisonous, they can even make a child ill if put into the mouth!

On the whole, therefore, it is better to choose a fairly open position away from the trees, although a wall or raised rockery may be used as a 'back-cloth' to afford some shade from the heat of the mid-day sun, or protect the pond from the vicious north and east winds — but make sure that the rays of either the morning or late afternoon sun can reach the water surface.

Whether a pond should be placed on high ground is a matter of personal preference — it does make it easier to empty a pond if it has to have the water syphoned out; it also tends to prevent water entering from the surrounding land. However, in nature most ponds are found on the lower levels: and, if possible, the ornamental pond should occupy a similar position — if only to make it easier to look down at the water. Rising ground does have the advantage of allowing two ponds to be built at different levels and connected by a tumbling waterfall. A water-pump will be found the easiest method of emptying any pond — irrespective of its level — and will also lift water from one pond to another to operate a waterfall.

DESIGN AND SIZE

Ornamental ponds may be formal or informal in shape; they may be sunk flush with the surrounding land or raised by being built on the land surface; or they may be part below and part above ground level. My own preference is for the latter type which allows a low wall to form part of the structure; an ideal place to sit and, more importantly, it acts as a safety barrier against small children falling into the water. A low wall will often cause an excitedly rushing child to veer aside, whereas a ground-level pond may give no warning until it is too late!

Formal ponds may be square, rectangular, circular or oval in shape. Such a pond is really only suitable for a formally designed garden where it will be complemented by the straight lines of precision-cut hedges, regimented herbaceous and rose gardens, and similar situations where the lines of formality reign. That is as it should be; for a pond must blend to form a part of the whole garden design, and the informal pond would be totally out of place in such a setting.

The true informal pond requires an informal setting of natural outlines and curves, semi-wild planting of gardens, and an avoidance of straight lines — the grounds, although tended, should not be obviously created but, instead, appear a creation of Nature. Such settings are not normally encountered in the smaller modern gardens of our times.

As a rule, modern housing estates tend to have smallish gardens and this somewhat restricts the style of garden design. Probably the most popular shape nowadays is a variation, to a larger or lesser degree, of the kidney outline. This design can almost always be adopted to blend in with modern garden layout, being almost infinitely variable.

Whatever the shape of the pond it must always be wider than it is deep. This depth may be as much as four feet, but should not be less than 18 inches; where the water is liable to freeze during cold weather the depth could, with advantage, be in the region of three feet to allow a safety margin for the fish. In fact, the well designed pond will provide a shallow area as well as a deep one.

Provision must be made for the plants by arranging shelves in the pond. If it is intended to put the plants in containers the shelves must be so positioned that the depth of the containers plus the growing length of the plants is allowed for. Where plants are to be grown in a permanent position in the pond the shelves must contain lips capable of holding a 3-4 inch (76-102 mm) depth of compost in position. The thickest area of submerged water plants, and thus the greatest area of shelving, should be at the shallow end of the pond. The fish prefer to spawn in shallow water and, as the water is usually warmer, young fish will congregate in the shallows and be protected by the growth of vegetation. Unfortunately, goldfish are cannibalistic and will eat their own eggs and any fish small enough to be caught. Even with the protection of plants many young fish will be lost — without them it is doubtful whether any would survive.

There is no such thing as the perfect design or size for a pond; so much depends upon the individual's personal ideas and, therefore, no two ponds are alike. However, theory dictates that *the larger the pond the better,* it will require less attention and hold a larger population of fish and plants. In practice this is not usually feasible — other members of the family may well demand that they be allowed to have a lawn and flowers; and so they should for an ornamental pond should not dominate a garden — nor should it be so small that it is insignificant. A small pond is subject to quicker fluctuations of water temperature than is one of larger proportions; neither the fish nor plants enjoy sudden variations in the temperature of their natural element. The answer is to allow the largest water surface compatible with the size of the garden. Possibly anything with a surface area less than 30 square feet (2.8 m²) is hardly worth the effort required to construct it.

The sensible way to decide the correct size and shape that would best suit a particular garden, and ensure that it blends in — as it should — is to draw a sketch. With a pencil sketch onto paper the boundaries and main features of the garden; if graph paper is used the drawing can be made to scale. If a cut-out of the proposed pond shape is made — the size being cut to scale — it can then be tried in various positions to decide how best it will fit into the whole; and also whether it is in proportion. When a satisfactory size, shape and location have been arrived at, it can be roughly marked out, life-size, by pouring sand (or even white flour) to the outline of the pond in its proposed position. Standing back the effect can be studied; if any slight alterations are thought necessary the line can be brushed out and re-marked.

EXCAVATION

If the pond is to be made of concrete the excavation should follow the line previously marked, but enlarged sufficiently to allow for thickness of the material (otherwise the internal dimension will be reduced accordingly); however, if a plastic liner is to be used no such allowance need be made.

Ideally ponds should be constructed during a spell of cool, dry, settled weather. Rain will create a muddy quagmire, and there is no pleasure in working under such conditions. Nor will a hot sun or cold wind be pleasant to work in. Concrete ponds are best started during the early autumn, before the frosts arrive; it can then be completed before

4

the onset of the winter. With the arrival of spring the pond will be ready for a final clean and can be planted early enough to allow it to settle down before the fish are placed in it.

The method of digging out the hole is a matter for the labourer*. It will be hard labour and may make the hire of a mechanical digger worthy of consideration. Although very expensive it will save many hours of hard work if a large area is to be dug out and so justify the cost. Provision of the plant shelves should not be overlooked. Shape the excavation, as work proceeds, into the desired shape of the finished pond with the shallow areas; but allowing for the thickness of the construction material.

Before rolling up sleeves and plunging the spade into the ground decide where the excavated soil is to be put. The amount of spoil will be considerable and should be deposited well away from the scene of operations, so that it does not impede the progress of the worker. Subsequently, if desired, it could form the basis of a rockery. If this is the intention be sure to keep the fertile top six inches separate.

MATERIALS AND CONSTRUCTION METHODS

Pond-liners. The use of plastic sheeting is the modern method of making ponds; it is much less arduous than mixing and pouring concrete, and allows the pond to be put into use immediately. The choice of liner is the factor which decides the permanency of the pond, and care must be taken not to puncture it.

Broadly speaking, there are three types of pond-liners. The cheapest and least satisfactory is **polythene.** Polythene has the great disadvantage of deteriorating after a few years; it rots above the water-line where it is exposed to the air. This material is really only suitable for temporary use and should be of at least 500 gauge quality and preferably black. Much more suitable for ponds are the tough, **nylon mesh reinforced pvc** liners. This material wears well and has a greater resistance to being punctured; it is very often available with a pebble design on one side and plain blue on the other. Best of all are the butyl liners which have an indefinite life and are very tough. Butyl has a great advantage in that it is possible to join it by electric welding, or the use of a special adhesive and tape, and so create various shapes. It is the

---

* For a large pond it may be worthwhile hiring a mechanical digger. This is expensive so make sure that a large area is to be excavated.

most expensive type of liner — but well worth the cost, in view of its virtually trouble-free long life. Being flexible, plastic liners are unaffected by ground movement, freezing, or the effects of contraction and expansion caused by temperature fluctuations.

In order to determine the size of liner required the length and width should be measured. Measure the maximum dimension of the base and up the two opposing walls to their highest points. Both total measurements should have *an additional 2 feet (610 mm) added,* this is to allow a 12 inch (305 mm) overlap all round, to be covered by the surround.

Having prepared the excavation, carefully remove any sharp stones or other objects that might make a hole in the liner. Next lay a 2 inch (51 mm) layer of soft sand over the bottom; an alternative is to line the excavation thickly with several newspapers. Lay the liner over the excavation, allowing it to drape down, checking that there is an equal overlap all round. Place a few bricks, or other weights, around the overlap to hold it in position.

The pond can now be slowly filled with water from a garden hose. As the weight of the water pulls the liner down, and moulds it to the shape of the pond, gently pull and ease the liner into position trying to disguise any folds or creases that may form. Care at this stage will add much to the appearance of the finished pond. Leave the weights to hold the flap in position until a permanent surround can be placed around it.

Although turves may be replaced over the liner overlap a far better method is to lay paving: this will make a firm area for walking on during inclement weather. Spread a layer of mortar under the paving to take out any unevenness of the ground, bed the paving onto this, allowing it to slightly overhang the edge of the pond, and then fill in the joints with mortar trowelled smooth.

When the paving has set firm and hard the pond should be emptied, to rid it of any slight impurities or fallen soil, and then refilled after filling the planting troughs with compost.

Fibreglass shells are preformed and available in various shapes and sizes. They tend to be expensive and are seldom of sufficient depth, even if they have a good water surface area. In fact, most are really too small for the well-being of fish. Installation merely requires a hole of sufficient size to accommodate the moulding, placing it into position and firming soil around it. Obviously it must be level — I have credited the pond builder with enough common sense to realise that *the ground*

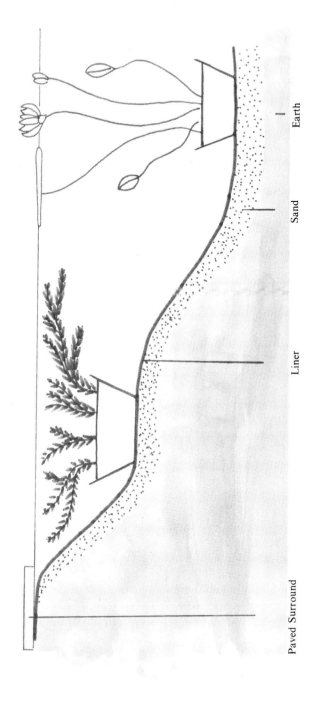

Figure 1.1 *Section Through 'Liner' Pond*

Liner ponds are usually made from plastic sheeting which must be laid over sand or layers of newspaper to avoid it being punctured by sharp objects in the soil

Paved Surround   Liner   Sand   Earth

7

for any type of pond must be levelled. A sloping water-line in a pond will look absolutely stupid and care must be taken that it does not occur.

Concrete ponds. If properly constructed this is the most permanent of artificial ponds; it can be built to practically any size, shape or depth. It requires a great deal of very hard labour but, in the years to come — after the aches and pains have been long forgotten — it will all have been worthwhile.

If the pond walls are nearly vertical, shuttering will be required to hold the concrete in position, and should be constructed of strong material that will not give with the weight of the concrete. It must be well braced and have spacers to hold the shuttering at least 6 inches (152 mm) away from the inner face of the excavation. These spacers are removed after the concrete has been poured, and the concrete must be tamped well down to remove any air-pockets. The base is laid after the shuttering has been removed, but before the poured concrete has really hardened, after which it is finished as described later.

Sloping walls allow the concrete to be 'battered' into place. This requires a stiff concrete mix which is thrown firmly against the walls and base; it should be firm enough to stay in place, and then is battered with the back of a spade. Continue over the whole area of the excavation, building a depth of around 3 inches (76 mm). The following day, repeat the process to build the concrete up to a 6 inch (152 mm) thickness. Any reinforcing material can be sandwiched between these two layers.

Whichever method is used, the concrete mix should be in the proportions of *1 part cement, 2 parts clean sharp sand* and *3 parts washed coarse ballast* — all measured with a bucket. Mix thoroughly in the dry state until the colour is uniform and free of streaks of grey or red. Make a depression in the agglomeration and then pour a little water on it, continue mixing and adding a little more water as required. The concrete should not be sloppy, a stiff consistency is required (and firmish if it is to be 'battered'), test by plunging and withdrawing the shovel — if it leaves ridges it is about right. The concrete must be laid as soon as possible after mixing.

As soon as the concrete has become firm, but not hard, a coat of the same concrete mix should be trowelled overall to a thickness of 1 inch (25 mm), this layer need not be too smooth and is better left a little rough. The following day a finishing coat should be applied to a thickness of ½-1 inch (13-25 mm).

The finishing coat, which is rendered over the complete face of the concrete, is a stiff mix of *1 part cement* to *3 parts clean sharp sand* plus a *waterproofing powder* — added according to the manufacturer's instructions. This rendering must be completed in one operation and trowelled smooth, care being taken to avoid or eliminate any air-bubbles that may appear. When this coat has set firm cover it with damp sacks, or something similar, to slow down the drying period. Within reason, the longer concrete takes to dry the harder it will be. Allow the pond to harden for about a week before filling it.

Estimated amounts of concrete required can be arrived at, for the above mixes, by allowing approximately 13 cubic feet (0.36 m³) of cement, 26 cu.ft. (0.74 m³) of sand, and 38.6 cu.ft. (1.1 m³) of ballast for each 100 square feet (9.3 m²) of 6 inch (152 mm) thick concrete. Calculating the pond area is done by measuring the length and width and adding twice the maximum depth to each. The two figures are then multiplied together to arrive at the square footage. To convert cubic feet into cubic yards, divide by 27.

New concrete contains a considerable quantity of lime which must be got rid of before the pond is safe to use. Lime is highly toxic and will prove fatal to fish and most plants. It is possible to apply various sealants to the concrete, to prevent the free lime entering the water. However, if these coatings become damaged the lime will be waiting to leach into the water with predictable results.

The oldest, and still the safest, method requires a little more hard work — but after the effort put into building the pond surely a little more energy can be found to complete the job! Fill the pond with water, leave it for a week, then, with a stiff brush, thoroughly scrub it all over. The pond is then emptied and any sediment removed. Refill and leave for a further week, at which time the process of scrubbing, emptying and refilling is repeated. Continue to give the pond this treatment for around eight weeks, then test the pH value*. If the alkaline content appears to be within a safe range a poor quality fish may be used as a final test. If at the end of a week the fish is still alive it can be assumed that the water is safe; if, however, the fish dies or the pH test gives a high alkali reading continue to change the water until it is safe.

Cement block and brick construction. These are ideal for constructing raised ponds. First make a **form** from battens slightly larger than

* See page 50 for explanation of pH value.

9

the outside measurements of the proposed pond. Pour a 1.2.3 concrete mix into the form to act as the foundation and base, making sure that it is level in all directions.

Whether using concrete blocks or hard house bricks they should be thoroughly soaked before use. Lay a line of mortar onto the concrete base after it has set, and commence laying the walls. For obvious reasons during this work use a spirit-level until the required height is reached. Leave the inside joints a little rough to act as a key for the rendering; the outside can, however, be neatly pointed — unless the exterior is to be rendered over.

Allow the mortar to set for a day before applying the rendering to base and walls in one operation — as described for concrete ponds. At this stage any capping can also be placed into position. It may be that, prior to rendering, the interior surfaces will require wetting — rendering is not successful if laid on a dry surface, and is liable to break away with time.

Cure the rendering, to remove the free lime, before putting the pond into commission.

Puddled-clay ponds. These were once the only way to artificially create a water-retentive area in which to keep fish. They require a great deal of skill, and are probably very tedious to construct. I have no experience of this type of pond and it would be very foolhardy to pretend that I have. For this reason and the fact that the modern methods are more acceptable, puddled-clay ponds are not covered.

A bog garden is best seen in conjunction with an informal pond where it can follow a natural contour, as a bog would in nature, and be in close proximity to the water. It is the ideal setting for many of the beautiful pond-side plants that enjoy marshy conditions.

The easiest method of constructing an area of 'bog' is to allow for it when building the pond. Build the pond oversize, extending to incorporate the area which will become the marsh area in the form of a shallow. This shallow portion needs to be of sufficient depth to allow a 6 inch (152 mm) layer of clinker of broken bricks and stones to be topped by 6 inches (152 mm) of loam and a final 2 inch (51 mm) dressing of clean gravel or chippings. It follows, therefore, that the minimum depth for the bog must be 14 inches (356 mm) — if the pond is to be of concrete the area will be excavated to roughly 22 inches (550 mm). When the concrete rendering is completed, build an irregular barrier (in keeping with the pond outline) leaving holes for the pond

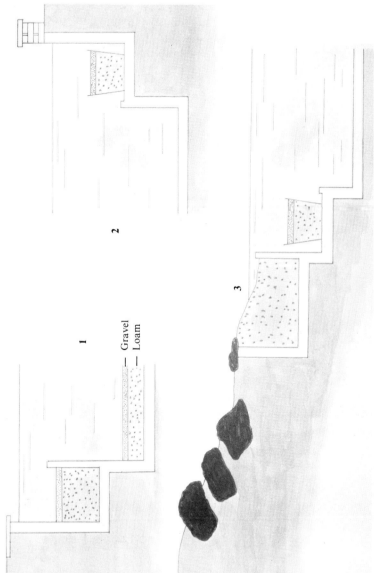

Figure 1.2 Sections Through Planting Areas of Concrete Ponds
1. Paved surround, with loam laid in trough and over base
2. Dwarf wall surround, with loam in container on shelf
3. Rockery, with Bog area filled with loam, and loam filled container on shelf

Gravel
Loam

11

water to penetrate the bog area.

The 'liner' type pond requires slightly different treatment — but equally simple. Make the bog-garden depression a little away from the main excavation leaving an earth barrier. Dish the barrier alongs its upper edge so that its lowest point is below the pond's water level so that water overflows into the bog-garden. The liner is then purchased large enough to drape into both pond and the bog area over the barrier.

It is essential to have these 'barriers' in order to retain the planting medium and prevent it washing into the pond.

Drainage and overflows may be worth incorporating and these should be built in during construction. Modern plastic plumbing pipes make this a fairly simple operation if given a little thought.

If there is reasonably easy access to electricity and a drainage point it may not be necessary to have a drainpipe in the pond — a water-pump and a length of hosepipe will quickly empty the pond and thus avoid any chance of a possible leakage. The overflow — which may be nothing more than an inconspicuous hole at the water-line — is necessary to keep the pondwater level from rising too high during heavy rain.

SURROUNDS

It is always preferable to have a dry, firm area around the pond upon which to stand. The surround may be simply a concrete path or be paved. Paving is by far the most popular, being either man-made or natural stone. Natural stone slabs look very attractive but the high cost of quarrying and haulage make them much more expensive than manufactured slabs. If paving is used it will add to the appearance of the pond if they overhang the pond edge, thereby hiding the concrete or liner overlap.

Old, hard housebricks can be used to make a path surround and, if laid to form an attractive pattern, will add character to the informal or semi-formal pond. As the colours of bricks come in many shades, it may be possible to find a type that matches any nearby brickwork.

Although a dry paved surround allows small plants to be grown in the joints it has been my experience that areas can become loose. I feel that, being so near to water, it is safer to have a firm based standing area. If top soil is removed to a depth of 3 or 4 inches (76-102 mm) a layer of concrete can be put down, and the bricks or slabs carefully

Plate 1 Similar Species of Carp

Top: Common Carp (*Cyprinus carpio*)

bedded to be level and flush with the ground.

If the pond has been let into a grassed area it will be found a big advantage when cutting the lawn, because the mower can be run over the solidly laid path. There is little chance of damaging the machine on a loose slab or brick, and edging will not be required so often.

ROCKERIES

Many good books have been written explaining how to construct a rock-garden. The following basic principles are provided as an aid to fishkeepers.

The well planned pond needs a background to complete the picture, and who would deny that a colourful rockery reflected in the pond is not a perfect 'backdrop'. Too often the garden pond is left without adornment — a flat uninteresting pool of water, which the owner audaciously describes as 'ornamental'. To be ornamental any object of beauty must be seen in the right surroundings and the 'ornamental pond' is no different. It should attract and give pleasure to the beholder, yet it should not force itself upon the eye — rather it should appear to be quite natural and uncontrived; it should blend with, and be at peace with, its surroundings.

Consider the aspect, seen across a neatly trimmed lawn, of a pond in which water lilies blaze; surrounded by gently bowing plants in a bog garden — backed by rock-guarded flowering alpines and heathers. Is that not truly ornamental?

But a rock-garden must be built with the same care that was devoted to the pond. To this end nature should be studied where, it will be noted, rocks are firmly planted in the ground and follow a definite stratum. Imitate Nature for there is no better teacher, and, above all, avoid putting the rockwork in regimental rows. Nature abhors straight lines so give the rockery irregularity of line.

The choice of rock is important; it must be hard and lime-free, the risk of alkali entering the pond cannot be risked. If a 'safe' local rock can be obtained it will obviously pay to do so; it may well be considerably less costly than rock which has had the cost of transportation added to its price. Select rock of the largest manageable size, but always remember that each piece will have to be man-handled into place and while the back may ache it should not be broken. It should hardly need saying that the rock must all be of the same kind.

To commence, the soil should be lightly loosened, so that the base rocks can be rocked to seat them firmly, at the same time imparting a backward tilt — this makes moisture seep into the soil, rather than running off.

Place the lower rocks into position, giving some a forward jutting position, and setting others back. Spread soil behind, on top, and between, stamp down firmly ready to receive the next stratum of rock which should be set back but following a similar juxtapositioning of the individual pieces. Continue until the rockery has taken form, never forgetting to imitate Nature. It is seldom advisable to exceed 3 feet (915 mm) in height, otherwise it may overpower the pond and prove difficult to maintain.

The planting of the rockery can be left to the creator, for one's preference may not be those of another. The range of alpine plants is wide, there are dwarf conifers of erect and procumbent growth, heathers and the like. The plants should be grouped into natural drifts and pockets of soil should be made, if necessary, to suit the needs of particular plants.

PLANTING THE POND AND BOG GARDEN

The planting medium most suitable for water and pond-site plants is a good turfy loam; the top spit from a meadow would be perfect — providing it has not been sprayed with any weed or pest-killer. It is not necessary to add any form of fertilizer, although others may think so, as there will be sufficient plant food in the compost. Place the loam into the containers, or the built-in trough, and gently firm down; cover with a 2 inch (51 mm) layer of well washed gravel or stone-chippings, to prevent the fish stirring the muddy loam into the water. Finally, thoroughly soak the beds ready for planting.

Before placing any of the plants into position they must be cleaned and sterilized, as fully explained in the section dealing with aquarium plants. This must be attended to if possible infection of the fish by disease or parasite is to be avoided with any certainty — it will also prevent the inclusion of snails for the reasons given elsewhere.

Pond Plants

The Queen of pond plants is the water lily, and this will be dealt with first in some detail, for it deserves lengthy consideration — as befits

14

such a popular and regal plant.

The water lily bears the same *Nymphaea,* bestowed upon it by von Linné, and is named after the Greek goddess of springs, Nymphe. The water lily was venerated long ages past, and was known to the Pharaohs. Flowers of the blue water lily (*N. coerulea*) and the Egyptian water lily (*N. lotus*) accompanied the Egyptian kings to their last resting place.

The cosmopolitan *Nymphaea* may be found in all temperature zones — except the very cold — but reaches its grandest in the warmer areas of the world. The world's largest aquatic plant was discovered in the tributaries of the Amazon during the early part of the 1900s. It is the Queen Victoria water lily which has leaf-pads capable of supporting a full grown man, such is their size.

Although American horticulturists have produced many beautiful hybrids none can compare with the Frenchman, Joseph Bory Latour-Marliac who, during his life time, produced a vast number of spectacular hybrids — a legacy that the modern water-gardener still enjoys — and died in 1910 taking his closely guarded secret with him.

Amongst the hybrids developed by this genius are plants suited to waters of shallow depth to waters of considerable depth — greater than would be found in the average garden pond. Of the varieties mentioned below, many will be attributable to that master-hand. The *Laydekeri* hybrids, for instance, were so called by Marliac after his son-in-law, Maurice Laydeker, and form a colourful group well suited to cultivation in shallow water.

To obtain a comprehensive catalogue of the many colourful water lilies, a subject which could alone become a book, one of the specialist water-plant nurseries should be approached for a catalogue of the varieties which they are growing. The following is no more than a list of the generally easily obtained and more popular types and are listed under the water depth which best suits them. Many of the water lilies best suited to deep water may also succeed in shallow ponds — although they may overpower the smaller pond — whereas those intended for shallower water will be unlikely to succeed in deeper water.

Depth 6″ - 12″ (152-305 mm) *Candida,* white with yellow centres; *Laydekeri Lilacina,* pink; *Froebelii,* bright red; *Graziella,* reddish-copper turning to orange-yellow; *Pink Opal,* deep coral

15

pink; *Pygmaea Helvola,* yellow.

Depth 12″ - 24″ (305-610 mm). *Albatross,* white; *Escarboucle,* crimson; *Esmerelda,* rose-white, mottled and striped deep rose; *Marliacea alba,* white; *Sunrise,* yellow; *Sultan,* cherry-red, stained white; *Vesuve,* purply-red.

Depth 24″ - 36″ (610-915 mm) *Nuphar lutea,* yellow; *Nymphaea alba,* white, the common water lily; *Picciola,* amaranth-crimson; *Virginalis,* snowy-white.

PLANTING

Prior to planting all dead leaves and stems should be removed and the roots trimmed. Cleaning and sterilizing must then be attended to.

The *Odorata* and *Tuberosa* types have long fleshy rhizomes which should be set under an inch (2.5 cm) of the planting medium leaving the crown only just exposed. Tubers of the *Marliacae* group are large and rounded with fibrous roots, these should be planted vertically with the roots well spread and the crown above the medium. The *Laydekeri* group have a similar, but smaller rootstock to *Marliacea* and are best set in a semi-horizontal position with the crown exposed.

Planting is best carried out between May and June, when the plant is starting into growth. Water lilies may be planted directly into the pond or in containers. Container planting is the better method for the average pond because it allows easy removal for trimming, when cleaning the pond. Moulded plastic containers are available in various colours and sizes, specifically manufactured for water lilies. Mix a small amount of bonemeal into a good turfy loam for the planting medium, and soak well after it has been firmed into the bed or container. The water lily can then be planted as described, weight the tuber down lightly to prevent it breaking loose and floating to the water surface. After planting it should either be lowered gradually to the bottom of the pond over a period of time or covered with around six inches (152 mm) of water. As the water lily grows, slowly increase the depth over a period of weeks.

Thinning out and propagation is by division of the rootstock during April and May. A sharp knife should be used to cut the tough rhizomes, each crown must be left with several inches of the tuber attached, and then planted in the normal way.

The water hawthorn *(Aponogeton distachyus)* is also worthy of

16

inclusion in the pond, if only for its sweet vanilla-like perfume that scents the evening air so delightfully, and is similar in mode of growth to the water lily. Originating from the South African Cape of Good Hope it has long been established in cooler climates. The elongated ovoidish leaves float upon the surface of the water and are green, becoming mottled with purplish-brown blotches. A forked spike carries the flowers which are snow-white with coal-black anthers. Seed is formed quite readily and young seedlings may sometimes be found floating in the water — they appear like small fine-stemmed grass — and these may be planted in small pots to grow on. This plant is a particular favourite of mine, and I have raised numerous plants from seed. Plant in exactly the same way as the water lily at any depth from six inches up to two feet.

Submerged Aquatics.

Having placed the specimen plants into position, attention can now be given to the submerged aquatics. The choice is not over plentiful but any of the following will prove most suitable:

> *Callitriche palustris* (Starwort). Spreads rapidly and enjoys cold water. The underwater leaves are linear, the floating leaves are lanceolate and form a rosette on the surface. Easily propagated from shoots and cuttings which take root quite quickly.
> *Ranunculus aquatilis* (Water crowfoot). Bears white flowers with a yellow patch at the base, borne on upright stalks which hold the flowers above the water surface. The submerged leaves are finely divided in stiff hair-like segments; the floating leaves, however, are kidney-shaped, divided into three lobes and three leaflets. Propagation causes little difficulty, cuttings rooting quickly and easily.
> *Hottonia palustris* (Water violet). Another flowering plant, it bears lilac-tinted spikes of flowers some 8-10 inches (203-254 mm) above the water surface. The fern-like leaves are pinnately pretinated into linear cuts and grow alternate upon branched stems. Propagation by division of the root-stock ensures that each cutting carries roots. Enjoys cold water and forms winter buds (turions).
> *Elodea canadensis; Elodea densa; Lagarosiphon muscoides; Ceratophyllum demersum; Myriophyllum spicatum; Myriophyl-*

lum verticillatum; Sagittaria and *Vallisneria,* together with *Fontinalis antipyretica* are all described under the section dealing with aquarium plants; they are equally suitable for planting in ponds. Planting is also the same as detailed for aquarium plants.

Although in a pond the plants must perform the same tasks as in the aquarium (purifying and oxygenating), not such a high density is required. Being open to the weather ponds have an advantage over the indoor aquarium: rain and wind will both help to keep the water refreshed and oxygenated. Plant at the rate of twenty to twenty-four plants for every square foot of the pond bottom-area, this should be sufficient vegetation to keep the water clear after they have become established.

Marginal Plants

Finally we come to the marginal plants, suitable for shallow water and the bog-garden. There are a great many plants in this class and I shall not attempt to list them all.

Do not try to grow too many different kinds or the effect will be lost. A few of each of your choice, grouped together as in Nature, will look far more pleasing. By the same token, select plants that are in keeping with the size of the pool. A small pond surrounded by some of the larger marginal plants will look completely wrong, and small plants of little height around a large pond would be very insignificant. If possible choose plants with different flowering periods to extend the season as long as nature will allow.

Planting must be firm, if necessary weight the plant until the roots have taken a grip, and do not plant deeper than the pale bottom portions of the plant which give a clue as to the depth at which it was previously planted. Plant between April and June.

These plants must also be cleaned and sterilized exactly as described for the other types of plants because they are just as capable of harbouring unwanted pests.

The following plants should be suitable for growing in the pond with about six inches of water over them and likewise be at home in the marshy conditions of the bog-garden — or any situation in between. They are:

Acorus calamus (Sweet Flag). Grows to 3 feet (915 mm). Scented.

Small yellowish flowers during June - July.

Butomus umbellatus (Flowering Rush). Height 2-4 feet (610-915 mm). Sword shaped leaves. Umbels of small rose-pink flowers during June - August.

Calla palustris (Bog Arum). Height 6-9 inches (152-229 mm). Heart shaped leaves. Creeping rootstock. White arum-like flowers April - June.

Caltha palustris (Marsh marigold). Grows to 1 foot (305 mm) and prefers moist conditions. Heart-shaped leaves. Butter-yellow flowers during April - May. Cultivated varieties are *alba*, 8 inches (203 mm), single white flowers; *nana plena*, 8 inches (203 mm), double-flowered; *plena*, up to 15 inches (381 mm), double golden-yellow flowers; *C. polypetala*, height 2-3 feet (610-915 mm), large leaves and yellow flowers up to 3 inches (76 mm) wide during spring.

Eriophorum alpinum and other hardy varieties. Related to *Scirpus*. 12 - 18 inches (305-457 mm). Flower heads are cottony or woolly in appearance.

Iris laevigata. Alba: Height 2 feet (610 mm). Sword-shaped leaves. White flowers June - September. *Atropururea:* violet flowers; the common form has blue flowers.

Iris pseudacorus. Alba: Height 2½ feet (762 mm). White flowers. *Bastardii:* 3 feet (915 mm), primrose flowers. *Variegata*, 3 feet (915 mm), yellow flowers.

Juncus effusus spiralis (Corkscrew Rush). 18 inch (457 mm) corkscrew - twisted stems; *vittatus* has 3 feet (915 mm) high leaves striped yellow.

Mentha aquatica (Water Mint). Height 1-4 feet (305-1219 mm), lilac flowers during August and September.

Mimulus lutens (Monkey Musk). Height 18 inches (457 mm), the flowers are golden-yellow spotted red and are produced all summer long. *M. ringens* has blue flowers and grows to 15 inches (381 mm). There are a number of other cultivated varieties, some with reddish flowers.

Myosotis scorpioides (Forget-me-not). Height 9-12 inches (229-305 mm). Sky-blue flowers May - July. Must be controlled.

Saururus cernuus (Swamp Lily). Height 1 to 2 feet (305-610 mm), heart-shaped leaves, dark green and up to 6 inches (152 mm) long. The flowers are white and fragrant during Summer.

Scirpus albescens. This rush grows to 3 feet (915 mm), the stems being variegated green and white. *S. cernuus* (syn. *Isolepis gracilis*). A tufted rush growing to height of 6-12 inches (152-305 mm), with drooping stems. This family includes, amongst others, the Bulrush — *S. lacustris* — which reaches a height of 6 feet (1829 mm).

Typha minima. A small reedmace with rusty brown pistillates, growing to 1½ feet (457 mm).

The following plants prefer a position that allows them to have around 3 inches (76 mm) of water over their growing point:

Alisma plantago-aquatica (Great Water Plantain). 2-3 feet (610-915 mm). Rose coloured flowers.

Glyceria aquatica (Reed Manna Grass). Height 4-6 feet (1219-1829 mm).

Glyceria aquatica 'variegata'. Height 18-24 inches (457-610 mm), White, yellow and green striped foliage.

Iris pseudacorus (Yellow Water Flag). Grows 3-5 feet (915-1524 mm) and bears golden yellow flowers.

Pontederia cordata (Pickerel Weed). Height 2 feet (610 mm). Arrow shaped leaves top the stems. Spikes of blue flowers during Summer.

Sagittaria macrophylla. Height 3 feet (915 mm). White mid-summer flowers.

Sagittaria sagittifolia (Common Arrowhead). Height 18 inches (457 mm). White flowers during mid-summer.

Sagittaria sagittifolia 'japonica' Height 2½ feet (762 mm) with white double flowers during mid-summer.

The *Sagittarias* will thrust up from a depth of 12 inches (305 mm) or more, some producing underwater foliage as well as the arrow-shaped above-water leaf.

Typha lattifolia (Great Reed Mace). Grows to a height of up to 8 feet (2438 mm). Dark chocolate-brown pistillates.

Apart from occasionally thinning to prevent any plant trying to over-run its neighbour, these plants only need cutting down to remove dead foliage during the winter to keep them tidy.

FILLING THE POND

When the planting of the pond, marginal and bog areas has been completed the pond must be filled with water. It is at this stage that eagerness can only too easily over-ride patience. Hurried, unthinking action can quickly undo all the care that has been taken; as rushing water jets through the hosepipe, causing it to whip uncontrolled, plants will be uprooted and the planting medium washed up in a great dirty cloud of mud. If that happens there will be no alternative other than to empty the pond, wash it out to remove the mud, replace the compost and cover it with re-washed gravel, and start planting all over again.

As the plants are put into place cover them with sheets of wet newspaper, to prevent the underwater plants drying out.

If the plants have been planted directly into the pond, cover all exposed planting medium with sheets of newspaper. Stand a large shallow pan in the centre of the pool bottom and lead the hose into it. Place a fairly heavy weight on the mouth of the pipe to hold it in position, but not so heavy as to prevent the water flowing freely.

In the event that the more common and popular method of planting in containers has been used, place the containers on one side outside the pond and cover with wet newspaper. The hose can then be weighted to the bottom of the pool, but facing away from the water lily — which should not be moved if it has been allowed to grow as recommended under that section.

Arrange for someone to turn on the water supply, while you watch the hose, and signal to them as soon as the water is flowing slowly and gently. The pond can then be left to fill very slowly to the required level with little fear of anything being disturbed.

Having successfully filled the pond, the sheets of newspaper can be removed, the hose, weight and pan lifted out and a check made that everything is as it should be, the last job being to slide the plant containers carefully beneath the water and into position. Again care is necessary to avoid the plants and medium swilling out. Finally, leave the pond to settle down for several weeks; this will allow ample time for the plants to root and establish themselves, and at the same time any chlorine in the water will dissipate into the atmosphere. Any soluble matter in the planting medium will also leach out into the water.

Before any fish are liberated into the pond, it should be emptied and given a final swill to remove any accumulation of sediment, mud or other unwanted refuse. It should then be refilled with the same care that was exercised after planting, and left for a further week for the water to settle down; it will then be safe for the goldfish to be introduced to their new home where, it is hoped, they will live happily and survive for many years.

FOUNTAINS AND WATERFALLS

Let me say at the very start: "The only place for a fountain is in the formal pond." Fountains are an obvious work of man; an artificiality that does not blend with, nor occur in, nature. Even in the strictly formal setting the fountain is not recommended because water lilies are not happy in the company of a fountain — they dislike the disturbance of the water created by the device. It will be found that in warm dry weather the level of the pond may fall quite rapidly, due to the high rate of evaporation which the spray from a fountain encourages. Nevertheless, for those who find the attraction of the fountain too hard to resist, a little guidance might be welcomed.

Fountain effects can be produced in a variety of patterns depending upon the types and number of heads being used. The height of the throw is dependent upon the capacity of the pump. The easiest type of fountain unit to install is the self-contained submersible, electrically-operated pump. Normally these pumps will throw a fountain pattern to a height of around 6 feet (1829 mm), which can usually be adjusted by a built-in flow regulator. At this height the approximate spread of the fall would be in a radius of 4 feet (1219 mm), this should be taken into account when positioning the fountain in the pond. A variety of fountain heads are normally available for attachment to the pump. In practice the pump is placed in the pond, possibly being raised on bricks, at such a height that the fountain head nozzle is just above the water surface.

The informal type of pond, with a rockery background, invites a waterfall. This is far more in keeping with nature, and beneficial to the pond inhabitants. As the use of an air-stone in an aquarium circulates the water, so does a waterfall for the pond; thereby presenting a greater body of water to the atmosphere where it will be oxygenated and odorous gases assisted to escape.

Who can deny the attraction of the sound of water rippling over rocks and cascading down to the water below. It draws the attention of the ear, and then the eye, as it beckons our approach.

However complex or simple the design of the waterfall may be it must conform to nature and be in harmony with its surroundings; a straight flight of steps is man's idea of a waterfall — not that of Nature. Consider those pools of the Highlands where water trickles down the hillside from one pool to the next, tumbling and gurgling over the rocks, and try to create in miniature what Dame Nature designed on the grand scale.

The course of the waterfall may be laid with butyl pond liner sheet, creating depressions and waterways in one piece to avoid any leakage, leaving a flap to be hidden beneath rocks and plants. It can then be disguised by having rocks carefully positioned in and around it; being sure not to obstruct the flow of water causing it to flood into the surrounding area.

Concrete may also be used, in the same proportions as used in the construction of the concrete pond. First line the course with polythene, to avoid water loss in the event of frost cracking the concrete at some future time, and shape the waterfall over this. Allow a thickness of around 4 inches (102 mm), and do not place any rock into position until it has set. Rockwork can then be cemented into position to give the appearance of a rocky water-course. The same care should be taken not to impede the water flow. This type of construction must, of course, be rendered safe, as was the pond. It is best, therefore, to build the waterfall immediately after the completion of the pond. If the waterfall is then allowed to operate continuously during the time that the pond is being cured, both pond and waterfall will be rendered free of alkali simultaneously.

Preformed basins and courses are available, manufactured in reinforced glass fibre and other plastic materials, in a wide variety of shapes and textures. Choose a type with a natural coloured finish. They are installed in a stepped fashion so that the water from each basin overflows into the next. All that is required is to mark out the course, excavate the site for each unit and then seat them level and securely into position, packing soil around them. As these are made from moulds it is necessary to use some ingenuity to disguise them. Concealing their edges with plants and overhanging rock is possible.

It is also possible to construct on-site waterfalls with fibreglass. Dig out the twisting water course and depressions and line it with polythene sheet. Over this lay the resin and glass fibre matting, building to a thickness of not less than ⅛ inch (8 mm) — a greater thickness is preferable — in layers and finish with the special paste and hardener. This produces a lightweight, easily repaired, waterproof course. The gifted can construct remarkably natural looking units in this way which only require overhanging slabs of rock to complete the effect.

Whichever method of construction is used the depressions and channels must have side walls of sufficient height to contain the water; too flat or shallow and the water will overflow and be wasted, requiring frequent 'topping-up' of the pond.

Water is lifted from the pond to the head of the waterfall by an electric pump through plastic tubing. The plastic pipe should have a ¾ inch (19 mm) bore and should be kept as short as possible to reduce friction — the longer the pipe the greater the friction and this will have a braking effect that will slow the flow of water. Moreover, it should also be kept reasonably straight, avoiding any 'kinks'. If rigid plastic pipe is used it can be buried under the soil and rocks and so hidden from sight. Tight fitting flexible hosepipe can be heated and forced over the pump end of the rigid pipe, thus making connection to the pump easier; if silicone rubber adhesive is first wiped around the end of the rigid pipe a watertight joint will result by joining together before the adhesive dries. To break the gush of water at the discharge end of the pipe is advisable. Carry the pipe over the basin to below the water level and place a piece of rock in front to hide it.

FILTERS

If desired a pond can be filtered and, if properly installed, this will maintain the water in a remarkable state of clarity.

One method, but expensive, is to install the type of filter used in the filtration of outdoor swimming pools following the makers instructions. These are usually known as 'high rate sand filters' and use silica sand as the filter medium — they are, of course, very efficient, but they require a powerful high capacity pump to operate a sufficiently high through-flow of water.

An alternative (which may be used in conjunction with the swimming pool filter) is to construct an 'under gravel filter' similar to those used in aquariums. Ideally, if this latter system is to be used, the pond should be constructed to allow 12-18 inches (305-457 mm) greater depth than would otherwise be required.

The filter should cover an area not less than one third of the surface area of the pond. With rigid plastic ⅜ inch (9.5 mm) bore pipe, 'tee' pieces and elbows, construct a frame to the required size. The straight lengths should be drilled with ¼ inch (6 mm) holes; the distance between the holes should gradually lessen the further they are from the pump connecting point. Make the connecting point by inserting into the frame a 'tee' piece to which a length of hosepipe has been joined. Space the long pipes about 8 inches (203 mm) apart.

Lay the frame in position on the bottom of the pond and connect to the pump. The perforated frame should then be covered to a depth of 18 inches (457 mm) with well-washed ¾ inch (19 mm) screened gravel. The filter is then ready for operating. The pump to be used should produce a water flow rate through the filter of around 10 gallons (45.5 litres) per hour, although, depending upon the size of the pond and number of fish, this may have to be increased. However, it should be capable of continuous running for full effectiveness.

The output from both filter systems, whether used individually or combined, can be connected to a waterfall which will be beneficial to the filtered water.

ELECTRICITY AND PUMPS

The installation of electric cables and power is the province of those who are skilled in such things — and never more so than when such work is to be carried to the outside — and is best left to the expert electrician.

Electricity in the garden is potentially dangerous, and can be lethal unless installed with a proper regard to safety. The correct type and quality of cable for exterior use is essential, and only those fittings approved by law, indeed, demanded by law, as being suitable for external fitting should be used.

The laws relating to outdoor wiring differ from country to country, but all have one thing in common — a regard for safety, stipulating the proper insulation and earthing of any outdoor installation.

Water pumps for ponds usually fall into two categories; the **surface type** and the **submersible.** Within those two categories there is a range in price, and power of output, for the different models.

The easiest type of pump to install is the submersible, which may operate direct from the mains or through a transformer. It is only necessary to connect the pump to whatever it is to operate, plug into the electricity, after placing the pump in the water, and switch on. Care should be taken when choosing the pump that one of adequate power is purchased. Consider the amount of work it will be required to perform and the desired amount of water it should turn over within a given time, then select accordingly.

The surface pumps are usually powerful, and expensive. These are placed outside the pond in a specially constructed housing or chamber as near to the water as possible. The container should be weatherproof and allow the pump to be below the pond water level, but at the same time they should be so built that they do not become waterlogged. Probably it is best to construct the container in waterproof concrete, below which is a well-drained sump. The base of the container should have one or more drainage holes to allow any accumulation of water to escape into the sump. Inlet and outlet pipes can be built through the concrete walls of the container. The lid should be a good fit and designed to prevent water penetration.

Make the container large enough to allow easy fitting of the connection pipes without undue difficulty; nothing is more annoying than receiving scraped knuckles through lack of working space.

It is a wise precaution to fit a stop-cock to the suction pipe, so that the flow of water from the pond can be halted when the pump is switched off or removed. If this is not done the pond water is sure to syphon along the suction pipe and flood the pump container.

Once the required housing has been constructed, the pump placed in position and connected to the inflow and outflow pipes, it only requires that a check is made to discover whether the pump needs priming — some do, others do not — before plugging into the electricity supply and switching on.

The use of electric water pumps has greatly simplified the movement of water in the pond. No longer is it necessary to lay water supply pipes to fountains and waterfalls, nor is it necessary to lay pipes to carry the surplus overflow of water to some drainage point. The water pump is a boon in another respect; no longer is it necessary to bale water by the bucketful from ponds, nor do we need a syphon. If a length of hosepipe is connected to the pump in the pond and led to a drainage point, we need only switch on and let the pump empty the pond for us!

CHAPTER 2

Aquariums and Equipment

FIRST CONSIDERATIONS

Before acquiring any fish the sensible person will give some thought about their accommodation. Where will the aquarium be located and what size should it be? It may be that it will be placed upon a stand; built into a bookcase or some other form of furnishing; built into an al cove or set into a partition wall between rooms. Whatever position is decided upon it should be reasonably permanent, adequately supported and easy to service. The size of the aquarium is important because fancy goldfish need plenty of room, as do most coldwater fish, if they are to be happy. The smallest tank that should be considered should not be less than 24″ x 12″ x 12″ (610 x 305 x 305 mm), anything smaller will be more trouble than it is worth. Obviously the larger the tank the more it will weigh and this could dictate the location most suitable for the aquarium. Whereas a solid floor would be perfectly safe, a timber boarded floor may be much too weak, unless it can be braced or the load spread to distribute the weight over a wider area. The easiest method of spreading the weight is to place the tank and its stand upon two strong battens that are of sufficient length to span at least two of the floor joists.

There is a long-accepted rule for calculating the number of goldfish that can be housed in any particular size of aquarium. The rule stipulates **a maximum of one inch (25 mm) of fish, excluding fins, to each 24 square inches (155 cm²) of water surface.** It must be stressed that this is the absolute maximum for novice fishkeepers and should not be exceeded. As the calculation relies upon water surface, and not the volume of water, it is obvious that if the above quoted tank were stood on end, so that its depth became 24 inches (610 mm), it would contain the same amount of water but only have a surface area of 12″ x 12″ (305

27

mm x 305 mm), thus only half the number of fish could be kept in it — as against the number in the aquarium with a surface of 24" x 12" (610 mm x 305 mm). There is no reason why an aquarium should not be deeper than 12 inches (305 mm), in fact 15 to 18 inches (380 x 455 mm) may give a more pleasing viewing aspect and suit some of the taller growing plants; however, the fish population must be based upon the area of the exposed water surface.

Using the rule of calculation it will be seen that an aquarium with surface measurements of 24" x 12" (610 mm x 305 mm) will have an area of 288 square inches (1858 cm²) which, divided by 24 square inches (155 cm²), allows a maximum of 12 inches (305 mm) of fish. If we hope for the fish to reach an adult size of, say, 6 inches (152 mm) it becomes evident the tank will only accommodate two adults. A surface area of 540 square inches (3484 cm²), (36" x 15") (915 mm x 381 mm), would accommodate 22 inches (559 mm) of fish.

Having decided upon the number of fish to be kept and the size of tank required, the total weight of the fully set-up tank can be estimated. The weight of the empty tank can be approximated by allowing 1 lb (0.34 kg) for each foot (305 mm) of 1 inch (25 mm) angle iron frame (if any), and 3¼ lb (1.47 kg) for each square foot (0.0929 m²) of ¼ inch (6.4 mm) thick glass, or 5 lb (2.27 kg) if the glass is ⅜ inch (9.5 mm) thick, (glass weighs around 13 ozs per square foot for each sixteenth of an inch thickness or 3.97 kg per square metre). Upon this basis the 24" x 12" x 12" (610 mm x 305 mm x 305 mm) tank will have an empty weight of about 38 lb (17 kg) if it has an angle iron frame or, if of all-glass construction it will weigh 26 lb (11.8 kg). To this must be added the weight of water and gravel. Water weighs approximately 10 lbs. per gallon (1 kg per litre). The gallonage can be arrived at by multiplying the length by depth by width (in feet) and multiplying the answer by 6¼, thus — 2' x 1' x 1' = 2; 2 x 6¼ = 12½. If this capacity of 12½ (56.8 litres) gallons is now multiplied by 10 lb we find that the water weighs 125 lb (56.7 kg). A tank with a width of 12 inches (305 mm) requires roughly 1 lb (0.45 kg) of gravel for each inch of length (25 mm) at a depth of two inches (51 mm), therefore a base of 24" x 12" (610 mm x 305 mm) will require, say, 24 lb (11 kg) of medium size gravel.

These calculations are now added together as follows:

Empty tank (all glass)	26 lb	11.8 kg
Water 12½ gallons (56.8 litres)	125 lb	56.7 kg
Gravel 2 inches deep (51 mm)	24 lb	11.0 kg
	175 lb	79.5 kg

28

Figure 2.1 *Water Surface Areas*

Both tanks are identical in size and water capacity; however, (a) has twice the surface area of tank (b) which allows it to accommodate twice as many inches of fish

It can now be seen that the weight is quite considerable for even this modestly sized aquarium and, of course, no allowance has been made for the support upon which it will stand!

It may be that the reader considers it unnecessary to bother with the problems of weight — perhaps, but it is not unknown for a fully set up aquarium to break through a floor of insufficient strength. If there is only the slightest doubt it takes little extra effort to make sure that such mishaps are unlikely to occur. These remarks should also be borne in mind when choosing or constructing a stand for the aquarium — unless it is being built into a wall.

The position in which the aquarium is to be placed is important. In the home it should form an attractive feature and be set at a comfortable height, high enough to avoid the attentions of small prying fingers of any younger viewers, but not so high that it cannot be seen when relaxing in a chair. Although light will be required if the plants are to make satisfactory growth, it should not be placed in such a position that it receives sunlight continuously for long periods. The ideal situation is one that allows only about one hour of sunlight to fall directly upon the aquarium. Too much sunlight will quickly cause glass to become obscured by a growth of green algae, a microscopic form of plant life; it may even turn the water green. Conversely, too little light will result in the plants dying; however, artificial light will supplement any lack of natural daylight. Although goldfish can be kept entirely under artificial light experience has proved that they do benefit from being allowed a certain amount of natural daylight and, where possible, this should be arranged.

Ease of maintenance is another factor that may well govern the position in which the aquarium is to be placed. It is essential that an electric power socket should be nearby. Electricity will be required to operate the lights and the air-pump, and obviously, in the interests of neatness and safety it is much better to avoid untidy trailing cables where possible. At fairly frequent intervals it will be necessary to clean the aquarium by scraping any algae growth off the front glass panel, syphoning accumulated sediment from the gravel, trimming or replacing plants, removing some of the water and adding fresh. These tasks are much easier to attend to if there is a convenient place to dispose of dirty water and obtain a fresh supply, without too much carrying being involved.

Another aspect that should be remembered when making the final decision of where to put the aquarium, is that it should not be situated near to a fire. In such a position the water temperature could rise quite rapidly during the daytime, and cool equally quickly at night when the fire goes out. Goldfish require an equable temperature where the rise and fall of the water temperature is a gradual process. If violent temperature fluctuations are allowed to occur the goldfish will surely suffer sooner or later. The goldfish is able to tolerate a wide range of temperatures, it will survive short periods of near freezing and live under conditions more suited to the freshwater tropical fish, nevertheless the transition from one to the other must be a slow progression over a somewhat prolonged period of time. During the warmer months of the year the goldfish is probably happiest in water that has a temperature of around 65° Fahrenheit (18.3° Centigrade).

The foregoing may, at first glance, appear to be a daunting list of requirements but, if considered logically, they are not. Moving an aquarium, after it has been set up, is not the way to enjoy keeping fish, therefore it is far better to weigh up all the factors prior to making the final choice of position. If these considerations are taken into account as far as possible, the aquarium will stand a good chance of succeeding, the fish should be happy, and there will be less likelihood of the tank having to be removed to another position — or, at least, not for some time.

CHOICE OF AQUARIUM AND CONSTRUCTION

Although the choice of aquarium must be a matter of personal preference, it should be stated that the larger the aquarium the easier it is to maintain. The greater the amount of water the less likely is it to be subject to sudden fluctuations of temperature, and pollution problems take longer to take effect. The greater the water surface the larger the population of fish that may be kept and fish always seem to do better the bigger the tank. The attraction of a large aquarium is undeniable if it has a carefully planned underwater scene of rockwork and plants, clear water and healthy, active, uncrowded fish.

Ready made tanks are available in one-piece moulded clear plastic, glass set in an angle iron frame, and all-glass construction. It is quite possible for the average handyman to build either the angle iron framed type or the all-glass tank without too much difficulty — if care is exercised. It is, of course, sometimes possible to buy second hand

31

aquariums and this can often result in a considerable cash saving, for new tanks are expensive and the larger sizes can be very costly indeed. If offered an old angle iron framed tank treat it with some suspicion, carefully check the frame to make sure that it is not too badly eaten away by rust, paying particular attention to the underside of the top frame. Leaks are not the problem they once were, provided the glass is sound, and can be sealed with one of the silicone rubber adhesives that are manufactured for aquarium use.

Plastic tanks, although leakproof, are liable to scratch and, apart from use as show tanks by exhibitors of fancy goldfish, are not often used by goldfish enthusiasts who much prefer the larger sizes of the other two types. Glass, of course, is less likely to scratch and tends to be clearer than plastic.

The angle iron framed tank was for many years the most popular of all types of aquarium, and with many aquarists still is. It is a sturdy method of construction that gives good support to the base so that the surface upon which it sits need not be as smooth as might be necessary for the 'all-glass' type. The frame can be made by most small engineering or welding firms. One-inch (25 mm) angle is suitable for tanks under 3 feet (915 mm) in length, tanks of larger size require angle iron frames of 1¼-1½ inches (32-38 mm). All welded joints must be ground flat and all angles of the frames should be square. The bottom glass should be cut to ⅛ inch (3 mm) less than the width and length of the inside measurements of the finished frame. The front and back panels need to be ⅛ inch (3 mm) less than the inner frame and ½ inch (13 mm) less than the depth, the two end panels will be ½ inch (13 mm) less than the depth and one inch (25 mm) less than the inside width. These measurements are based upon the use of quarter-inch (6 mm) thick glass.

Suppose, the construction of a 24″ x 12″ x 12″ (610 mm x 305 mm x 305 mm) tank is used as an example. The angle iron frame will have 1 inch (25 mm) flanges, and have a thickness of approximately ⅛ inch (3 mm). If the outside measurements agree with the example size the inside will be reduced by the thickness of the frame and thus be 23¾″ x 11¾″ x 11¾″ (603 mm x 298 mm x 298 mm). Glass will, therefore, be cut as follows — base 23⅝″ x 11⅝″ (600 mm x 295 mm); front and back panels 23⅝″ x 11¼″ (600 mm x 286 mm); and panels 11¼″ x 10¾″ (286 mm x 273 mm).

Before glazing the frame it must be thoroughly cleaned, and all traces of rust removed, to leave a bright metal surface. Grind flat all welded joints and fill any hollows with metal filler paste to form a smooth surface. Prime the metal on all faces with cellulose primer. When dry the primed frame coat should receive two or three coats of cellulose aluminium undercoat. Finally the frame can be given two coats of cellulose gloss enamel in the desired colour. The care and attention given to painting the frame will have a great bearing upon how well it will resist rusting; the better the quality of paintwork the longer the frame will last. The best type of cellulose for this purpose is 'brushing cellulose' which results in a thicker coat than spraying.

A metal glazing putty will be required to bed the glass into the frame, around 4 lb (1.8 kg) will be needed, or one of the specially pre-pared aquarium glazing mastics may be used. Work a quantity of the compound in the hands until it becomes smooth and soft. Sufficient should then be placed around the bottom inside edge of the frame to allow a surplus to be squeezed out, but still leave roughly a quarter-inch (6 mm) thickness between glass and frame. Place the base glass into position upon the putty, and firmly press down to remove all air-pockets. Next insert the front and back panels in exactly the same way. Finally glaze the two end panels into position. Unless the putty is very soft, the tank can then be placed on a smooth level area and slowly filled with cold water. Leave for twenty-four hours, during which the water pressure will squeeze out surplus putty. Before carefully empty-ing it, fill up and leave for a further day. If no leaks have developed it can now be put to use in its permanent position. Alternatively, as an added safeguard, the inside glasses may be cleaned with carbon tetrachloride to remove all trace of grease and then polished with crum-pled newspaper to remove any smears. Having obtained perfectly clean surfaces, for about 1 inch either side of the butting joints, the joints can be over-sealed with silicone rubber adhesive. This will delay the tank being used for a further 24 hours, however, it will make it vir-tually permanently leakproof.

The 'all-glass' tank has become the most popular form of aquarium, with no frame to rust it allows unobstructed viewing of the contents and is aesthetically ideal for use in the home. Easy to construct, this type of tank can be built to almost any size — provided that glass of adequate thickness is used — and may even be in the form of a three-sided tank, to fit into a corner. Having no frame it is essential that the base sits upon a flat, smooth surface over which a half-inch (13 mm) layer of expanded polystyrene has been laid to level out any uneven-

Figure 2.2 *All - Glass Tank*
Made with adhesive silicone rubber, which makes strong water-tight joints and holds the glass panels securely in place

ess. The padding cushions the bottom of the tank against any stress that might cause a fracture when filled with water. If seating the tank upon an angle iron stand it is only necessary to place the padding along the top edge of the stand to avoid direct contact between the stand and the tank.

The glass panels of the tank are bonded together with one of the silicone adhesives that are made for aquarium use. Avoid the use of non-aquarium sealants — they contain toxic elements that can leach into the water and kill the fish. The silicone rubber adhesive is immensely powerful when used with any material that contains silica — such as glass. When cured it is capable of withstanding extremes of heat and cold and has a pliable, rubbery feel. Although the material bonds the glass firmly it nevertheless has a flexibility that allows minute movements, due to vibration and temperature changes, without leaking.

Tanks up to 36 inches (915 mm) long can be constructed of ¼ inch (6 mm) thick glass; anything longer or wider than 12 inches (305 mm) needs glass that has at least a thickness of ⅜ inch (9.5 mm). Decide the

Figure 2.3 *Framed Aquarium*

size of tank required and have the base cut to the length and width. The front, back and end panels will sit upon the base, therefore, if the height is critical, the thickness of the base must be deducted to arrive at the correct cutting size. Have the front and back glasses cut to the same length as the bottom glass. The two end panels will fit between the front and back, thus the cutting size will be the width of the bottom glass less the combined thickness of the front and back panels. The glass must be cut absolutely square and clean.

Before any attempt is made to assemble the aquarium the glass panels should be cleaned, to ensure good adhesion at the joints.

A little ammonia in warm water will remove much of any film or smears that may be on the glass; it can then be dried. Use a solvent, such as carbon tetrachloride, to clean the cut edges and a one-inch (25 mm) strip on both faces around the edges of each panel. Finally, polish with crumpled newspaper to remove all traces of fingerprints or other smears and the glass is then ready for assembly.

The construction must be carried out on a flat surface. This can be a strong table or the floor, over which several layers of newspaper have been spread. Commence by laying the base glass on the work surface and support the back panel in an upright position near to the back edge of the base. Apply a continuous thin line of adhesive to the top face of the bottom glass, near the back edge where the back panel will be set. Carefully lift the back panel and place it upon the sealant, making sure that it is flush with the cut edge, and support it in position. Next run a similar line of the sealant along the end of the base and continue up the back panel, to seat the end panel in position. Check one of the end glasses, to be sure you have it the right way, and carefully lower it into position to make good contact with base and back. Again ensure that the panel is flush with the cut edges, and then tape to the back glass with a strip of adhesive tape to hold it in place. Treat the other end glass in the same way and secure it with tape. It now remains to run a continuous line of sealant down the cut edges of one end panel, along the base and up the cut edge of the other end panel. Carefully place the front panel into position and tape to secure. Check the assembly to make sure that it is square and the panels correctly lined up, remove any surplus adhesive carefully with a damp cloth, and leave to cure for 24 hours.

When the silicone rubber has set it must be oversealed to provide maximum security against leakage. Run a continuous but fairly narrow line of the sealant along all internal angles then, with a moistened finger, gently smooth the rubber to neatly seal the joints and remove any air-pockets that may have formed. Pay particular attention to the corners, being absolutely sure that they are properly sealed. The tank must now be left for a further 24 hours. In the meantime measure the inside of the aquarium and have cut two 2 inch (51 mm) wide strips of glass, the same as that used in the tank, to fit the length of the inside front and back. These are required to add strength, and prevent any 'whip' in the upper area of the long panels. If the aquarium is over 36 inches (915 mm) in length it would pay to obtain a similar glass strip to span the tank across the centre, from front to back. Smooth the edges of these strips with either a fine grinding stone or disc, or alternatively 'wet-and-dry' abrasive paper may be used with plenty of water.

Support the glass strips so that they rest roughly an inch (25 mm) below the top edge of the tank, then remove them and run a thin line of adhesive along the two short ends and one long edge. Some care will be required when replacing them into position to avoid smearing sealant over the top inch of glass — if this does occur it can be left to set and then be scraped off with a razor blade. After the 'bracing strips' are firmly set in place, which will take another 24 hours, all external edges of the tank should be smoothed, to remove any sharpness and danger of cuts, by the same method that was used to smooth the glass strips. Finally, finish by running a bead of sealant along the angles between glass strips and the aquarium. At this stage, if desired, strips of Formica can be glued around the top outer face of the aquarium with the silicone rubber adhesive, to mask the 'bracing strips' — these Formica strips need be no deeper than 1¼ inches (32 mm) and will give a neat finish to the tank. Allow one more day for the adhesive to thoroughly 'cure', then flush it out with water and it is ready to use.

A note of caution must be sounded — *wet glass tanks are very slippery.* Never carry the tank by the internal 'bracing strips', see that it is completely empty before attempting to move it and, if possible, have the assistance of a second pair of hands. The rubber seal is likely to leak if it is cut, therefore do not use a razor blade to clean the inside of the glass — it is too risky!

LIGHTING

Whatever form of artificial light is used it will need to be installed in a cover of some type. Lighting hoods can be bought to accommodate either tungsten bulbs or the more popular fluorescent light strip. Usually they are constructed of metal and rest across the top of the aquarium, but it is a fairly simple matter for the average 'do-it-yourself' person to devise a suitable hood. However, electricity and water are a dangerous combination and it is absolutely essential that they are kept apart. The lighting must be protected from condensation and the method normally employed is to use a cover-glass. A cover-glass is simply a sheet of glass that rests across the top frame of the tank and apart from protecting the lights, stops fish jumping out, keeps dust and tiny fingers from entering and helps to slow down the rate of evaporation. In the case of the 'all-glass' aquarium a panel of glass, slightly smaller than the internal measurements of the tank, can be made an easy fit to rest upon the 'bracing strips', and if strips of glass, or small rubber bungs, are cemented to the glass with silicone rubber adhesive, it makes removal very simple. With the cover-glass in position the lighting hood is stood upon it and so protected from any condensation.

The amount of artificial light required to maintain the health of plants is important and approximately determinable by multiplying the length of the aquarium by 3¼. This gives the wattage needed to light the tank for ten hours each day, which is about the right period of lighting for an indoor aquarium. The calculation is made in inches and applies to tungsten light sources, either bulb or strip, and should be divided by 4 to arrive at the fluorescent light figure — selecting the tube nearest to that figure. Taking the 24 inch long tank as an example: 24 x 3¼ = 78. The tungsten wattage could thus be two 40 watt bulbs. If, however, fluorescent light is required, the figure of 78 would be divided by 4, resulting in a suggested wattage of 19.5. The nearest fluorescent tube would be 24 inches long and have a wattage rating of 20 — it would therefore be ideal for the length of the example tank.

It must be said that some fishkeepers find plants do best under a combination of the two types of lighting. A method which I have found successful merely requires that the wattage of each be halved. Under this arrangement the 24 inch (610 mm) tank would have a 40 watt tungsten light together with a fluorescent tube of 8 watts. Both would be easily accommodated in the light hood and could be placed one behind the other; this would ensure an even distribution of both types of light, if desired each could be independently switch-controlled.

A complaint that is occasionally made against the use of tungsten light is that it is short-lived and gives off heat that can raise the water temperature, unlike fluorescent light, which is cool and has a long life. Despite these objections it should be remembered that they gave trouble-free service for many years before there was any real alternative, and the goldfish did not appear any the worse. If using any form of tungsten lighting it is a simple matter to drill a few holes in the hood, over the light, to allow the heat to escape; this will be assisted if the hood is slightly raised from the cover-glass to allow a free-flow of air.

Discovering the ideal combination of light intensity and length of time the tank should be lit is very much a matter of trial and error. It is not difficult to arrive at the combination most suitable for a particular aquarium; it relies upon observation — noting the results produced and adjusting the time/light intensity accordingly until the right conditions are achieved.

Too much light will encourage an excessive growth of algae that will start to cover plants, gravel and rockwork in a green blanket. Reduce the wattage of the artificial light (if necessary screen some of the natural daylight), and see if there is any improvement — if not then reduce the wattage further or cut down the period that they are alight.

Too little light results in yellowing, thin, leggy plants that will soon rot and die unless the lighting conditions are improved. If the lights are burning for 10 hours each day it must be that the light intensity is not strong enough, so increase the wattage to a level that encourages the satisfactory growth of plants without producing an overgrowth of algae.

The ideal to aim for is one where the various plants grow and produce sturdy green new growth, but where the algae remain within reasonable bounds and do not discolour the water or smother the aquarium plants in a dense blanket of unsightly green matting. Unfortunately even when the right lighting conditions have been found it will not suit all plants; some demand more light than others, and there will invariably be certain types that will fail. Again this is a matter of trial and error, but it is a simple matter to replace the failures with offshoots or cuttings from the successful plants.

FILTRATION

Although not strictly essential, filtration will help to preserve the water clarity, remove some elements that could otherwise build up into a contributory pollution factor and, also, impart some slight movement to the water — which is itself beneficial to some degree. It is, therefore, very worthwhile installing some form of filter to help take care of conditions within the aquarium.

Filters are available in a wide range of prices and types, but they all rely upon the mechanical movement of water to make it circulate through the unit. No matter how expensive or sophisticated the filter may be, they will all rely upon one of two methods to accomplish their task (some may combine both methods). The first relies upon 'mechanical filtration' and is the older of the two methods. This type of filter consists of a container in which is placed a suitable medium that removes particles from the water as it passes through the filter. The simplest type comprises a small container with a perforated bottom that is positioned inside the aquarium. A quantity of nylon floss or glass wool is placed inside the filter to trap and retain any small particles of matter. A tube leads from a little distance below the filter and up into the filter, from where the water is discharged above the filter medium. A smaller tube is connected into this larger tube, and is known as an air-lift; in operation the small tube is connected to an air-pump. The pump forces air along the small tube where it emerges, in the form of bubbles, near the lower end of the larger tube and rises up that tube. In the process the rising bubbles carry water, between them, up the tube and this is discharged into the filter from where it quickly seeps through the filter medium and thence back into the aquarium via the perforations. This type of filter is referred to as an 'inside filter'.

Much more popular are the 'outside filters', which in many cases are hung on the outside of the aquarium — though some are free-standing — and also employ a filtering medium. In the majority of models an 'air-lift' is used which consists of a rigid tube in which an 'air-stone' is fitted. The tube is shaped to bend over the top of the aquarium and discharges water into the filter. The filter box usually has a compartment from where the filtered water is carried, via a syphon tube, back into the aquarium. There are two, or perhaps three, other compartments that contain the filtering medium. The normal practice is to lightly fill the first compartment with a material such as nylon floss to remove suspended matter. The second compartment is filled with 'activated carbon' to remove certain of the dissolved elements. The remaining compartment, if there is one, is filled with some other filter material. To operate, the filter box is first filled with water, the syphon tube is filled and placed into its respective compartment. Finally, an air-line is attached from an air-pump to the air-stone and the pump switched on. From the porous air-stone a mass of fine bubbles rush up the air-lift tube carrying water to the first compartment. The water passes through the compartments, being filtered as they do so, to emerge as cleaned water which is syphoned back into the aquarium. Many of these filters are extremely effective and will clean a tank of green water quite quickly.

More sophisticated, and a great deal more costly, are the 'power filters' which incorporate their own built-in water pumps. These filters have some advantages over the simpler types; they can, for example, pump quite large amounts of water. In the larger models this can be up to 500 gallons (2273 litres) an hour. They tend to be quieter in operation and, with some models, can be situated a little distance from the aquarium. Often the filter materials are pre-packed ready for immediate placement in the filter body which is often totally enclosed.

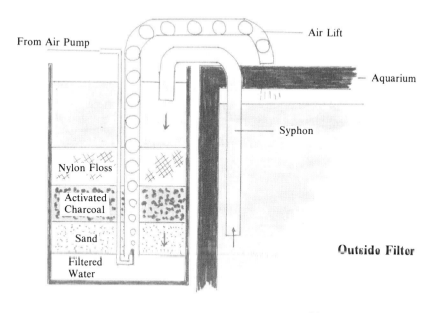

From Air Pump

Air Lift

Aquarium

Syphon

Nylon Floss

Activated
Charcoal

Sand

Filtered
Water

Outside Filter

Undergravel Filter

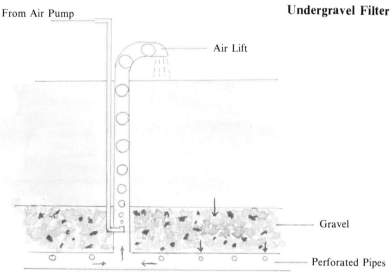

From Air Pump

Air Lift

Gravel

Perforated Pipes

Figure 2.4 *Airlift Filters*
The top diagram illustrates the mechanical type of filtration. The lower illustration depicts a biological type of filter

Normally the manufacturers of these filters will have available a number of different filter and water-conditioning materials to suit various needs.

All 'mechanical filters' require regular servicing, the frequency depending upon the conditions of the aquarium and how often the filter is used. The filter medium will not last indefinitely and will require replacing when it becomes too dirty and clogged to filter the water efficiently.

The alternative to 'mechanical filtration' is 'biological filtration'. It will help the reader to understand the latter system if I first describe what is meant by 'biological filtration'.

The biological purification of the aquarium water depends upon bacteria. These micro-organisms can be found in all natural stretches of water, where they live by breaking down animal and vegetable matter — for example they will convert poisonous nitrogenous substances into nitrates, which in moderation are harmless and are an essential form of plant food. Aerobic bacteria are the organisms that perform this essential work and, to survive, need a plentiful supply of dissolved oxygen in the water. In order to ensure the success of this system it is necessary to try to duplicate Nature, in other words, keep the fish population below its maximum and do not overfeed but, regrettably, few will observe those requirements. What, then, can be done to help the situation if the fish are at maximum density and are sometimes overfed? The answer can be found in the water purification methods of the municipal bodies; there large colonies of bacteria are grown in thin layers over the surface of materials such as clinker and coke. Biological filtration is, therefore, a method that encourages the development of a thriving colony of bacteria that will break down harmful elements and render them innocuous.

'Undergravel filtration' makes use of biological purification, it has been proved to be most efficient and requires little, if any, maintenance. Perforated plates, or a grid of perforated plastic tubes, are laid on the bottom glass of the tank and connected to an air-lift. Medium size gravel is then spread to a depth of two inches (51 mm) over the base. When connected to the air-pump and switched on, water is drawn through the gravel bed carrying with it dissolved oxygen. The action of the water will also draw suspended matter into the gravel where the bacteria will break it down. The food and dissolved oxygen will promote the bacterial colony, which will form around the individual small stone particles. Once the colony has formed and reached maximum efficiency it will continue to purify the water indefinitely as long as the air-pump continues to operate the filter.

Despite the use of filtration it is still advisable to keep the accumulation of sediment down by syphoning it out of the aquarium, and at the same time a partial change of water will be very beneficial. These partial water changes will prevent a build-up of nitrates or other chemical salts that could become harmful to the fish. Should the aquarium water become a pale golden-yellow colour, when seen in a bright light, it is reasonable to suspect that there has been a build-up of these unwanted chemicals and approximately 25% of the water should be removed and replaced with clean fresh water, making sure that both waters are at roughly the same temperature.

AIR PUMPS

Air pumps range from the cheap and shoddy up to very expensive precision engineered instruments. Two types are available — the piston pump and the diaphragm vibrator pump. The piston pump falls into the higher price category and may have one or more pistons. It is a very reliable piece of equipment that will give sterling and constant service for many years, provided that it is given the necessary lubrication as required. It is also very quiet in operation, unlike some vibrator pumps which can be fairly noisy.

The vibrator pumps may have one or two diaphragms and one or more outlets. There are various design differences between the various models, and spares are usually available, such as valves and diaphragms. These pumps range in output from those suitable for a single aquarium up to powerful models that are ideal for use in a fish-house, where a heavy output of air may be required to serve a number of tanks.

Air pumps are required to operate many types of aquarium filters; they are also used to force air through 'air-stones'. Air-stones are usually made of a porous ceramic material which is attached to the air pump by means of a length of flexible plastic tubing. It is often stated that the fine cloud of bubbles that rise to the surface from an air-stone adds oxygen to the water; however, this is not strictly true. What actually happens is that the bubbles cause currents that impart an 'up-and-over' movement to the water. This water movement helps to remove

Figure 2.5 *Vibrator Type Air Pump*
Has rotary knob for adjusting the output of air

carbon dioxide by carrying it to the surface where it dissipates into the atmosphere. In turning over the water a greater volume is exposed to the air which allows a large proportion of oxygen to be absorbed. It is at the water surface that these gaseous exchanges take place, therefore the greater the volume of water exposed to the air the greater will the gaseous exchanges be. It should not, however, be a reason for increasing the density of the fish population.

Control of the air supply may be built into the pump or by means of either a clamp on the air-line or an adjustable valve let into the line.

Unless care is taken, water will syphon back into the pump when it is switched off. To guard against this happening the pump must either be placed at a higher level than the aquarium or, alternatively, a non-return valve must be incorporated into the plastic air-line.

ANCILLARY EQUIPMENT

Although not really necessary, a thermometer allows the fishkeeper to keep an eye on the aquarium water temperature. By glancing at it first thing in the morning and again last thing at night it will be possi-

Plate 2   Water Plants
Top: **Lagarosiphon**   Water Lily
Bottom: Water Hawthorn   **Common Yellow Water Iris**

Figure 2.6 *Piston Type Air Pump*
Ideal for the aquarist who needs a continuous output of air to a number of aquariums

ble to estimate the amount of temperature fluctuation that is taking place. It is an unfortunate fact that aquarium thermometers are not calibrated as accurately as they could be; however, the mercury types do tend to be a little more accurate than the spirit types. The fact that the thermometers do not give clinical accuracy need not cause undue concern; they will be near enough to indicate whether the water is getting too warm, and operate well enough to calculate the variation between early morning and night-time temperatures.

Outside-fitting thermometers may suffer from the fact that they are not immersed directly in the water and could be influenced by the atmospheric temperature, or read unduly high if warmed by the sun. Those types that are placed inside the aquarium are probably preferable; being in direct contact with the water they are not so liable to suffer from other influences; the water will act as a buffer and help prevent a falsely high or low reading being given.

Feeding rings are very useful items of equipment that prevent dried food spreading over the surface of the water. By restricting food to a specific place the fish will learn to gather near the 'ring' at feeding times. The fact that the food does not spread indiscriminately around the aquarium enables the fishkeeper to ensure that the fish are eating the food and not allowing any to go to waste, this obviously helps to reduce the possibility of pollution due to overfeeding. Feeding rings may be either free-floating or fixed to the tank glass by means of a suction-cup. The fixed type are to be preferred because they can be positioned in one of the front corners; in this position it becomes an easy task to syphon out any uneaten food.

Cleaning equipment need consist of nothing more than (and be as cheap as) a length of hose-pipe and a plastic scouring pad. The pad will clean the inside glass of an aquarium without causing damage to the silicone rubber seal, and is easily replaced when it is worn out. A length of half-inch (13 mm) bore hose-pipe is ideal for syphoning mulm from the floor of the aquarium, it is also useful for emptying the water from the tank. If the reader does not feel inclined to start the syphon by sucking water through the pipe, perhaps receiving a mouthful of water from the tank, there is a quite simple method that can be employed. First fill the length of hose-pipe with fresh water, place a thumb over each end of the pipe to prevent the water escaping, then, holding the lower end over a suitable container such as a bucket, immerse the upper end in the aquarium water. Release the thumb first from the upper end and then from the lower, and the syphon should then operate. Take care that the pipe is kept below the water surface — if, even for a moment, it is allowed to suck in air, the syphon action will cease and have to be restarted. The flow of water can be regulated by pinching the hose at its upper end, and can be stopped completely by placing a thumb or finger firmly over the open end beneath the water — this will allow another person to empty the container without the syphon having to be restarted each time.

'Vacuum cleaners' are very effective, if care is taken not to stir up the sediment by moving them over the gravel too quickly. Basically these cleaners are air-lifts, as described in the section about filters, and consist of a narrow-bore air-pipe that is sealed into a larger diameter rigid plastic pipe. The working end of the pipe is fashioned into a 'fish-tail' while the other end is connected to a container, usually a washable bag. Although some models contain their own built-in battery-powered motor, the majority are operated by attaching a length of flexible plastic tube from the cleaner to an air-pump. Simple to use, the air-pump is switched on and the fish-tail end of the cleaner is slowly and carefully passed over the gravel; the 'air-lift' action of the cleaner causing sediment to be sucked up and discharged into the container bag. If the cleaner is held too close to the bed it is possible that gravel may be picked up; however, this can be returned when the container is emptied. No maintenance is required other than to swill the bag during and after use.

Nets are available in a range of different sizes and are necessary pieces of equipment. The experienced fishkeeper will often prefer to catch fish by hand, but it is a skill not recommended to the novice. The use of a net will ease the task of catching slippery fish and help to avoid accidents. Be slow and deliberate, sudden rushes will scare the fish and are liable to uproot plants. When the fish is caught, tilt the net as it is brought out of the water, to close the top and trap the fish in a fold; this will prevent the fish jumping out again. Withdraw the net and, gently supporting the fish with the free hand, make the transfer by lowering the net into the water and allowing the fish to swim out.

'Planting sticks' and tongs may, or may not, be considered as necessary equipment. I leave that decision to the reader (I much prefer to use my hands). Knitting needles could serve the same purpose.

Books about goldfish are few — and good books even fewer — and of those that are available many can be positively misleading for it is apparent that the author has little, if any, practical experience and knowledge. Discriminate and select with care, for there are one or two good books available. Choose books that will truly contribute something to your knowledge and understanding of the goldfish and its care. An informative, reliable book will become a source that can be referred to and will add much to the interest that is derived from keeping goldfish. Whether the reader's enjoyment is in one or two ornamental aquariums, a garden pond or a more extensive fish-house and the cultivation of fancy goldfish — or perhaps the exhibition of fish in competitive open shows — the fact remains that something more can always be learned. A good book can help to increase knowledge, or suggest alternative methods and ideas, and is therefore a worthy adjunct to a fishkeeper's equipment.

Patience, although not tangible, is a very necessary requirement. There is an old saying: "Patience is a virtue, seldom in a woman and never in a man!" If the fishkeeper does not have patience, then the virtue must be cultivated. Too often the novice will try to rush things, and become impatient when things start to go wrong. It must always be remembered that it is Nature that we are dealing with and Nature refuses to be rushed. Too often haste can lead to mistakes, whereas planning, care and attention to detail and a willingness to await the results will bring success in due time.

CHAPTER 3

The Aquarium Environment

The various elements that go into the aquarium must be given careful consideration for not only do they affect the final appearance and durability of the miniature underwater world of the 'furnished' aquarium, they also have a profound effect upon the well-being of the fish. The most innocent but attractive-looking stone could contain a poisonous substance which, if placed in the aquarium, could result in the death of the inhabitants.

WATER

So far as the fish are concerned, water is by far the most important element and must be considered in some detail. Most people are aware that water is known scientifically as H_2O and that it can be either salty or fresh: fresh water can also be either soft or hard. To the average person that is the sum total of their knowledge of water. However, water almost always contains some impurities which often are quite harmless; however, certain others can be a real hazard to fishlife. Ranked amongst these harmful elements must be additives that are put by the various Water Authorities into water intended for domestic consumption . For this reason it is not always advisable to draw water from the mains supply and place the fish directly into it.

Normally water drawn from the main domestic supply can be made safe by the simple process of allowing it to stand for a few days. Chlorine, the most commonly used additive, is seldom of sufficient strength to harm the fish (unless they are continuously exposed to it) although eggs may be killed. Chlorine will dissipate into the air and this can be speeded up by pumping air through an air-stone into the water with sufficient force to make it turbulent. After three or four days the water should be perfectly safe to use. Some writers advise the use of chemicals to nullify the chlorine; but this is merely replacing one chemical with another.

Probably the best source of water would be from either a stream or pond in which fish are known to be living, if the risk of possible water-borne fish disease is thought to be worth taking. Rainwater from an old water-butt or tank may be suitable but rain can, and does, pick up impurities as it falls through the atmosphere. When rain has fallen over a town it will, more than likely, be polluted by smoke and other noxious matter. Only in an area miles from any town is it reasonable to consider collected rainwater to be safe for use in the aquarium.

Roughly speaking, fresh water is either neutral, acid or alkaline and these can be measured, the result being known as the pH (potential hydrogen) value. Absolutely neutral water has a reading of 7.07, and water either side of this is either acid or alkaline. If the reading is less than 7.07 the pH value indicates acid; the lower the reading the greater the acidity. Conversely, the higher the reading above 7.07, the greater the alkaline content. The full range of pH values extends equally on each side of 7.07, graduating from 0.3 to 14.5. The pH value of water is very easy to ascertain by using one of the various kits that are available; a sample of water is taken and a small quantity of a special solution added, the water is then agitated until it changes colour. A comparison of the coloured water is made against a colour scale and the figure read — this figure denotes the pH value.

Apart from pH testing kits it is also possible to obtain kits for testing the carbonate hardness and general hardness of water, and kits are also available for checking the nitrite content. In fact, it has become far too easy to test water for various things; it is all more trouble than it is worth. For a great many years goldfish enthusiasts managed to keep their fish successfully without recourse to testing the water, in any event an alteration to the water characteristic may well do more harm than anticipated — especially as most rely upon the addition of chemicals. My advice is to accept the water as it is, draw it from a healthy source and leave it to mature for a few days before use. Adopt this simple approach and neither you nor the fish are likely to encounter any problems.

Many writers are fond of extolling the 'magical properties' of 'old water' which, they firmly declare, is the perfect water for goldfish. No doubt they mean well, and such water may or may not be suitable, but such statements are open to question. Water that has stood for a long time is not necessarily healthy water; by the same token it may not be unhealthy. If it has stood in a dark place without plant or fish-life and, perhaps, overhung by trees it should be viewed with suspicion at the very least. Of course, if by 'old water' the writer means water that has stood in an aquarium for some time, and the aquarium contains only a few fish, the plant growth is plentiful, and regular maintenance has been carried out, then, yes, that water, though 'old', would indeed be healthy.

'Healthy water' is difficult to describe: it has a sparkling, beautifully crystal-clear clarity with a faint greenish-amber tint. It 'smells sweet'! The appearance is very different to the clear water that is freshly drawn from the main domestic water system. Unhealthy water may be recognised by its lack of clarity and faint bluish hue. This type of water lacks essential mineral salts and is not suitable for aquarium use. Often the water in a newly-filled pond or aquarium will become cloudy within a short time. This is not, normally, a sign that the water is unhealthy, for a number of changes in the appearance of the water may occur during the maturing process. Chemical changes in the planting medium will cause the water to become opaque. After a time the opaqueness will change to green due to the presence of free-floating algae, and because new water tends to be alkaline it is particularly susceptible in a pond. Aquariums are not quite so liable to such drastic changes, in fact, there may be no noticeable change. If the fishkeeper is patient the condition will, in time, right itself as the plants take hold and multiply. There are chemicals that can be used to rid the pond of the 'greenness' but, at best, they are only short-term remedies and the trouble is almost sure to return. Algae are present in all waters, the 'spores' are air-borne, so the problem cannot be avoided by natural means. I recommend that Nature be allowed to bring her own cure. Given sufficient time the water will become acid, plants will grow and so reduce the light and certain other elements that the algae require. It takes time for the water to assume the desired clarity that is so impatiently awaited — but clear it will. Be prepared for a certain clouding of the water to occur during the early part of each year, this is the natural order of things. During the winter plants will have died down, minute organisms died, and wind-blown debris entered the water and rotted down, all helping to provide the right conditions for the rebirth of the algae. With longer days and rising temperatures higher forms of life will re-establish themselves and the water will clear. These remarks apply to the open pond: the aquarium is a much more protected environment and should remain perfectly clear after it has become established.

POLLUTION

Pollution can be due to any number of factors but the most common is lack of care and maintenance. Black, evil-smelling areas of the gravel, or planting medium, from which gaseous bubbles occasionally rise to the surface is a certain indication that food or some other material is rotting. The offending medium must be removed without delay and steps taken to see that the condition is avoided in future — probably by cutting down the amount of food and making sure that any which is given is eaten within a few minutes. Turbid water which has a milky appearance heralds serious trouble: if fish have not died they soon will, unless urgent action is taken. Excessive quantities of unconsumed food will help to bring about this sad state of affairs, as will a great quantity of rotting detritus and other material. The whiteish appearance is due to fungoid growths that have arisen from the rotting nitrogenous matter. Sometimes called 'sour-water', this condition can occur at any time of the year. In the pond it will most often appear during the summer when the decomposition is speeded up by the higher temperatures. The only remedy — which must be applied immediately — is to empty the pond or aquarium completely of the offending water, together with any rotting matter, and refill with clean fresh water; which will certainly prove that 'prevention is better than cure'.

Brass, bronze and copper will poison the water, as will the leaves and/or berries of laburnum, laurel, holly and rhododendron. The results of allowing any of these into the water could well be the death of the fish, therefore the answer is perfectly obvious — avoid them!

Having discussed water in some detail, the elements that go towards the 'setting-up' of an aquarium can now be given consideration.

GRAVEL

In the ornamental aquarium a planting medium will be required in which to root the plants. The type of medium will have an effect upon the water; resulting from its acid or alkaline content the nature of the water may alter accordingly. Red builders' sand is not suitable because it is exceedingly difficult to wash to a sufficient state of cleanliness and nearly always causes trouble. Very fine silver sand also has disadvantages, not least being the ease with which the slightest movement can make it swirl around. Pebbles and builders' chippings have the disadvantage of being too large and creating cavities in which food can become lodged beyond reach of the fish, and so lead to pollution. Sea shore sand and grit will be difficult to rinse free of salt and could have an adverse effect upon the plants. Gravel or sand from a natural water that contains fish may be suitable; however, it does carry the risk of contamination, unless thoroughly sterilized and cleaned, and is probably best left where it is. Crushed coral, such as is used in marine aquaria, is most unsuitable for the freshwater tank because of its very alkaline nature.

A sand or fine grit with a pin-head size grain is really the smallest particle material to use in a goldfish aquarium, but it may be too small if an 'under-gravel' filter is to be used because it could clog the filter perforations. The best, most widely used, and easiest to obtain medium for the aquarium is the commercially prepared 'aquarium gravel'. Offered in both loose and pre-packed form, it is available from most aquatic-pet dealers, and usually has a grain size around ⅛ inch (3 mm). The size of this gravel is ideal and allows easy percolation of the water, without clogging an 'under-gravel' filter; plant roots have no difficulty in penetrating and forming a good anchorage. It is small enough to prevent uneaten food lodging beyond the reach of the fish, and it does not swirl around.

From whatever source the planting medium is obtained it will require washing, even the pre-packed gravel will contain fine dust that must be got rid of. It will be found a daunting task to try to wash the gravel in bulk and the end result will not be satisfactory. By far the easiest is to wash a little at a time. A bucket and a shallow pan, such as a hand-bowl, will be required together with a source of running water. Place a small manageable quantity of the gravel into the pan and cover with boiling water, stir the gravel thoroughly to free any obstinate matter, and then pour off the dirty water. The pan of gravel should then be thoroughly washed under a stream of running water, pouring off any floating debris, and continuing until the water runs clear. The washed gravel, when cleaned, should be free of any sediment. This can be checked by placing it in a large glass jar of water and agitating vigorously. If the water clears immediately after you cease shaking the jar, the gravel is ready to be used; if not, it should be given a further wash.

Although it may take some time the whole of the gravel must receive this thorough washing before it is placed into the aquarium. Cleanliness, which is said to be next to Godliness, is essential to the well-being of the aquarium and the fish; it should not be under-estimated.

Gravel which has been discoloured by pollution can be re-used if it is thoroughly washed and then spread thinly to dry in the fresh air and sunlight. After a time it will be found that the discoloration will bleach out and it is then safe to use.

It is possible to purchase specially treated or manufactured gravels in a wide range of bright, sometimes startling colours. Let those who wish use them — no doubt there is a place for these garish, unnaturally coloured products, but it is not in the goldfish aquarium! Bright colours, yes, but let the fish provide them.

ROCKS

Rockwork can add interest, if it is kept in proportion and not over-done, by helping to create a natural looking underwater scene. It can be utilised to hold the gravel at different levels and hide such objects as air-stones. Rock can improve the attraction and appearance of the ornamental aquarium for, as with all good ornaments, the attraction of the indoor aquarium should be in its beauty. The rock must be selected with care for it must not be so large that it overpowers, nor so small that it is insignificant, it must be chosen to blend into the overall picture and give a look of permanence to the scene.

Not all types of rock and stone are suitable for the aquarium. Some may be soft and will break down and disintegrate with time and the action of the water. Others may be dangerous because of their chemical composition which will allow harmful elements to leach out into the water. Some soft sandstones fall into the first category, while such as limestone and marble are to be avoided because of their high alkaline nature which will have an adverse effect upon the water and, sooner or later, prove fatal to the fish. Marble will, in fact, release so much alkali that it will form a whiteish deposit upon the plants and gravel.

Rock such as hard waterworn sandstone, Westmoreland, Somerset and York are quite safe. Granite, slate, tufa and pumice stone are also safe and can be used to good artistic effect. It is also reasonable to assume that rock and stones from waters inhabited by fish are safe to use — the fact that there are fish indicates that any harmful substances have leached out long ago.

When selecting the rock study it carefully. It should be well worn with no sharp edges that might damage the fish — notice that in Nature water-covered stones and rocks are almost always free of jagged or sharp edges; they tend to be worn smooth. Consider the dimensions and shape and visualise it in the aquarium. It must be of the right proportions and sit upon a wide base that will prevent it toppling over. Need it be said that if more than one rock or stone is used they should be of the same type?

ORNAMENTS

The goldfish tank is a freshwater aquarium and as such will contain freshwater fish and plants — ideally it will set out to represent a section of natural life in a freshwater pond or stream. It is extremely unlikely that deep-sea divers or sunken galleons would be encountered in even the deepest freshwater lake or river and yet many are the fishkeepers who do not seem to realise this — judging from their aquariums.

Plastic divers, mermaids, sunken galleons, treasure chests, windmills, water-wheels and such unrealistic items, by their addition, make the owner unworthy of the aquarium. Such bric-a-brac should be left where it is — in the dealer's store.

It may also be said that all sea-shells should be excluded from the goldfish tank; they are things of the sea and would not be found in fresh water. Over a period of time these shells will turn the water alkaline, some quicker than others, and are of no benefit to the aquarium aesthetically or otherwise.

The fish, plants, rock and gravel are the only suitable and correct ornamentation necessary in an aquarium. I strongly suggest that it should remain so.

BACKGROUNDS

It is more often than not an advantage to blank out the rear glass of an aquarium, and perhaps even the side panels, to restrict the amount of light entering. Often the wall-paper, or something else, is visible through the back of the aquarium and detracts from the impression intended. If the back is screened in some way the effect is greatly enhanced by restricting the vision to the interior of the aquarium.

The very simplest method, and the one which I and many others favour, is to paint or spray the outside of the rear glass with a pale blue or green enamel paint. In very bright situations the two end panels are also painted so that light can only penetrate through the front and top of the tank. Paper backgrounds are also made for this purpose, but care must be taken that the insidious diver or galleon is not also depicted. I once made a quite attractive background by cutting out the pictures of various leaf-plants from magazines, and pasting them onto a light blue paper. If one cuts carefully around the printed plants they can be arranged to form groups and thickets and so build up a picture. The completed background is then pasted to the outside of the glass, being sure to exclude all air-bubbles.

Another type of background is manufactured from plastic or fibre-glass and is usually in the form of a rock face. These fit inside the aquarium and thus slightly reduce the internal area.

I have seen a very effective external background that was made by coating the glass with a clear varnish over which dry sand was spread a little unevenly. When the varnish had dried a further coat was applied, this time in a curved line down the sides and bottom margin of the glass, and sand again spread thickly over the wet varnish. After both coats had thoroughly hardened the surplus sand was brushed off and finally a coat of pale blue emulsion paint was applied to cover the back completely. The completed effect had the appearance of a sandy-walled river bed.

None of these methods of reducing light and view are really necessary because Nature will eventually cover the inside glasses with a dressing of algae and this, if it is wished, can be left to form its own background.

AQUARIUM PLANTS

Plastic plants can be bought but these never look anything but what they are and, serving no useful purpose, should be left out of the gold-fish aquarium.

There are not as many coldwater plants available as there are for the tropical aquarium, nevertheless there are enough varieties to suit the demand of most coldwater fishkeepers. Some can be grown in both cold and tropical tanks, so the difficulty is, therefore, to find those which have been grown under cold conditions, for they will stand the best chance of survival in the goldfish aquarium. Probably the best place from which to acquire plants is a nursery that specialises in the cultivation of water plants; if it is possible to make a personal visit so much the better — the conditions under which they have been raised can then be seen — failing that, obtain their catalogue and order through the post. It is also possible to buy plants from a dealer; however, there may not be a very large range to select from. Avoid plants that appear yellowish or spindly and leggy and try not to choose from plants that are in a tropical aquarium, or heated water. Ideally the plant should be sturdy and a healthy green with a good root system, unless it is a cutting. To obtain the best effects the plants should be grouped in drifts and clusters, as they would be found in Nature, and a suggested minimum number of plants can be based upon one plant to every four square inches (26 cm²) of the aquarium base — in other words a 24″ x 12″ (610 mm x 305 mm) area would require around 72 plants. Keep these facts in mind when planning the number of plants of each variety that are to be purchased.

Aquarium plants are required to perform a number of functions; they must be decorative yet sturdy enough to resist the attention of the goldfish; they must help to oxygenate the water; their roots must purify the gravel; they must absorb impurities. Additionally they must provide a browsing area for the fish; a receptacle for the eggs of spawning fish; and shelter for fry and small fish. If the plants are to perform their task satisfactorily they must receive the correct intensity of light; the planting medium must suit them; the character of the water must be to their liking; and there must be an adequate food supply (this being supplied from the fish droppings). The novice fishkeeper should not therefore be surprised, or lose heart, if some of the plants fail to do well or die. It is logical that the conditions of the aquarium will not be to the liking of all varieties of plants and these will not flourish; however, other types will be quite happy in the conditions provided by the aquarium. Losses can be made good from the successful plants or other varieties can be tried. For a time it will be a matter of experimentation — a case of trial and error — until a successful combination of suitable plants is arrived at.

The type of water plants required for the aquarium are known as 'submerged aquatic plants' and the following is a list of the more easily available sorts.

Elodea canadensis is an excellent oxygenator that consists of a much branched stem thickly dressed in narrow lanceolate leaves. It grows well in the company of *Vallisneria* with which it makes a good contrast. A fast growing plant that makes few demands, it does need bright light if it is to succeed. Sold as cuttings, it will propagate and root quite easily from segments broken from the main stem.

Elodea densa is similar to, but stouter than, the previous plant. The single main stem is sparsely branched and the narrow lanceolate leaves grow into whorls around the stems. Easily grown from cuttings it requires good light intensity if it is to succeed.

Lagarosiphon muscoides. Very similar to *E. densa;* it is distinctly tubular in appearance. The branched stem is thick — but tends to be fragile — and encircled by dark-green crispate leaves. Given lots of light, especially during the winter months, it grows well with *Vallisneria* and *Ludwigia.* Propagated in the same manner as the *Elodeas.*

Ceratophyllum demersum (Hornwort). A favourite of many goldfish keepers; it has a distinct seasonal cycle and tends to die back in the winter. This plant has the curious habit of never developing roots, although it may develop a lightish-coloured shoot that will penetrate the gravel, and therefore needs anchoring down. The main stem is many-branched, dark green and stiffish, the older portion becoming bare of leaves. The leaves are rather 'needle-like' in appearance and arranged in whorls around the stems — they are very brittle and the plant should be handled with care. A good oxygenator, the plant does best at temperatures in the lower 60°F (15°C) region.

Myriophyllum spicatum is, in my opinion, a better subject for the aquarium than the previous plant. It is also known by the common name of Milfoil and is widely spread throughout much of the world. Branched stems carry whorls of four or five feathery, pinnate leaves that are olive-green in colour, the stems being reddish-brown. Propagate from cuttings; it forms a strong root system and requires a very good intensity of light. Under the right conditions it is an excellent oxygenator and will make good growth.

Myriophyllum verticillatum is another Milfoil which may succeed if the water is a little too acid for the former type. In fact, these plants prefer a pH value of 7.5 to 8.0.

Ludwigia palustris. A very good contrast plant that will root from cuttings. The thick articulated stem, which branches into side-shoots, carrying opposed sessile leaves. The blades are thick and smooth, bright green on the upper surface, the underside may be dark green to wine-red. During the winter period this plant will often shed the lower leaves as part of its vegetative cycle. Allow sufficient light and it should do well in the aquarium.

The above water plants will all be sold as cuttings; buy at least six to form a group. The individual stems should be very firmly inserted into the gravel and weighted down. The easiest method is to obtain lead wire from the plant dealer and attach a small strip to the stem — take care that the plant is not bruised as this may cause the stem to rot.

In the case of the following, the plants should possess a healthy root system. When planting make a shallow depression, spread out the roots, carefully cover and lightly firm down. An important point to observe is that only the roots should be covered, the growing crown must be kept above the gravel otherwise the plant may rot. Remember that the success and appearance of the aquarium will rely to a large extent upon the power of the plants to survive and multiply — rough treatment will lessen their ability to adopt to their new environment.

Sagittaria subulata will adapt to a variety of aquarium conditions and is very popular for this reason. The leaves are ribbon-shaped and may be bent or curved; unlike *Vallisneria* the apex of the leaf is not dentate. Young plants grow on runners from the short rootstock of the parent plant. It will establish itself fairly readily in the less-well-lighted position and thus makes a good background plant. There are three forms of this plant: *gracillima* has leaves about 3 feet (915 cm) long; *natans* may form floating leaves. The under-water leaves are around 12 - 13 inches (305 - 330 mm) long; *pusilla* is the smallest form with leaves approximately 4 inches (102 cm) in length and can, therefore, be kept towards the front of the aquarium.

Vallisneria spiralis is similar, in some respects, to *Sagittaria.* The leaves are grass-like and arise from a short root stock from which runners grow to develop young plants. The ribbon-shaped leaves reach a length of between 8 and 36 inches (203 - 915 cm) and terminate in a tiny dentation in the tip. *V. spiralis* is an old, long-established aquarium plant which can adapt to a variety of conditions. It is an excellent background plant that will help to impart a realistic look to the aquarium. It enjoys plenty of light, especially sunlight. There is also *V. torta* which has spiralling twists to the leaves. An attractive plant but not as hardy in the coldwater tank as *spiralis.*

Eleocharis acicularis (Hair Grass). If this plant takes to the aquarium (unfortunately it does not accept all conditions) it will form a carpet of green, the threadlike 'foliage' forming a grassy cover over the base. The filiform stalks arise from a creeping root stock to form tufts. Each grasslike stalk develops tiny bunches of roots and is self-supporting.

Fontinalis antipyretica is not a rooting plant, it is a water moss with branched stems and leaves. The leaves fit closely around the stem and are dark olive-green to brownish in colour. It is usually found in cool flowing water attached to solid objects. If collected from the wild it must be thoroughly and carefully cleaned and sterilized to rid it of any parasites. If possible transfer both the moss and the object to which it is attached. This moss has the habit of attracting sediment and may require rather frequent swillings.

Floating Plants. These are far better left out of the aquarium. It is unlikely that they will add anything to the charm of the underwater picture — due to the viewing angle they will be seen from below — and will, more than likely, grow to such an extent that the submerged plants will be deprived of essential light. Some people claim that the fish will eat floating plants. I can only say that, although some may be eaten, the plant will invariably grow at a much faster rate than it is consumed.

CLEANING AND STERILIZING

Second-hand aquariums. These should be filled with water to which 'Dettol' has been added, and stirred, to turn the water milky. An alternative is to dissolve crystals of potassium permanganate in hot water, by shaking in a well stoppered bottle, and then stirring into the tank water until it becomes a deep, dark claret. The tank should be left to soak for 24 hours, during which any parasites will be killed and hardened dirt or dry algae will have softened. Empty the tank and refill before thoroughly scrubbing out, repeat until the tank is cleaned to your satisfaction, making absolutely certain that all traces of the chemicals have been removed.

Gravel and Sand. The only way to sterilize these is by thorough boiling. The use of chemicals is not recommended because of the difficulty of being sure that all traces are subsequently removed. Cleaning has been described previously under the heading 'gravel'.

Rocks and stones will be easier to clean if they are given a good soaking in hot water first. Use a stiff brush and thoroughly scrub to remove all dirt and foreign matter. This is best done under running water, being sure to pay particular attention to any holes, hollows or crevices. Not only must all loose stone and dirt be removed but also any worm-like creatures, snails, snail eggs or other jelly-like matter, together with any suspicious material that is not part of the rock or stone. Sterilize for 24 hours in a strong solution of potassium permanganate, as described for aquariums. A final scrub will make everything clean and safe. It is quite likely that the rock will have become stained but this will clear after a time.

Plants. First swill and remove any suspicious matter, as described above, together with any hairs or algae. Gently remove yellow and dead leaves, at the same time cleaning up the roots. Having got the plants as clean as possible they must be sterilized for it is surprising how many unwelcome pests and parasites will have escaped even the most careful scrutiny. Potassium permanganate can again be used but in a much weaker solution; use only sufficient to turn the water pale pink and soak for two or three hours. Finally, wash under running water, by gently rubbing the leaves and stems with the thumb and finger, before placing into a container of clean water.

'SETTING-UP' THE AQUARIUM.

Having considered, in some detail, the elements which go into the 'furnishing' of an aquarium we can now take the most important step of creating the ideal home for the goldfish. The best position has been chosen, a strong supporting stand awaits, and the correct size tank now waits for attention. Despite any eager impatience to see the aquarium planted, and fish swimming in the beautifully created 'under-water heaven', the impatience must be resisted. An aquarium that has been hastily planted stands little chance of becoming an object of attraction, whereas careful planning, attention to detail, and a willing-ness to progress slowly will bring its own reward and give a great deal of pleasure for many years.

Before commencing it will be of help if a number of different sketches are made of possible layouts. Give some thought as to the best position for the rocks and commit the idea to paper. Decide what plants should be where, and their variety. Mark down the clumps and drifts; arrange the plants around the rocks. Revise, study the draw-ings, and revise again until it is thought that the best design has been arrived at. If the drawings are made to scale it will be possible to esti-mate the number of each type of plant that will be required. This is no different to the methods employed by the professional gardener when planning the layout of a garden — how much more important it is when creating a miniature world in which creatures live!

The appearance of the tank is all important, clean it thoroughly making sure that all smudges and smears are removed, dry it to a spark-ling clarity. Not until the tank is quite clean should it be placed upon the stand. The all-glass type must have a layer of expanded polysty-rene placed between the stand and the tank to prevent the two being in contact. Check, with a spirit level, that the tank is level in all direc-tions; nothing looks worse than an aquarium in which the water level appears to slope — if nothing else it shows a lack of care.

If 'under-gravel' filtration is to be employed the unit should be installed at this stage. Arrange the perforated plates, or tubes, to cover the bottom of the tank according to the maker's instructions. Measure the amount of flexible plastic tubing required to reach from the filter to the air-pump. Cut the required length and connect to the air-lift of the filter — drape the other end over the top of the tank so that it is out of the way of further operations.

Carefully clean the gravel, as explained under that section, and place it into the tank a little at a time. It is unwise to tip the whole amount into the tank haphazardly as this could, due to the sudden stress, result in the tank springing a leak or perhaps cracking the bottom glass. Spread the gravel evenly over the base, building up gradually to a depth of 2 - 3 inches (51 - 76 mm) at the back and sloping gently down to the front. By sloping the gravel the sediment will be encouraged to gather near the front, from where it can be easily syphoned. Next the well-cleaned rocks can be positioned. Carefully place the rocks into the approximate position, then stand back and consider the effect, move the pieces around until they look right and appear natural. When the positions are satisfactory, carefully and gently work the rocks down into the gravel so that they look as though they have always been there. Smooth the gravel surface and lightly firm it with the palm of the hand. It is useless to create artistic undulations because the goldfish will only level it by their habit of rooting in the gravel for food. The reason for setting the rocks into the gravel, apart from making them look more permanent, is to prevent uneaten food or other matter getting trapped below them.

Filling the tank is not merely a case of pouring water onto the gravel — to do so would undo the work that has already been carried out by swirling the gravel around. First cover the gravel with a sheet of newspaper, upon this stand a deep plate. Water can now be slowly poured into the plate from where it will overflow onto the paper and, provided the water is not poured too fast, the paper will prevent the water disturbing the gravel. As the level of the water rises the paper may float up around the plate but it will still protect the gravel. When the tank is sufficiently full the plate can be removed, and the paper slowly and carefully slid out of the water. Within a short time it will be found that small bubbles will form upon the gravel, rocks and inside faces of the tank glasses. These are bubbles of undissolved oxygen that will slowly be absorbed by the water, surplus oxygen being dissipated into the air. Allow the tank to stand for a day after which a hosepipe can be used to remove about fifty per cent of the water, at the same time gently syphoning out any sediment that may have settled over the rocks or gravel.

If it is intended to incorporate an air-stone it should be done before planting. Cut sufficient flexible plastic air-line to reach from the pump to the air-stone, allowing enough to lead the tube down one of the back corners and be buried, out of sight, below the gravel. If possible, hide the air-stone behind one of the rocks, endeavouring to mask both the tube and stone to avoid the intrusion of any artificiality in what, it is hoped, will appear to be a natural — if miniature — section of a pond or stream.

Planting the aquarium completes the scene and must, therefore, be treated with careful attention to detail. Plant in groups and drifts, as would occur in Nature, trying to screen the rear corner angles. Step back and study the effect as each group is planted; if the position does not look right — alter it. Continue until the plants have all been positioned, always checking the appearance of the growing picture. The completed scene must be pleasing to the eye. To continuously alter the position of the plants from week to week will quickly spoil the look of the aquarium. Be patient and get it right first time, remembering to leave sufficient swimming space for the fish.

Refill the aquarium by placing a sheet of newspaper over the lowered water surface and gently pouring water onto it. Having filled the tank to the required level, fix a thermometer in place, and connect the filter and air-stone. Finally, put a 'cover-glass' over the top of the tank and stand the lighting hood on it.

The electrical equipment should be connected to a convenient point and all wires neatly hidden. It is possible to purchase connection-boxes that are specially made for aquarium appliances. The air-pump and lights can be connected into the individual switch points, giving full control of each, and the box is then placed in a convenient, but unobtrusive, position. Connection to the electric supply is by a single cable which allows the fishkeeper to make the installation safe and neatly tidy; an essential requirement for the indoor aquarium.

The completed 'set-up' is by no means ready to receive any fish and must be allowed to settle down. Fishkeepers who cannot exercise patience will find that the fish will uproot the plants and spoil the whole effect — all the careful planning and work will very quickly be undone. It is often a failing of the newcomer to the hobby of fishkeeping that instant success is expected; however, such expectations are seldom realised — the more experienced fishkeeper seldom rushes things.

Allow the aquarium to settle down for a period of 7-14 days, during which the plants will become established by producing new roots to anchor themselves into the gravel and, thereby, be less likely to be pulled loose by the fish. Very often the leaves of some of the plants will turn yellow and die, this is to be anticipated. The fishkeeper need not be alarmed by this natural occurrence for it will soon put itself right and new leaves and shoots will appear if there is sufficient light and the planting has been properly done. Bruised and badly planted plants will not be so likely to recover from the shock of being transplanted. Ideally, the best time of the year to plant an aquarium is during the early spring, when the plants are beginning to make new seasonal growth and therefore stand the best chance of recovery.

During the waiting period any chlorine and excess undissolved oxygen will be eliminated from the water, which will become safe for the well-being of the fish. This process can be greatly assisted by running the filter or air-stone, thus causing a larger amount of the water to be exposed to the surface where the gaseous exchange takes place.

The use of a layer of soil, peat or any other material, beneath the gravel is not recommended, because it can bring many troubles in its wake.

A wise precaution is to gently pull each plant, before placing the fish into the tank, to ensure the plant has anchored itself. It sometimes happens that the roots of a plant will die, but the visible part of the plant will continue to extract nourishment from the water through its leaves. The plant may appear to be alive and healthy when it is, in fact, dead. Where a dead terrestrial plant would do no harm other than to be unsightly, in the restricted confines of an aquarium the dead plant is a real danger to fish, for it will eventually pollute the water unless removed.

A suggestion, made in many books, is to include snails in the life of the aquarium. The usual reason given is that, being scavengers, they will help to keep the aquarium clean by eating any food that the fish overlook. Such advice can be misleading and may lead the novice to think that they will prevent the water being polluted by uneaten food. In practice it is better not to include snails. Some snails will eat living plants — an undesirable trait — and the amount of snail droppings will outweigh any food that they may consume. All snails will eat the eggs of fish, and some can be hosts to fish parasites. In the aquarium the snail population will increase quite rapidly, and once introduced snails are very difficult to get rid of. Additionally, dead snails will help cause pollution. In my opinion snails should be rigidly excluded from the aquarium, they are of no benefit and are much more trouble than they are worth. The fishkeeper is by far the best regulator of the aquarium conditions. Control of light intensity, offering only sufficient food to be immediately eaten, regularly syphoning over the gravel, filtration and periodic partial water changes will ensure the best chances of the aquarium remaining in a healthy condition. This is the responsibility of the fishkeeper, and the condition of the aquarium relies entirely upon the correct attention being given to the maintenance of the aquarium at all times. Regular attention will reveal any trouble that may be manifesting itself — a dying plant or a sick fish should be removed — and steps can be taken to remedy the situation before it gets out of hand.

CHAPTER 4

Maintenance

CONSIDER HOW

In nature no pond is truly permanent, for having made the pond Dame Nature then conspires to eradicate her work. Leaves are blown into the water where they decompose; submerged and marginal plants die and rot; wind-blown dust and other matter finds its way into the pond. In their various ways each eventually becomes silt at the bottom of the pond. Dying vegetation around the margin of the pond falls and becomes compost, which allows the pondside plants to advance little by little into the water. In so doing the banks are extended and the water surface reduced. Behind the steadily marching marginal plants the ground becomes ever more firm, to be colonised by the terrestrial forms of ground cover.

The reduction of the surface area combined with the ever decreasing water depth leads to a faster and faster rate of evaporation of the water. Eventually the combination of thickening bottom silt, encroaching pondside banks and vegetation, and the rapid evaporation rate will lead to the complete loss of the pond. The most that may remain to show that it once existed could be nothing more than a damp hollow. It may take a great many years, but fade the pond will. The only pond which may survive is one that is scoured by a strong through current from a stream or small river — but that type of water is not a pond in the context of this section, which is to do with a totally enclosed self-contained body of water.

Much is made of the so-called artificial balanced pond, but is there such a thing? It pre-supposes a self-sufficiency; an inter-dependent self supporting system that requires no outside assistance. Oh, that such a system could be devised but, alas, it cannot be — not in the restricted world of the average ornamental pond. Neglect to feed the fish and they will suffer for, despite a common belief, there is little likelihood that there will be enough natural food to support a number of fish. Failure to remove decomposing debris will sooner or later result in pollution, with consequential loss of fish.

In nature each form of life fights for dominance, in one way or another. Creature preys upon creature, each intent upon trying to survive. 'Eat or be eaten — kill or be killed' is the law of the wild, and so an uneasy balance is arrived at. However, that is not the sort of ruthless balance that is wanted in the ornamental pond; therefore we must exercise control over the pond to ensure the well-being of the fish and maintain the pond's appearance.

ROUTINE JOBS

Realising that the ornamental pond cannot be left to take care of itself the water-gardener will develop a method of routine maintenance. Daily inspections will be made to ensure that all is well — fish do die and, occasionally, some other creature may fall into the water and drown. The routine periodic pruning of plants takes less time than is devoted to the annual pruning of ornamental shrubs, and cleaning the pond is less laborious than digging a vegetable plot. Such routine maintenance is essential to the continued success of the pond and should not be neglected.

No matter how carefully designed or perfectly made a pond may be, no matter the consideration that was given to stocking it with plants and fish, despite how well it has settled down, or how long it has been established, the time will surely come when something will go amiss and require urgent attention. Daily inspections will immediately reveal any trouble and allow action to be taken in time to avoid a possible catastrophe. Attention to the following will guide the novice and perhaps others along the right path. (I can do no more than indicate the right direction, I cannot insist that it be followed!)

ANNUAL CLEANING

This can be undertaken during either spring or autumn, in fact, there is no reason why it should not be carried out twice yearly. It is surprising the amount of detritus that can be deposited on the bottom of a pond during a period of six months. If the major overhaul is made during the spring it would, no doubt, be beneficial to drain the pond in the autumn, remove the accumulated debris, and then refill with fresh water. This would provide clean conditions, reducing the possibility of noxious gases building up when the pond is frozen over, thus improving the fishes' capability to cope with the coldest months of the year.

Equipment required will be a long-handled net; container for the fish; a stiff scrubbing brush; and some utensil with which to bail out the silt.

Commence by lowering the water to a level that will ease the task of catching the fish, which should be netted and carefully placed into containers of clean water. Make sure that the water in the containers is at the same temperature as that in the pond, also move them out of harm's way — it is only too easy to knock over a bucket of fish in a moment of forgetfulness.

When the fish have been safely caught and placed well away from the working area, the plant containers (if any) should be slid out of the pond. Gently hose them down with a jet of water to remove as much blanket-weed and sediment as possible. Remove dead leaves and stems and pick off any strands or mats of algae, to leave the plants and containers as clean as possible. Cover with wet newspaper, to prevent them drying, and place in a cool shady spot that is sheltered from any wind. The remaining water should then be removed to reveal the liquid sludge of bottom silt.

Take care when baling out the silt, keep a watchful eye open for any fish that may have buried themselves in the sediment. If possible strain the muck through a small mesh sieve to be sure that no fish is accidently lost. The dark, strong-smelling sludge can be disposed of on the garden where it will help to enrich the soil. Although potentially harmful in the pond the silt is beneficial to terrestrial plants, and the strong smell will quickly disappear when exposed to the air.

Repeatedly scrub and hose down the pond interior to get rid of sediment and algae, removing the accumulated water in between the flushings. If a filter is incorporated in the pond, connect the hose and backflush until the water runs clear. It will be necessary to drain the water from the pond, as it is backflushed through the gravel-bed.

Pick over any plants that are planted in the pond with the same care as described for the container grown plants.

Partially refill and empty the pond a few times to ensure that as much as possible of the remaining fine sediment is removed. The pond is ready for refilling when any sediment quickly sinks and the water is clear, without any trace of cloudiness.

The plants in their containers can now be replaced and the pond refilled with fresh water. Allow the water to run in slowly making sure that it does not disturb the planting medium. If it is a warm, dry day the wet newspaper should be left over the plants to protect them; the paper can be removed after the water level has risen above the plants.

Before replacing the fish the opportunity can be taken to give them an inspection. Look carefully for any sign of disease or parasite infection and, if necessary, place suspect fish on one side for attention. (Diseases and their treatment are covered in Chapter 9.) If all is well, as hopefully it will be, the bucket of fish can be carefully stood, or floated, in the pond to allow the water temperatures to equalise. It then only remains to turn the container on its side to allow the fish to swim free.

I am well aware that not everyone agrees that an ornamental pond requires an annual clean-out, and many ponds remain uncleaned for many years with, seemingly, no ill effects. In the larger ponds it may not be so essential due to the greater volume of water being better able to withstand the threat of pollution, but the possibility is always there, and even they would be the better for a periodic clean-up. I have had it said to me that the bottom silt is 'good for a pond', an observation with which I most strongly disagree — it is rather like suggesting that we humans would be better off if our homes were never cleaned, our refuse never removed, and our excreta left where it fell — what utter rubbish. The bottom of a pond consists of similar aquatic matter! The average ornamental pond does most definitely need the annual attention of its owner; and deserves such attention if it is to remain healthy and retain its ornamental appearance, otherwise it can deteriorate into a stinking mess of dead fish and rotting vegetation.

CONTROL OF PLANTS AND THEIR PESTS

Given the right conditions all water-plants will establish themselves and then commence to extend their territory. As always the strongest will be the most successful and, unless strictly controlled, will overpower their weaker neighbours.

Control the rampant growers by removing any adventurous offshoot or seedling. Take out excessive growth by thinning and pruning;

where possible remove the older plants to allow the younger growth to develop. The young plants will be stronger and more vigorous than the older which may be near the end of their life.

Where a plant reproduces by means of runners, it is best to sever the young plant as soon as it has rooted by cutting the runner near the parent stock; this avoids the older plant being weakened unduly, and also encourages it to propagate further plantlets.

Tuberous rooted plants should be divided by having the newer portions separated from the old rootstock, making sure that it has roots attached and a growing crown.

At times the quality of the various plants may begin to deteriorate, when that time arrives the plants should be lifted, the young, vigorous growth selected and replanted in a newly replaced planting medium.

On no account should insecticides or any form of chemical be used to control insects found in or around the water garden. They could, and very likely will, prove harmful to the fish. DDT is lethal to fish in as little as eight grains in a thousand gallons of water   at least if it does not kill them they will be seriously upset. Any insecticide containing this chemical must be avoided like the plague. Bordeaux mixture and nicotine spray are equally, or possibly more toxic than DDT. Beware the application of insecticides anywhere in the vicinity of the pond because the wind could carry them into the water, with fairly predictable results.

Various insects may at times attack the leaves of water lilies and other aquatic plants; fortunately they seldom reach uncontrollable limits.

The brown china-mark *(Nymphula)* lays its eggs amongst waterside vegetation during June and July, when it deposits rows of eggs on the underside of water lily and other leaves. The greenish-yellow caterpillars feed upon the leaves from which they cut oval-shaped pieces. Weight the leaves below water level so that the fish can easily reach the larvae.

Galerucella grisescens, the orange coloured water lily beetle, is about the size of a ladybird. Although not a true aquatic beetle, it lays its yellowish eggs on the underside of water-plant leaves. The beetle and its eggs are readily eaten by fish, as are the reddish-black water lily aphis *(Rhopolosiphom)* which may be controlled by flushing them into the water. Use a strong jet from a hosepipe for a number of days, at intervals, until the problem is cured.

71

SNAILS

In my opinion snails can become a great nuisance in the ornamental pond and are better excluded. An excess of snails, especially if they are of the genera *Lymnaea* or *Physa* (the pond snail and bladder snail respectively), will feed freely upon the underwater vegetation and can cause considerable damage to the plants. Unlike most of its kind the great pond snail *(Lymnaea stagnalis)* presents an even greater hazard in the ornamental pond. Whilst most snails prefer to be vegetarian, this latter snail will also consume decaying animal matter — which might be applauded were it not for the fact that they have also been known to attack living animals such as newts and small fish!

Once snails gain entry to a pond it is virtually impossible to destroy them completely. They can be crushed as and when they are within reach, and the fish may eat the flesh. Some may be caught by floating a lettuce leaf on the water surface and removing it when covered by a number of snails. Far better than cure is prevention by making sure that no snails are accidently introduced into the pond.

BLANKET-WEED

This type of alga can be particularly obnoxious and troublesome, as can the type that forms tangled masses of hair-like growth. If allowed to go unchecked these pests will quickly choke the water plants and strangle the life out of them. Whenever it appears it should be raked out, or a twiggy branch can be twisted in the water, to gather it around the branch. Take care when removing the growths that no small fish have become enmeshed in it. On no account be tempted to use any form of chemical control.

Leaves and other matter will be blown into the pond during the year; during autumn, in particular, a great many leaves will fall upon the pond surface. Each day they should be skimmed off with a net. Not only do they spoil the appearance of the pond, but some of the leaves might be poisonous and a danger to the fish. If allowed to remain they will rot in a very short time, and an excess of decomposing vegetable matter will give rise to pollution of the water, the putrid condition eventually proving fatal to the fish.

TURBID WATER

If the pond water develops a milky aspect, however slight, it is certain that the water has become badly polluted. Net the fish, if they are still alive, and drain the pond. Remove the cause of the pollution, clean and refill with fresh water. Make sure that the condition is not allowed to re-occur.

OXYGEN EXHAUSTION

Fish gasping at the water surface is usually evidence of a shortage of oxygen in the water. Although hungry fish may rise to the surface when someone approaches the pond, to beg for food, they do not remain there. Oxygen starved fish will remain permanently at the surface and leave only if frightened, returning almost immediately.

An over-large fish population; decomposition of matter; or an over-abundance of submerged plants; any one, or all may be the cause for a depletion of the oxygen content. During a hot, dry spell the water in a pond that is over-crowded may be depleted of oxygen to a level that is too low to support the fish. Bacteria in decomposing matter require oxygen and can effect the oxygen level to a marked degree. During daylight plants take in carbon dioxide through their leaves and convert it into oxygen which is released into the water. However, during the hours of darkness this process ceases, instead the plant takes in oxygen. Thus too many plants may lead to an excessive build-up of carbon dioxide and a lowering of the oxygen content in the water. This will result in the fish suffering from insufficient oxygen, but the condition will normally right itself with the return of the daylight.

The oxygen content of the water is also related to the water temperature: the higher the temperature the lower the content; but this is usually only a temporary condition and need cause no alarm.

If it becomes evident that there is a continuing lack of the essential oxygen immediate steps must be taken to remedy the condition. Relief may be given, as a temporary measure, by giving a partial change of water. This must not be relied upon as a permanent cure — it is not! Seek the cause, whether it be an excess of plants or decomposing matter; check that the seemingly healthy plants are indeed alive and strongly rooted. If, after a general tidying and renewal of the water, the condition returns, and the fish again hang at the water surface gulping air, it is obvious that the number of fish must be reduced.

OVER-FEEDING

It is a sad fact that the novice (and some who should know better) tend to over-feed their fish. The exact amount required depends upon a number of factors, such as the water temperature; the number of fish; and their size. As a rule of thumb the fish should never be given more than they will quickly eat within about ten minutes. The fish may be fed three times daily; one feed in the morning, another at mid-day, and a last feed a few hours before the sun goes down — these feeding times may be reduced to only one or two, but the amount of food must not be increased. The fish will not eat more than they require at that moment and the uneaten food may ultimately become a possible cause of pollution.

During the warmer months of the year the fish will be active, but as the weather cools the activity of the fish lessens until, during the cold months, the fish become semi-dormant. The warmer the weather the more the fish will eat, the colder the weather the less the appetite. After the winter, therefore, no food should be given until the spring when the fish become more active. Commence by offering a little at weekly intervals, increasing as the fish becomes more lively until it is feeding readily every day — this may take some weeks. With the approach of winter the feeding routine should be reversed. Start to reduce the number of feeds during the autumn.

Do not be tempted to feed during the winter, even if a day of warm weather does encourage temporary activity; the fish will come to no harm, and be all the better for a winter rest.

ICE AND SNOW

It is seldom that a pond will freeze solid in winter, provided it has a depth of at least 18 inches (457 mm) (a greater depth provides a better margin of safety) due to a peculiar property of fresh water. On cooling fresh water contracts and becomes denser until it reaches a temperature of 39.2° Fahrenheit (4° Centigrade). If cooled further, it begins to expand again and becomes lighter. Thus with the onset of freezing conditions, the colder water from the surface sinks and warmer water from below rises to take its place. This continues until the whole body of water reaches 39.2° F; further cooling results in the colder water remaining at the top, where it freezes. The deeper water, however, remains at 39.2° F, while the layer of frozen surface water acts as a blanket and slows down further cooling. Even in the most severe conditions there is usually an unfrozen area of deeper water in which the fish can survive.

Ice covering the surface of the pond will prevent the escape of noxious gases, which can prove harmful. In order to allow the gases to escape, a hole must be kept open in the ice. Never break the ice haphazardly because the broken pieces may freeze into an even greater thickness. Even more important, blows from a hammer can kill the fish by concussion. A far safer method is to either drill one inch (25 mm) holes or melt a hole in the ice. Draw off a few inches of water to create an air space below the sheet of ice, then cover the hole with straw, or something similar, to prevent cold air freezing the lowered water level. The hole will admit oxygen and allow the gases to escape. Check the hole each day to ensure that it remains open.

As already explained, plants need light in order to survive and produce oxygen. If snow covers the frozen water surface it will cut out the light and prevent it reaching the plants. This, in turn, will prevent the plants performing their essential function and they may even die. Snow must therefore be swept off the ice every day. The danger of 'winter-kill', as it is known, is greater when snow blankets the ice and prevents the plants receiving sufficient light.

It is possible to purchase specially made 'pond heaters'. These are very like aquarium heaters, and may be connected to an electricity point. It should be of only sufficient wattage to keep an open hole in the ice during freezing weather, when placed just below the surface of the water; it should not be so high that it prevents the fish hibernating.

PREDATORS

Fish may be taken from the ornamental pond by a number of different types of predator: bird; animal; reptile; and even humans have been known to steal fish. In the town the cat is probably the greatest menace of all and the feline thief is hard to deter. My own method is to drill and plug the outer wall of the pond and drive in brass screws almost to the head. A net with one inch mesh is then stretched over the pond and anchored by the screw heads. This may detract from the appearance, but not greatly so, and it has ensured the safety of my fish for many years. An additional benefit is that the net will prevent many leaves entering the water.

FROGS, TOADS AND NEWTS

These creatures may decide to take up residence in the ornamental pond, and, provided they are not too numerous, they may be welcomed. During the time that they are present they will give added interest to the pond.

Occasionally a male frog may seize a fish in its nuptial embrace (the poor deluded creature) which may kill the fish. However, it is not that common and the lively faster fish are not often caught in this way. The risk only exists during the frogs' breeding season.

When small, the tadpoles of the frog will be eaten by the larger goldfish; however, they will not have an appetite for the toad tadpoles and they will be ignored.

A LITTLE ECOLOGY

The plant life of a wild pond is normally divided into several distinct communities, each more or less confined to a particular zone, as follows:

Zone 1 Marshy area some distance from water.
Zone 2 Swamp adjoining water.
Zone 3 Marginal-mud in shallow water.
Zone 4 Water surface.
Zone 5 Deepish water.

Each zone is colonised by a different form of plant although these may vary from pond to pond depending upon conditions.

Marsh plants are not true aquatic plants although they prefer moist conditions in which to root. They are known as **hygrophytes.**

The waterlogged soil in which they grow is usually rich in mineral salts but low in oxygen. Marsh vegetation makes lush growth and generally is characterised by large leaves. Their structure is spongy and plentifully supplied with aerating tissue in which to store air.

Swamp plants prefer to root in ground that is covered with water for most of the year, drying out only during the driest part of the growing season. Generally these plants are tall with a strong tuberous rootstock. They root firmly in the mud and form dense communities by means of the creeping rhizomes.

76

Plate 3   Fish Ponds
Top: Ornamental Pond with Waterfall
Bottom: Semi Raised Pond

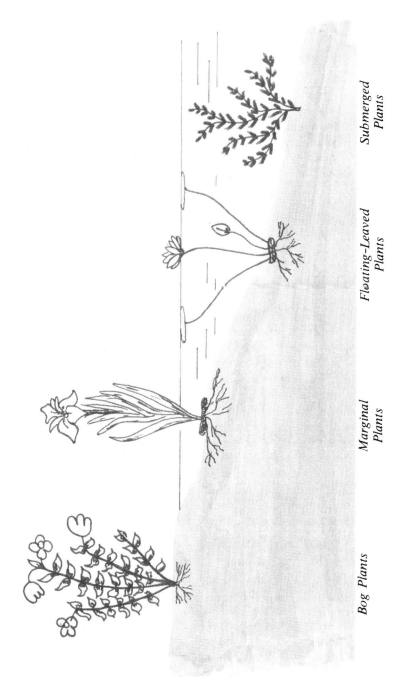

Bog Plants   Marginal Plants   Floating-Leaved Plants   Submerged Plants

Figure 4.1 *Section of Pond Margin*

The remaining zones are populated by the true aquatic plants —
hydrophytes — which will only survive by growing in water.

Marginal plants have leaves that either float on the water surface or
stand above it. Typical of these plants are the water lilies, which adjust
the leaf and flower stems to rising water depths. *Sagittaria sagittifolia*
and *Potamogeton natans* are also typical.

Floating plants. These float freely in the water, the roots being used
for balance and the assimilation of dissolved substances from the
water. The most commonly encountered of these plants are the *Lemna*
species which tend to inhabit very foul water. It is common to find that
ponds covered with 'duckweed' rarely contain much in the way of animal life. *Hydrocharis morsus-ranae* (Frog-bit); *Stratiotes aloides*
(water-soldier); and *Utricularia* (bladderwort), although varied in
form, are all members of this group of plants.

Submerged plants. This is probably the largest group of plants and
are totally submerged; they root firmly in the mud and obtain oxygen
and carbon dioxide from the water. A fair amount of their nutrients is
absorbed from the water, while the roots absorb mineral salts from the
mud. The species in this group are diverse and varied but most are
good oxygenators.

The ability of the submerged aquatic plants to build, by photosyn-
thesis, a store of organic material from inorganic substances provides
a source of food for aquatic animals. The oxygen they produce and the
absorption of carbon dioxide are of great value to the wellbeing of the
habitat.

The simple plants that inhabit the fresh water ponds are usually
thought of as algae, but there are many forms of microscopic plant-life
present in such waters. Apart from algae, these include bacteria and
fungi.

Although individually too small to be seen, when for some reason
large numbers are produced the congregated mass attracts even the
least observant eye. Floating blue-green algae produce 'water-bloom';
vast numbers of certain forms of green algae will turn water into 'pea-
soup'; the activity of bacteria in some ponds can produce an almost
overwhelming stench. All are familiar results of the effect of these
minute plants.

The importance of these organisms should not be underestimated,
either in the context of water or of land. Were it not for the action of
these 'simple plants' our world would become over-burdened with

dead life of all forms. Algae are the first link in a food-chain. Using chemical water substances and light energy they build up their own structure; in so doing they make available food for the herbivorous animals, and, indirectly, carnivorous creatures. Bacteria and fungi are responsible for the breaking down of dead animal and plant matter, converting organic substances into nutrients that can be used by plants.

Algae may be composed of a single cell, some are irregular masses of cells, others are single rows of cells forming filaments, and others are complicated multi-celled structures. All algae possess chlorophyll, although the presence of other pigments may combine to give the appearance of blue-green, red or brown.

Blue-green algae (myxophyceae) are the most primitive of algae. The cells are usually formed into masses of filaments which may be blanket-like. It will also grow as a bluey-green slime on solid objects, or it may appear as round blueish-green lumps of jelly.

When conditions are right, usually during late summer, some species may rapidly multiply and float to the water surface to form the scum commonly called 'water-bloom'. Poisonous substances produced by the algae may kill fish.

Yellow-green algae (Xanthophyceae) form dark green mat-like masses, rough to the touch, on the mud of well-aerated ponds and the damp earth near by. It may also appear as tiny green balls on the mud of shallow ponds.

Green algae are a large group which includes *Cladophora* — the 'blanket-weed' — which can grow into quite large masses. It also includes the *Spirogyra* which can be found in most stretches of fresh water, free floating and looking like green cotton wool. Another member of the group is *Zygnema,* free floating single celled algae, it is drawn to the surface by bright sunlight.

Bacteria. These are the smallest living organisms and are single-celled. The structure consists of a central protoplasm around which is a membrane. Most bacteria are incapable of voluntary movement and must rely upon wind or water. However, some are capable of self-propulsion through a liquid by means of tiny threads called 'flagella', which they lash vigorously to impart motion.

Bacteria may be **parasitic** and live on live vegetation or animals;

saprophytic bacteria feed on dead animals and vegetation. In both cases the food is broken down by using ferments, or enzymes, which they produce. They can thus obtain the material they require and convert it into other substances which they release. The food material is absorbed in solution through the membrane.

The first stage of breaking down the dead matter is to convert it into carbon dioxide, water, ammonia and various ammonium compounds. Other bacteria then oxidise the ammonia into nitrites, still others oxidise the nitrites into nitrates, which then become available as plant food.

Most bacteria require oxygen to maintain their life. Under certain conditions the decomposition of the organic matter by **anaerobic** bacteria will result in the production of sulphurated hydrogen, with the familiar smell of rotten eggs. Methane gas may also be produced, causing bubbles to rise to the surface.

Aerobic bacteria cannot exist without oxygen, but anaerobic bacteria have the ability to exist in the absence of oxygen. Some bacteria can live under either condition.

Fungi, like bacteria, do not possess chlorophyll. Both **parasitic** and **saprophytic** forms exist, and each can be found in fresh water.

Best known are the *Saprolegniales* which are mostly saprophytic; however, some are parasitic. The parasitic *Saprolegniales* are the best known, and the most obnoxious, for it is these which are responsible for the fungus diseases which affect freshwater fish. The fungus appears, first, as small whiteish patches on any part of the fish, especially where there is a wound. It can spread quite rapidly to cover large areas, and can cause the death of an infected fish.

Molluscs . This phylum is a large one whose members may be found throughout the world. In this phylum are found the *Gastropoda,* the class which includes the snails. *Gastropoda* of the freshwater belongs to two sub-classes, *Prosobranchia* and *Pulmonata.*

The most obvious characteristic of *Prosobranchia* is the horny plate called the operculum which is attached to the foot; from this they are known as operculates. When they withdraw into their shells, the operculum fits over the opening and closes it.

Prosobranchia operculates breathe by means of a gill that is attached to the mantle. They mainly live in clean, well-oxygenated waters. With the exception of *Valvatidea,* both male and female individuals exist.

The freshwater pulmonates have no operculum nor do they have a gill. Although able to extract a certain amount of dissolved oxygen by diffusion through any tissue that is in contact with the water, they obtain their main supply of air by taking it in at the water surface. They have a small tubular structure through which, when at the surface, they draw air into a 'lung' cavity. This cavity lies between the mantle and the dorsal wall of the body. Due to their ability to breathe atmospheric air they can live in water conditions that might not be suitable for the gill-breathing operculates.

Each pulmonate snail contains both male and female organs *(Hermaphroditic)* and are capable of self-fertilization. The usual mode of reproduction, however, is by the union of two individuals.

A snail consists of a soft body which shows no segmentation; the front part of the body carries a mouth and a pair of sensory tentacles with eyes at the base; it is therefore called the head although there is no distinct head; behind the head is the foot. The major part of the body is always inside the shell; this visceral mass extends into soft folds forming the mantle.

The eggs of snails are encased in a jelly-like substance and are attached to aquatic plants and firm surfaces such as stones. The minute snails hatch out as perfect replicas of the adult.

Essentially vegetarian, snails will feed on algae and living submerged water plants; it is known that some will also consume animal matter. Should the snail population increase to the extent that there are too many snails and too little green food, it is obvious that the underwater vegetation is likely to suffer a great deal of damage.

Insects form an integral part of the pond fauna, the population may well include some that are savagely predacious. These, however, will be considered elsewhere.

The artificial pond is almost always much smaller than a large wild natural pond. However, if an effort is made to understand the elements and forces that are at work in natural waters we are in a better position to understand the forces which are at work in our man-made ponds. This knowledge can then be applied to control the various factors, so enabling us to preserve the looks and healthy conditions of the ornamental pond.

In 1887 an American biologist, S.A. Forbes, wrote a paper entitled *The Lake as a Microcosm.* In it he stated: "It forms a little world within itself — a microcosm within which all the elemental forces are

81

at work and the play of life goes on in full but on so small a scale as to bring it easily within the mental grasp."

The aquarium is an even smaller microcosm. However, much that applies to the pond can apply to the indoor aquarium.

It can, perhaps, go wrong much more easily and quickly than the larger body of the pond, unless care is taken. The care of the aquarium need not become a tedious task if attended to regularly.

In order to preserve the looks of the ornamental aquarium it is only necessary to syphon mulm periodically from the gravel, occasionally stiring the top layer lightly to prevent it becoming clogged. Clean algae from the glass so that the interior does not become obscured behind a wall of green. Carefully examine the plants to ensure that they are still alive and healthy, and if necessary thin them out. Having attended to those elementary jobs and syphoned out the dirty water and sediment, the aquarium can be gently refilled with clean fresh water, making sure that its temperature is the same as that in the aquarium.

Devote a few minutes of time to the routine of maintenance and the microcosm of the ornamental aquarium will be preserved, for, as with many things, care and attention are well repaid.

CHAPTER 5

Anatomy of the Goldfish

GENEALOGICAL CLASSIFICATION

The **Chordata** is the phylum which contains all those species which have a backbone — the vertebrates. Man is, of course, a member of this phylum. The **Chordata** includes the following groups:

Cyclostomata	Round-mouthed lampreys.
Pisces	The fishes.
Amphibia	Amphibians, including newts, frogs and toads.
Reptilia	Lizards and snakes.
Aves	Birds.
Mammalia	Those that suckle their young.

We are most interested in the second of these — *Pisces.*

Pisces comprises over twenty-thousand species and is divided up into a number of orders and sub-orders. This enables the various species to be classified according to their relationship.

The first step down the phylum **Chordata,** towards the goldfish, is the *Ostariophysi* order, which serves to distinguish a thousand or so species that differ from the other orders by having a chain of small bones connecting the air-bladder with the ear.

Just as the best families have a 'family tree' so does the great family of **Chordata.** The *Ostariophysi* is the strong limb of the 'tree', this forks into two main branches — the sub-orders, *Siluroidae* and *Cyprinoidae*. The first of the branches embraces the catfish family and is of no interest to us. The second branch however, does concern us; it divides into two family branches one of which is the *Cyprinidae* — this is the carp family.

83

The carp family is the largest of the fish families; the *Cyprinidae* comprise around two thousand species and occupy most of the world's water. *Cyprinidae* are distinguished by the following characteristics: the head is naked; the mouth is toothless, protactile, and the upper jaw is formed by intermaxillaries; there is no adipose fin; and, most important, the lower pharyngeal bones are well developed, falciform and sub-parallel to the bronchial arches. Although not having true teeth, its tooth-like processes are highly modified gill-bones, known as pharyngeal teeth.

The 'family branch' of *Cyprinidae* divides into numerous smaller branches — the genera — and these further divide into the species.

The genus in which we are interested is the one called *Carassius;* it contains two species — *Carassius carassius* (Crucian Carp) and *Carassius auratus* (Goldfish). The 'linear tree' of the goldfish is therefore:

Phylum	**Chordata**
Class	*Pisces*
Order	*Ostariophysi*
Sub-order	*Cyprinoidae*
Family	*Cyprinidae*
Genus	*Carassius*
Species	*Carassius auratus*

It is important to note that the goldfish is a distinct species; it is not, as has been claimed, a variation of the Crucian carp. J. Travis Jenkins, D.Sc., Ph.D., in writing about the carp family in 1950, in his text book *The Fishes of the British Isles* states the differences which separate them. "Crucian carp: Dorsal spine feeble, finely serrated. Edge of dorsal fin convex, 6½ to 9 scales between origin of dorsal and lateral line. Goldfish: Dorsal spine strong, coarsely serrated. Edge of dorsal fin straight or concave. 5 to 6 scales between origin of dorsal and lateral line." On page 285 he writes: ". . . but Tate Regan considers it (the goldfish) a separate species, distinguished from the Crucian Carp by the fact that the body is more elongate, the dorsal fin highest anteriorly . . .; the scales are large, 25 to 30 in the lateral line (28 to 35 in the Crucian Carp)."

Though closely related it is, nevertheless, a distinct species and not descended from the Crucian Carp; nor is it a sport of the Common Carp *(Cyprinus carpio)* which, unlike the goldfish, has barbels at the corners of its mouth.

Although it is possible to breed the goldfish and Crucian Carp together, there would be no merit in such a cross; there would be no advantage to either the breeder or the hybrids which were so produced. It would surely be a worthless venture.

THE SCALES

The scales of fish are the present-day remnants of the heavy, enamelled 'armour-plate' which earliest-known fossil fish wore. As fish evolved they became more active and faster swimming, and the continuous mail-like covering had to become much more flexible. This was accomplished by breaking it up into smaller sections, and in time these smaller sections evolved into the protective scale covering which the majority of present day fish wear.

Goldfish scales are evenly curved, smooth and flexible. When the newly hatched fish first emerges from the egg it is totally devoid of scales. Within a short time, however, minute scales appear in the skin and form a complete covering by the time the fish has grown to half an inch (13 mm) in length. No matter how large the fish grows during its life-time, the number of scales will remain constant. Except to replace a missing scale, no further scales will develop.

Fish scales are dead material, similar to the human fingernail. At the appointed age of the baby fish, little scale nuclei are formed under the skin, of such a size that by just touching each other they manage to cover the body of the tiny fish. Each scale is composed of two layers : a flexible, fibrous lower layer, and an upper brittle layer formed by a deposit of clear bony dentine. The lower layer is formed in sheets across the underside of each scale, but the upper layer grows only at the edge, so that whilst the diameter may increase, its thickness does not. For this reason a scale is always thickest immediately under its original scale plate.

The forward end of each scale is embedded in the dermis and the free after-end develops to cover the front end of the scale behind it. The free end of the scale is therefore the only visible part, although it is smaller than the size of the complete scale.

As the fish grows, the scales must also grow in order to continue to overlap the scales behind them. This is done by the individual scale adding new rings of dentine around its edge, in much the same way

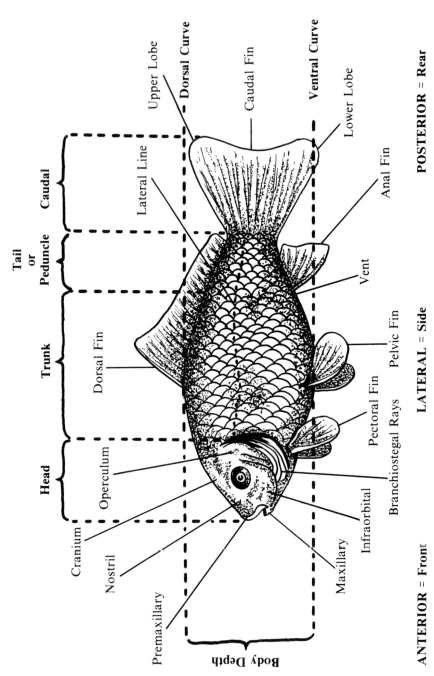

Figure 5.1 *External Features of the Goldfish*

ANTERIOR = Front   LATERAL = Side   POSTERIOR = Rear

86

that a tree grows. Where this new material is added to the after-end of the scale it shows in irregular, poorly marked accretions. Fortunately the larger portion has clearly defined rings on it throughout its life.

Whereas a tree adds a ring for each year of its life, the growth of fish scale rings will vary according to the seasons, the food supplies and the activities of the fish. A skilled observer can tell not only the age of the fish, but how many times it has spawned, and the length it reached in each year of its life.

In summer, when the water is warm and food is plentiful, a fish tends to feed well and grow rapidly. This means the scales must grow quickly to keep the fish covered so the rings are therefore widely spaced. In cold weather food is scarce and the fish grows slowly, if at all. This results in rings which lie close together and a dark band, called the annual check, appears. By counting the number of annual checks the age of the fish can be determined.

The scales, which are transparent, are bedded in the dermis and provide protection to the body of the fish, covering the fish from behind the gill-covers to the root of the tail. Scales are absent from the head which is bare.

THE SKIN AND PIGMENTATION

The skin is composed of two layers: the thin, cellular, **outer epidermis,** and the **inner dermis** which is composed of connective tissue in which are blood-vessels and nerve-fibres. The epidermis covers the head and body-scales of the fish, it produces a mucus — it is this which makes the fish feel slimy to the touch — the secretion acting as a protection against diseases and parasites, and it also reduces friction. Beneath the dermis there is a layer of fat (adipose tissue) and muscle (myotomes).

The dermis contains a substance called guanine — a reflective substance that lies just under the scales and also at a lower depth. This light, reflective substance is a white material which collects in clusters of crystals known as iridocytes.

In addition to the iridocytes, the dermis — and to an extent the epidermis — contains colour pigment cells known as chromatophores, these being disposed at different depths within the tissue. These pigments may be red-orange, yellow or black (the pigments are the same in all fish, no other pigments having been discovered). The red-orange and yellow pigments, known as lipochromes, are liquid, while the black are called melamines. The pigments are relatively large cells of irregular, ramified shape, containing the colour-matter inside themselves in the form of droplets or grainlets. They are capable of concentrating all the pigment into a tiny spot in the centre of each cell, or of expanding it out all over the cell. It is possible for some cells to expand at the same moment that others are contracting.

Although the scales appear opaque they are, in fact, transparent. If we think of a mirror we can then understand that if the transparent scale is looked upon as the glass, and the reflective iridocytes as the backing, we have a good light-reflecting surface.

All varieties of goldfish, no matter what shape they may be, can normally be placed in one of three groups — **Metallic, Nacreous** or **Matt** — depending on the amount and disposition of the reflective tissue. These groups are often referred to as 'scale groups', but this is erroneous, as will be seen, and should be more correctly known as 'reflective groups' — for each group depends upon the amount of reflective shine exhibited by the individual fish.

Metallic group. This group has a metallic shine due to there being normal placement of the iridocytes, giving full reflection over the head and body.

Nacreous. In this group most areas lack the upper layer of iridocytes allowing the deeper layer to show. This lower layer of reflective tissue appears as a mother-of-pearl shine (nacreous). The individual fish therefore exhibits a nacreous shine and, possibly, a few scales with metallic shine; these scales should be as few as possible.

Matt. An absolute lack of shine, due to a complete absence of reflective iridocytes, is the mark of fish in this group. All regions of the head and body have a matt appearance.

Colours. As explained earlier the pigments in goldfish are red-orange, yellow and black; to these must be added the red pigment (haemoglobin) in the blood.

The red-orange and yellow pigments are found in the epidermis and the dermis — the red and orange tending to be in the area just below the scales, while the yellow is just above the scales. The black pigment is found in the epidermis, dermis, adipose tissue and myotomes. In the upper region the pigment appears black, in the next lower it is slate-blue, in the adipose tissue it is a bright blue, and in the lowest layer of tissue it shows as a brilliant blue.

Haemoglobin is responsible for the pink body colour of most matt fish and some nacreous fish; it is also responsible for the deep red colour of the gills of matt and some nacreous fish. This red is due to the concentration of blood in the gills showing through the translucent bones of the opercula.

Due to the pigments lying at differing depths it is possible for them to overlap and thereby create a variety of colours other than those of the pigments.

The **Metallic** group of goldfish may be reddish-orange or yellow. In the absence of pigment they will be silver; due to the reflective whiteish tissue showing through the transparent scales. Within this group, also, are wild olive coloured types (these are fish which have not changed to the reddish-orange or yellow colour, and is due to black pigment combined with the other pigments). The young of this group, when first scaled, are olive in colour, after a time this darkens to almost black. As the fish develops the black will begin to recede deeper into the tissues, and as it does so the other pigments will be revealed. Eventually the black pigment will be so deep in the tissues that it cannot be seen. During this colour change the fish may be reddish-orange, yellow, silver and black — that is an extreme example of multi-coloration in the metallic group — but more often it is a single colour plus a non-permanent black.

The **Matt** group are usually pink with black eyes, but it is possible to find fish with colours similar to those in the next group. Due to the lack of reflective tissues the intensity of colours will appear different.

The **Nacreous** group, being the most colourful, may exhibit either a single colour or a number of different colours as follows: whiteish-pink, yellow, orange, red, blue, violet, brown and black, and any multiplicity of those colours.

GENETICS

Any of the three groups is capable of cross-breeding with another. The Matt and Metallic groups will breed true if bred with fish from their own group. However, the Nacreous group will not breed one hundred per cent true, whether crossed with fish from their own group or not. Breeding a Nacreous fish to another Nacreous fish will, in fact, produce a percentage of each of the three groups in the resulting young.

The following table of possible crossings, together with the percentages of each scale group into which the young will fall, will clearly illustrate the point:

Nacreous x Nacreous = 50% Nacreous, 25% Matt, 25% Metallic
Nacreous x Matt   = 50% Nacreous, 50% Matt
Nacreous x Metallic = 50% Nacreous, 50% Metallic
Matt x Metallic   = 100% Nacreous
Matt x Matt   = 100% Matt
Metallic x Metallic = 100% Metallic

ANATOMY

A fish is normally described in four parts, which can be distinguished as the head, trunk, tail (peduncle), and fins. The boundary between the head and trunk is determined by the gill opening, and between trunk and tail by the vent.

The skeleton of the goldfish basically consists of a backbone supporting the skull, and providing attachment for the ribs and support for the fins (limbs). The vertebrae of the backbone are so arranged that they allow flexibility of the body, especially in the region of the tail. The first four vertebrae are modified to such an extent that they appear to be almost part of the skull. They have certain curiously shaped elements on each side which provide contact between the ear and the air-bladder, known as the Weberian ossicles. The rear end of the backbone is modified to form the structure of the caudal fin rays.

The skull is made up of a number of bones. The *cranium* is a box-like structure in which the brain is contained, a large opening at the back allows the spinal cord to pass out backwards. Other apertures allow egress of the nerves to nasal organs and the eyes. Appended from both sides of the cranium, behind the eye openings, is a chain of bones (the *suspensorium*), and the lower jaw is hinged from the lowest of these bones. The lower jaw consists of three bones on each side; the upper jaw has four bones — a *premaxillary* on either side and, behind each, a *maxillary*. They move forwards when the jaw opens. The mouth, which is roofed by flat bones forming the *palatine arch,* is toothless. Food is masticated by the eight 'teeth' on the *pharyngeal bones* which bite against a horny pad at the base of the skull, at the entrance to the gullet.

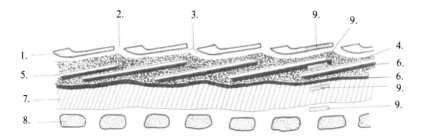

Figure A *Metallic Group*

Normal placement of reflective tissue below scales and deep in the dermis produces the well known metal-like shine of the common goldfish

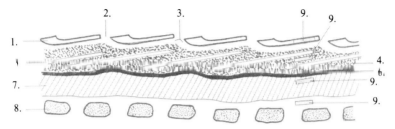

Figure B *Nacreous Group*

The upper layer of reflective tissue is missing, allowing the lower layer to show dully through the dermis and scales. This results in the fish having areas with a mother-of-pearl shine

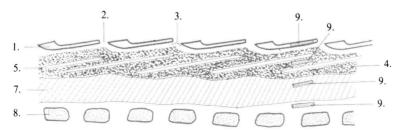

Figure C *Matt Group*

A complete absence of reflective tissue gives a matt appearance to the scales of the fish

Figure 5.2 *Sections Through The Lateral Line — Reflective Groups (Skin Tissue)*

1. Epidermis. 2. Lateral line pore. 3. Lateral line canal. 4. Dermis. 5. Scale. 6. Reflective (iridoctyes) tissue. 7. Adipose tissue. 8. Myotomes — muscular tissue. 9. Chromatophore levels.

The eye-openings are surrounded externally by a ring of *circumorbital bones,* which contain channels for certain sensory canals. Behind these, hinged to the cranium, are the *gill covers* — composed of four flat bones that are plainly visible — known as the *operculum.* The operculum, which protects and covers the gill-cavities, is raised and lowered during the process of breathing.

There are five *gill arches,* four of which support the gills. The first is the *hyoid arch,* and consists of large flat bones that form a strong frame for the gill-cavities. The gill arches also have a series of sabre-shaped bones *(branchiostegal rays)* that open like a fan below the operculum to protect the gills. From the junction of the hyoid arches a bone projects, from near the chin, forward into the mouth, supporting what may be called the tongue, whilst another bone passes backwards, forming a firm connection with the shoulder-girdle. Each gill-arch comprises a number of slender bones which are suspended in a chain below the cranium, and linked together below. The elements of the last arch are greatly enlarged, and sickle-shaped, bearing four rows of strong flattened tooth-like processes — these are the *pharyngeals.*

The shoulder-girdle consists of the *pectoral arches,* which are attached to the back of the skull on each side, and meet below. Each arch is made up of several bones joined together, and supports a pectoral fin. Set further back, on the belly, is a pair of *pelvic fins,* supported by two flat *pelvic bones.* The pelvic bones are not attached directly to any part of the skeleton.

The *fins* are supported by *rays,* each ray being built up from short segments of bone, which are very flexible. Each ray of the dorsal, caudal and anal fins are actually double and are formed by elements from each side of the body. Most of the rays are branched, but in some of the fish the first one to three may be spine-like and stiff, due to the bone segments being firmly united. The fin rays are hinged upon their supporting bones, to allow movement in one or more directions.

Movable bones are bound together with *ligaments,* and generally cushioned against shock by *cartilage.*

It must be mentioned that in the more fancy varieties of goldfish, where the caudal and anal fins are divided to form separated twin caudal and anal fins, the doubled bone segments of the fins' rays have separated. The resulting double fins are therefore much weaker than are the rays of the normal single fins.

The *muscular system* of the goldfish is not over-complex, consisting mainly of two muscle masses along each side of the central axis. One mass lies above and the other below the axis, and each consists of an upper and lower section. The muscles are in segments known as *myotomes,* the number of segments corresponding to the number of vertebrae. The *dorsal mass* is attached to the back of the skull and extends the full length of the body. The *ventral mass* is weakly developed at the forward end and shows the strongest development in the region of the tail.

The *dorsal* and *anal* fins are controlled by a number of small muscles which expand or contract the fins. The muscle which controls the expansion, or elevation, is the stronger. Therefore, in a healthy fish, the dorsal and anal fins are seldom folded. The *caudal* fin is controlled by similar muscles which are also used to move the upper and lower rays from side to side. The front pair of *pectoral* fins perform a number of movements and thus the controlling muscles are strong and complex. Those of the *pelvic* fins are small, merely being required to spread the rays fan-wise.

The *muscles of the skull* perform a number of functions, such as operating the gill system, moving the eyes, opening and closing the mouth; these muscles are therefore quite complicated.

The main *senses* of the goldfish are those of touch, taste, smell, 'hearing', and a sort of 'sixth-sense' (this 'sixth-sense' is situated in the lateral line). It must be said that there are differences of opinion with regard to the exact nature of these senses; however, it is obvious that they differ from those of land animals which live in a completely different environment.

The organ of *smell* is not used for respiration, but it does have the faculty of smell, which either attracts or repels a fish when it is near certain odours.

The sense of *taste* is no doubt slight, but the goldfish does have a peculiar organ on the roof of its mouth, which may be an organ of taste since it is richly provided with taste buds and nerves.

We know a little more about the *sight* of fish. In all fish, the skin of the head passes over the eye, becoming transparent where it enters the orbit. The eye is subhemispherical, the cornea being quite flat, so that when the fish swims there is no resistance to the water and, being level with the head, is less liable to suffer injury.

The structure of the *eye* shows clearly that, compared to our vision, the fish is short-sighted. Instead of being lens-shaped the lens of the fish is globular or spherical, and the range of perfect vision can be little over three feet (915 mm). Adjustment of the sight to a greater or lesser distance is not accomplished, as in land animals, by an alteration in the shape of the lens, but by the aid of a special muscle which moves the lens further away from or nearer to the retina. This may give only imperfect vision over a range of thirty feet (9 m).

It is thought that the goldfish does have a sense of *touch,* probably being most sensitive around the lips of the mouth.

The *auditory organ* in fish is much simpler than in man. In fish the external ear and middle ear are non-existent, and the inner ear consists only of a labyrinth with three semi-circular canals. The vestibule of the labyrinth is dilated into one or more sacs that contain the ear-stones, or *otoliths.* As already explained, this arrangement is connected to the air-bladder. There is no cochlea. It is precisely those parts of the human ear in which the actual hearing apparatus is situated that is missing in fish, therefore they cannot hear in the sense that we do. The auditory organ in fish is mainly a balancing organ. They are, of course, sensible to vibrations. When the labyrinth is damaged or injured, the fish loses its power to balance the body. The otoliths grow from year to year by the accretion of layers of calcium carbonate, and allow a means of estimating the age and growing of a fish by a skilled observer, as do the scales.

Along the side of the body will be found a series of perforated scales known as the *lateral line.* These scales cover a canal which runs along both sides of the body under the skin, extending from the start of the caudal fin to the head, over the head in three branches, over and under the eye and along the lower jaw. This canal is filled with mucus. Put very simply, the lateral line is a sense organ that enables the fish to determine changes in direction and strength of currents in the water. It is thought that fish can sense vibrations through the lateral line — the 'sixth-sense'.

Just behind the shoulder girdle lies the *liver,* a large dark red gland. Bedded in the liver is the *pancreas;* its duct enters the *intestine* close to the *bile-duct.* Near the *stomach* is the *spleen.* The *kidneys* are long and thin, deep red in colour, immediately below the *vertebral column.* Their duct (the *ureter)* passes down the back end of the abdominal cavity.

The *gullet* is situated immediately behind the last pair of *pharyngeal slits.* A duct connects the gullet (oesphagus) to the *air-bladder,* which

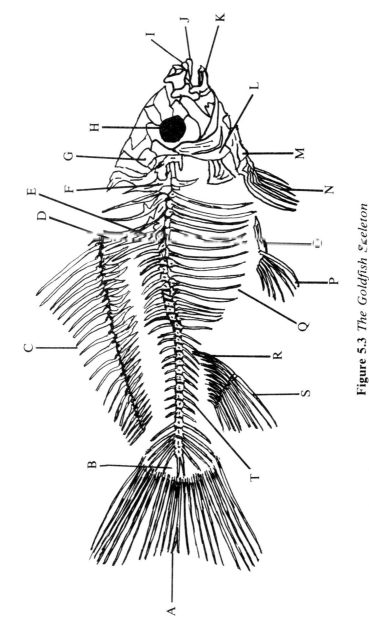

Figure 5.3 *The Goldfish Skeleton*

A. caudal fin; B. hypural bones; C. dorsal fin; D interneural; E. neural spine; F. vertebra; G. post-temporal (provides pectoral arch attachment); H. orbit; I. maxillary; J. premaxillary; K. lower jaw; L. pharyngeal bone; M. coracoids; N. pectoral fin; O. pelvic bone; P. pelvic fin; Q. ribs; R. interhaemal bone; S. anal fin; T. haemal spine lies below the vertabral column at the centre of gravity. It is a membranous sac constructed in two lobes, of which the hind lobe is perhaps slightly the larger — at least it is in the normal common goldfish. The bladder contains oxygen, nitrogen and a small amount of carbon dioxide. The hind lobe normally contains the higher proportion of oxygen.

The air-bladder is a most important organ to the fish. Apart from acting as a reservoir for oxygen, it also serves two other functions. By adjusting its contents the fish is able to alter its specific gravity, so that it can float at any desired level without difficulty. The second function is the part it plays, as already mentioned, in the auditory system of the fish.

The *stomach,* an extension of the alimentary tract, lies just below the liver and is connected to the coiled *intestine,* which occupies a position in the lowest part of the body cavity — uncoiled the intestine would be approximately four times the length of the fish — and this, in turn, leads to the *anus.*

The *digestion of food* is performed in a different manner to that of the higher vertebrates. Fish 'bolt' their food; there is no true chewing or mastication. Food is passed from the mouth to the pharyngeal teeth and the gullet. From the gullet it passes through the stomach, where the solid matter is acted upon by an acid medium; various enzymes reduce the food to a liquid state; it then passes into the intestine. The intestine has a number of appendages *(pyloric appendages),* which secrete an enzyme, and also increase the absorptive surface area of the intestine. The enzymes reduce the liquid food to a state that enables the nutritive substances to be absorbed through the walls of the intestine. Nutritive material is passed into the blood, and the indigestible matter is passed out, as faeces, through the *anus,* a vent just in front of the anal fin.

The *blood* of the goldfish contains haemoglobin and is, therefore, red in colour. The red blood corpuscles when leaving the heart are deep red *(arterial blood);* but during the circulatory process, the blood will gather carbon dioxide and become bluish-red *(venous blood).* The red blood corpuscles in the goldfish are oval in shape and fewer than in the blood of mammals. There are also white amoeboid corpuscles in the blood of fish. The quantity of blood is comparatively small and bears only a small relation to the body weight — about one sixty-third.

Blood containing carbon dioxide passes through the veins to enter the *heart,* which is rather small. The heart lies forward in the body, in the *pericardial cavity* (a special chamber), below the gullet. The blood is received into a single *auricle,* and is pumped out by a single muscular *ventricle.* The heart, therefore, deals only with the venous blood, which is pumped along the *ventral aorta,* through the *arteries* and spreads out over a large area in the *gills.* There the red corpuscles discard the carbon dioxide and replace it with oxygen. Having made the gaseous exchange the oxygenated blood passes along further arteries into the great *dorsal aorta,* which lies below the vertebral column and branches off to supply blood to all parts of the body.

Fish do not have the ability to regulate the temperature of their blood, as do most other animals, which therefore varies with the water temperature. For this reason fish are known as poikilotherms. It stands to reason that sudden and violent temperature changes will, more than likely, distress the fish.

Respiration in fish is accomplished by means of the *gills* which are highly vascular structures. The blood is circulated over the branchial *almellae* and the blood is aerated. During this process there is a gaseous exchange, whereby oxygen replaces carbon dioxide. The quantity of oxygen utilised by fish is far less than that required by higher vertebrates, so that passive fish, such as the goldfish, can live in water that would have too low an oxygen content to suit others.

Fish do not drink. All the water which is taken into the mouth passes over the gills and out of the gill-openings. Water is prevented from entering the alimentary canal because the pharynx contracts and the water is driven through slits in the pharynx and out through the gills. At the same time the *gullet* contracts to close it tightly, so that no water can pass into the alimentary canal. Should food, however, touch the closed gullet, no matter how lightly, the gullet immediately relaxes to pass the food. A negligible amount of water may also pass through with the solid matter.

The *nervous system* of the goldfish is a comparatively simple affair. The main centre is the *brain,* with lobes. From the front lobe (the *presencephalon),* the *olfactory nerves* pass forward to the nasal organs. On either side is a large optic lobe, giving rise to the *optic nerve* which is responsible for sight. Below is the *infundibulum,* a lobe from which is suspended the important ductless *pituitary gland.* Behind the optic lobes, on the upper side, is the *cerebellum,* or hind brain, which co-ordinates muscular activity in response to stimuli received through the senses. Below the cerebellum is the *medulla oblongata,* which enters

97

the spinal chord where it leaves the cranium. In the region of the medulla are five *cranial nerves* on each side. Along the spinal chord a similar pair of nerves is situated, above and below, at each vertebral segment. The nerves divide, root-like, to serve all parts of the body in a complex manner.

Nerve fibres either control the muscular response, or they are sensory, conveying stimuli to the brain or other centres.

Locomotion is achieved mainly by flexion of the lateral muscles, particularly by the strong muscle in the tail causing the caudal fin to sweep from side to side with a twisting motion, between the upper and lower lobes, rather like a stern sculling oar. The movement not only imparts forward propulsion but also tends to push the head down. The action of the gills tends to push the fish forward too.

The *pelvic fins* act rather like the elevators of a submarine. They are used partially to adjust the angle of the fish. The *dorsal* and *anal fins* are intended to stabilize any rolling motion that the *caudal fin* causes. The *pectoral fins* act as brakes, and are used in a similar manner to a canoe paddle. When the fish is resting they are used to counteract the movement imparted by the gills. When the fish is moving it can alter direction by raising one or other of the pectoral fins and spreading it into a fan. When stopping it extends both fins and this presents maximum water resistance, quickly bringing the fish to a halt.

From what has been written it can now be seen that the fish is a creature perfectly adapted to its environment — it merely asks that the fishkeeper provide the best possible environment.

Before leaving this section the differences between the two sexes should be explained.

The reproductive organs consist of ovaries in the female, and testes or milt in the male (hard roe and soft roe, respectively, as they are sometimes called). The ovaries are yellowish in colour and have a granular texture. The testes have a soft, creamy texture and are much paler in colour. Both ovaries and testes occupy much the same position in the body of the fish, lying just below and behind the air-bladder. They are paired and elongated in shape, and connect to the kidneys. As the breeding season approaches and the female becomes 'ripe', the ovaries become enlarged, filling the body cavity to such an extent that the body of the female can become visibly swollen.

The shapes of the male and female goldfish vents are slightly different to each other; a difference which the keen-eyed may be able to

98

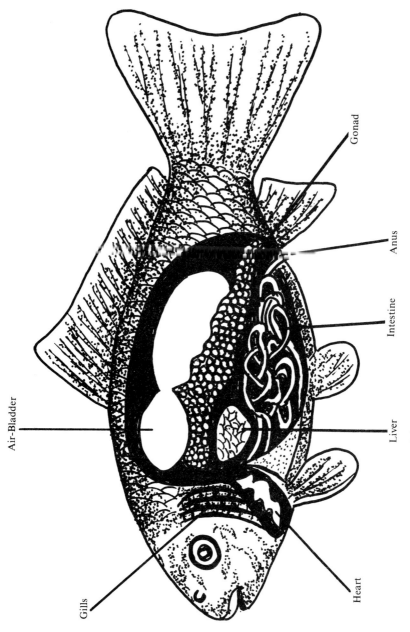

Gonad

Anus

Intestine

Liver

Air-Bladder

Gills

Heart

Figure 5.4 *Main Internal Organs of the Goldfish*

99

discern. The vent of the male is small and oval in shape and is very slightly indented. That of the female is larger and more round and slightly protuberant. During the breeding period the female vent becomes distended, larger and more protuberant in readiness to expel her eggs.

The most obvious and easily recognised sexual difference can be seen when the male is in breeding condition. At this time the front rays of the pectoral fins become thicker and tiny white pimples, about the size of a pin head, develop on them, which are known as tubercles. The tubercles also appear on the gill-plates. Although it is not unknown, the females do not usually develop tubercles. It is therefore possible, during the breeding period, to differentiate between male and female with reasonable accuracy.

The germ-cells, or gametes, are fragments of protoplasm containing nuclei that develop into ova in the ovary and spermatozoa in the testes. The unfertilised egg consists of living protoplasm, and a quantity of yolk, enclosed in a protective membrane. The yolk (non-living foodstuff) collects at one end of the egg, known as the vegetative pole, and the protoplasm at the other end, which is the animal pole. At the animal pole a tiny pore, the micropyle, pierces the protective membrane. Sperm fertilizes the egg by entering the micropyle, which then closes behind it — allowing only one spermatozoon to enter.

Before release the eggs are very small, but upon being released the egg swells by an osmotic intake of water. After the egg has swollen it is approximately 1/16 inch (1.5 mm) in diameter. The goldfish egg is demersal adhesive; in other words, the egg is heavier than water and therefore sinks, it is also covered with a sticky substance by which it adheres to whatever it comes into contact with during its fall through water.

The further development of the fertilized egg will be explained in the section which deals with the breeding of goldfish; however, in order for the egg to become fertilized the sperm must enter the micropyle before or during the intake of water. Once the egg has swollen it is no longer capable of being fertilized and dies.

CHAPTER 6

The Goldfish

THE HISTORY AND DEVELOPMENT OF THE GOLDFISH

There seems to be some doubt about the earliest date that the goldfish was first cultivated on a serious scale. Not being a student of the historical origin of the goldfish I must rely upon others more learned in the subject.

In 1971 Dr. Yoshiichi Matsui, Professor of Fish Culture at Kinki University, in Japan, wrote a booklet under the title of *Goldfish.* In the book he wrote that, according to ancient Chinese records, the first coloured fish were discovered around 265-316 AD, and the Chinese began breeding the fish about 700-800 AD.

Dr. Matsui wrote a further book, *The Goldfish Guide,* in 1972. In that he states that the time is generally put in the Sung era, which was somewhere around 1000 AD, although old poetry of the period, circa 800 AD, mentions goldfish.

A classic book, *The Goldfish,* was published in 1948. The authors, Messrs. Hervey and Hems, remark that references to goldfish being kept as pets during the T'san Dynasty of 616-907 AD, leave them unconvinced. They, like Matsui, consider 'safe ground' to be the Sung Dynasty. For, they say, the literature of the Sung, contains many references to goldfish, thus proving that the goldfish had become a popular pet from the eleventh century onwards. They write: "Finally, the evidence of the *Meng Liang Lu* goes to show that before the end of the thirteenth century (1276) gold, silver, red, black, and mottled fish were being bred and sold in Hangchow." According to Dr. Matsui, two areas of China compete for the honour of being the first to produce red goldfish — the district of Che Chiang Chen, and the district of Chiang Su Chen.

The date that the first goldfish reached Japan is also somewhat in-

101

definite; however, it is reasonably certain that by 1500 AD, they had become established in that country. The Japanese icthyologist Mitsukuri wrote in 1904 that there was a record of about 1500, in which it was noted that some goldfish had been taken from China to Sakai, near Osaka, Japan. It seems that two centuries were to elapse before the Japanese began breeding goldfish — the honour of being the first to breed the goldfish in Japan is accorded to Sato Sanzaemon of Koriyama, during the Hoyei era of 1704-1710.

By the end of the seventeenth century the goldfish had become widespread throughout the East. Engelbert Kampfer wrote of his travels in the Far East, between 1691 and 1692: "In China and Japan, and almost all over the Indies, this fish is kept in ponds."

The dates of the Chinese goldfish reaching Europe are much more definite, for there are records of 1611, 1691 and 1728, or so Matsui states.

It is known that by the middle of the eighteenth century the goldfish had become widespread in England, in fact, Horace Walpole (Earl of Oxford, 1717-1797) was constantly presenting goldfish to his friends.

About 1750, goldfish arrived at the French port of Lorient. They were imported by the French East-India Company during the last days of the French monarchy. So great did their popularity become that, in 1780, Billardon de Sauvigny published his *Histoire Naturelle des Dorades de la Chine,* which contains plates of eighty different sorts of goldfish.

Prior to this, von Linné (1707-1778) produced his book *Systema Naturae* in 1758, in which the goldfish was first zoologically classified as *Cyprinus auratus.*

By 1754 the goldfish had reached the Netherlands — it had already become known in Italy — where they were placed into ponds on the estate of Count Clifford and that of the Lord of Rhoon, but they do not appear to have bred. Job Baster was the first to breed goldfish in Holland, from fish imported from England, during the winter of 1759-60, in his Zeeland ponds.

Scandinavian countries knew of the goldfish by the beginning of the eighteenth century — it was there that von Linné received his goldfish specimen.

By the end of the eighteenth century the goldfish was flourishing in the Russian climate. In 1791 Prince Gregory Alexandrovitch (Prince Potemkin) used goldfish in bowls to decorate the fabulous Winter

Gardens, where he gave a banquet for Catherine the Second.

Available records show the goldfish as arriving in America in 1874, although it is conceivable that some may have arrived earlier. Admiral Ammon is said to have imported them from Japan. The goldfish made rapid progress in America and by 1889 a goldfish farm was established in Maryland.

Having devoted some time to the recorded spread of the goldfish from its ancestral home in China to other lands, let us now give some consideration to how the many fancy varieties evolved from the original wild form.

One has only to think of the many variations in colour, finnage, body-shape, and head and eye development, to realise that the goldfish must be a very "plastic" creature to be capable of such a wide diversity of form. Yet, if left to go its own way, it will quite quickly revert to its original wild ancestral type. It is only by controlled selective breeding that the various fancy varieties are maintained, improved and new forms established.

Although there is no firm evidence to tell us when the first divergence from the wild uncoloured goldfish occurred, nor when the first change in body and finnage was noted, it is possible that such fish arose from time to time but were not considered of any great interest to the Chinese of more than a thousand years ago.

At some stage, however, these unusual types were noticed and, with foresight, gathered into special compounds. With the infinite patience of the Chinese race they began to breed these abnormal fish. Interbreeding and cross breeding the fish, as each new character appeared, created greater divergence from the normal.

Some individuals would exhibit abnormally shaped bodies, there would be variations in scales, colours, fins and eyes. By careful selection and breeding features were fixed or, perhaps, combined. As each variation arose it was separated and cultivated to emphasise the new feature. And so with diligence and patience the Chinese began to create new forms of goldfish. Over many years the foundation of the many varieties became established. This careful breeding has continued, unbroken, over the centuries, right up to the present day. In fact, modern China has government establishments — often in a zoo or park — where the goldfish is bred, and the creation of new varieties attempted.

Little is recorded of the early Chinese goldfish, the earliest reference seeming to be in the *T'ing Shih,* around the year 1200. About 1276 Wu Tzu-mu published his *Meng Liang Lu* in which he mentions Tortoiseshell Fish being sold in Hangchow, and he also mentioned gold, silver, and other coloured fish. By the late Ming period (1369-1644) a large number of multi-coloured fish had apparently been developed. T'u Lung wrote in 1590, or thereabouts, describing various coloured fish, which are thought to be early fancy goldfish. Various other Chinese writers made references to goldfish in the following years — P'eng Ta-i and Chang Ch'ien-te being two such.

It is certain that many fancy varieties of goldfish were being bred by the sixteenth century. It is quite possible that the telescope-eyed goldfish was known by the early part of that century. In the *K'ao P'an Yu Shih* (circa 1590) reference is made to fish with ink-black, snow-white, scarlet, purple, agate and amber eyes; and later to 'red protuberant'. There is little doubt that the telescope-eyed goldfish was well known by the mid-eighteenth century. The proof is in a scroll sent from Peking to Paris in 1772, which depicts a number of this type of fish. This particular variety was the subject of considerable literature between 1872 and 1900, by which time it had become well known in the Western World. The Chinese had begun breeding many fancy types, of different colours, by the seventeenth century. The first illustration of a fish with no dorsal fin was in 1726, when it appeared as part of the *Tu Shu.* On the Peking scroll several of the fish have markedly fat, round, short bodies without dorsal fins. A fish somewhat similar to a Celestial goldfish, with up-turned eyes, is also shown upon the scroll.

The nineteenth century marked the decline of the Manchu Dynasty (1644-1912), and, what with foreign wars and internal strife, there was a lessening of interest in the various luxury arts and crafts within China. The cultivation of goldfish then passed more to the Japanese, who developed many new varieties.

In his book *Goldfish Guide* Matsui informs the reader that the date of the first goldfish to reach Japan from China is somewhat vague, but that it is fairly certain that they had become established by 1500. This is confirmed by the Japanese ichthyologist Mitsukuri, as already mentioned. Matsui also mentions in his booklet *Goldfish* that at present more than twenty different varieties of goldfish are bred in Japan. The source of the initial breeding stock was obtained from China and consisted of Wakin (something like the common goldfish but having a double caudal fin), Maruko (a double caudal finned fish lacking a dorsal fin — possibly the ancestor of the Lionhead), Ryukin (a fish with double caudal fins, very similar to the modern fantail but with much longer fins), Demekin (a black, telescope-eyed fish, having twin caudal fins it was the forerunner of the modern Moor), and Oranda shishigashira (similar to the modern Oranda, but with very limited head growth).

From the Chinese importations a number of mutations are said to have appeared. Matsui lists them as Peacocktail (Jikin), Nanking (Nankin), Lionhead (Ranchu) Narial Bouquet (Hana Fusa), Ironcolour Fringetail (Tetsu Onaga) and Tamagata (Yamagata Kingyo). By cross-breeding, it is stated, such varieties as the following were produced: Watonia, Tosa (Tosakin), Golden Blearyeye (Kinranshi), Autumn Calico (Shukin), Red Marked Calico (Shubunkin), including Tsugaru Calico and Hiro Calico, Calico (Kyarico), and Dutch Calico (Azuma Nishiki).

From these original importations, and the mutations, the Japanese goldfish breeders have produced many varieties that have become well known to Western goldfish enthusiasts. Probably the best known of all being the Lionhead. There is absolutely no doubt the true Lionhead was developed by the Japanese in the nineteenth century; however, Matsui claims that a type of Lionhead — which he calls *Buffalohead* — is depicted in a group of Chinese drawings of around 1429.

Probably the forerunner of the modern Lionhead was the Osaka Buffalohead, which was a mutation of the imported Maruko. This was a smallish fish with a well spread twin caudal fin. It had a downbent tail (caudal peduncle), and a normal head without any sign of the raspberry-like growth (hood) which is the distinctive feature of the Lionhead. This fish was first produced in Osaka — hence its name — where it continued to be bred until the late 1940s, when at the beginning of the war it was allowed to die out. A show programme for Buffaloheads was printed in 1862, for a goldfish show held in Osaka. (That show is believed to have been the very first Japanese goldfish show.)

American goldfish keepers, in Philadelphia, developed the modern type of Veiltail from the Ryukin (which reached their country in the late 1800s), and created a deep bodied fish with long, square-cut, divided double caudal fins and twin anal fins.

Shortly before that, during the early 1800s, the American Hugo Mulertt developed the Comet variety of goldfish.

During the early 1920s specimens of a type of Shubunkin reached

105

England and from these Messrs. L.B. Katterns and A. Derham bred the type known as the London Shubunkin. The Americans produced a type with long flowing pointed tails, and large numbers were sent to England. By crossing these types, and with much selective breeding, members of the Bristol Aquarist Society developed an English variety of the Shubunkin — the Bristol Shubunkin — with an enlarged flowing caudal fin, the lobes of which were rounded. In 1934 the Society produced the first show standard for the Shubunkin which they had created, and which became universally popular.

Despite the foregoing being but a 'potted' version of the history and development of the fancy goldfish it serves to prove that, even though there may be some gaps, it has a recorded pedigree covering almost one thousand years (which is probably more than can be claimed for any other animal) and may thus be thought of as a 'Regal Fish'.

British aquarists long ago took the fish to their hearts, and have continued to breed many of the different varieties. Always striving to improve the quality and characteristics, their present-day strains of fancy goldfish are now amongst the best and hardiest in the world. Of recent years there has been a reawakening of interest amongst American fishkeepers who, no doubt, will soon build up their own strains to the position they once held.

THE GOLDFISH VARIETIES

Probably the first variety to deviate from its wild ancestor, and the progenitor of the many diverse forms of fancy goldfish, the common goldfish has been, and still is, the delight of countless children and adults alike. It has served to introduce many to the wider interests of the fishkeeping hobby, being well able to withstand the maltreatment of confined quarters (a glass goldfish-bowl is not the place to keep fish), poor food given in either too little or too great a quantity, dirty water and the consequent many changes of water and temperature that the inexperienced owner is apt to subject it to. Equally at home in the indoor aquarium or the more rigorous conditions of the outdoor pond, this fish has remained popular with many fishkeepers. So well known is this fish that a description would hardly seem worthwhile, but not to do so would be most remiss for it is, despite its title and what some may think, a fancy goldfish. It is, therefore, with no apology that I include this 'common goldfish' with its more illustrious relatives — common in form it may be, but Royal by lineage!

106

Common Goldfish. A good specimen should have a well-proportioned sturdy look about it, with a moderately curved back from the peduncle to the head and a corresponding ventral curve to the underside of the body. The head should be short and wide, with a small mouth, without any trace of 'snoutiness'. The highest point of the back is above the pelvic fins, and at this point the dorsal fin commences. The caudal peduncle is short and strong, supporting a short, shallowly forked, caudal fin. Pectoral, pelvic and anal fins are of moderate size, paddle-shaped and carried stiffly. The eyes are bright and of the normal iris type.

The scales of the Common Goldfish have a bright metallic appearance (metallic group) and cover the body and peduncle in an even pattern of rows, overlapping like the tiles on a roof (imbricated) starting at the junction with the head and running back to the caudal joint. Self-coloured reddish-orange, orange or yellow are generally preferred to the variegated types, however, red and silver, reddish-orange and yellow, or yellow and silver, are not uncommon. Black may also be exhibited, but this is not a permanent colour and will disappear with time. White (or pearl) fish are not highly thought of by most fish-keepers.

London Shubunkin (Nacreous group). Has exactly the same body, head and finnage as the Common Goldfish — of which it is a variation — but lacks the reflective tissue and metallic shine. The transparent scales allow a multiplicity of colours to be seen. Ideally the background colour should be a bright forget-me-not-blue, interspersed with patches of red, yellow, brown, violet and black, over which there is black speckling. The colours should spread into the fins. Fish that are a single self-colour, or pinkish-white, are not considered to be of any value. Suitable for pond and aquarium.

Bristol Shubunkin (Nacreous group). A slim, streamlined fish, the depth of its body being less than half its length and the head less than one-third. The dorsal fin commences on the high point of the back and is almost as high as the body is deep. The pectoral and pelvic fins are long and well developed. The caudal fin is the main feature, being single and well developed with large rounded lobes. The fin should be carried without any sign of drooping. A very attractive fish, probably the most colourful variety, it is also very hardy and does well in both aquarium and pond.

Wakin (Metallic group). This is the 'common goldfish' of Japan.

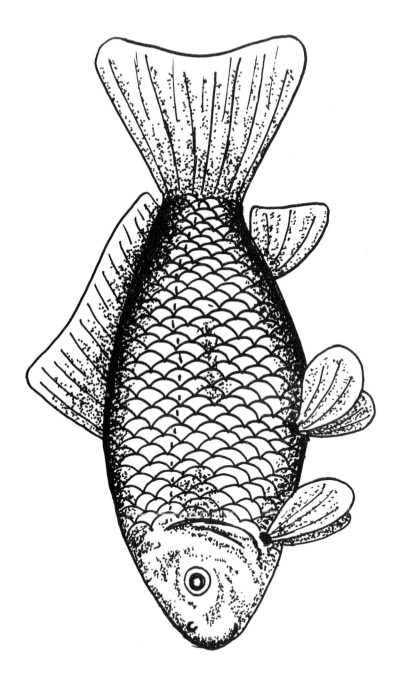

Figure 6.1 *Common Goldfish*

Plate 4   Further Fish Ponds
Top: Sunken Pond
Bottom: Natural Pond

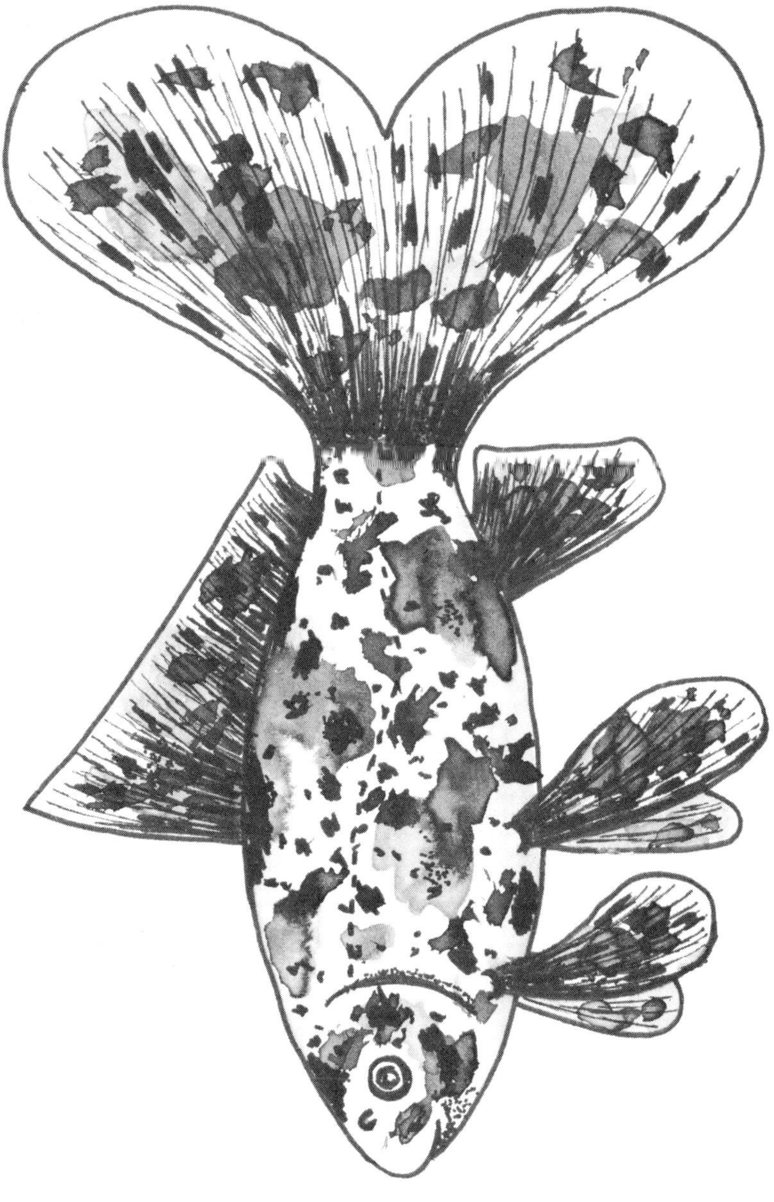

Figure 6.2 *Bristol Shubunkin*

With a similar body shape to the Common Goldfish and short fins, it has a double caudal fin. Although not as common as the metallic type, there is also a nacreous form.

Jikin. The Peacock Tail. (Metallic group). A very old variety developed from the Wakin. Apart from the caudal fin, the fins and body are the same as the Wakin, although slightly compressed vertically and somewhat thicker in the region of the belly. The best specimens have a silver body with red lips and fins — but perfect placement of the red is very rare. The distinguishing feature of this fish is the caudal fin. Seen from behind it is 'X' shaped, and the peduncle is broad. The axis of the caudal fin is almost perpendicular to the axis of the body. Only a very small percentage of the young fish are likely to resemble the parents — even from the oldest of strains.

Ryukin (Metallic group). Japan's second most popular variety. In this fish is seen the first real deviation towards the short, deep-bodied types. The body is short, deepish and moderately compressed often with a pronounced hump at the junction with the head. The fins are longer than those of the Wakin, the caudal is forked and divided into two fins, the anal fins are also paired. The Ryukin is popular with professional fish breeders because of its hardiness and ease of management, and the high percentage of good progeny which it produces. Suitable for pond or aquarium.

Fantail (Metallic and Nacreous groups). The Western version of the Ryukin. It is found in both normal and telescope-eyed form. The Fantail can best be described as an egg-shaped fish; it is not so deep bodied as the Ryukin and should have no trace of a hump to its back. The dorsal fin rises from the high point of the back to a height of about one-third of the body length. The pectoral, pelvic and double anal fins are short and paddle shaped. The caudal fin is of medium length, moderately forked, the twin fins should be carried stiffly without drooping.

The English aquarist, Mr. Arthur Boarder, developed an excellent strain of metallic Fantails which has greatly influenced the modern British variety. Suitable for aquarium or pond.

Demekin. Telescope-eyed fish (Metallic and Nacreous groups). 'Kuro Demekin' is a velvety black due to an excess of melanic pigment. Some tend to turn red with age. 'Aka Demekin' is the red metallic type. 'Sanshoko Demekin' is the nacreous form. The eyes protrude greatly from the head. The body shape and finnage is very similar to the Ryukin.

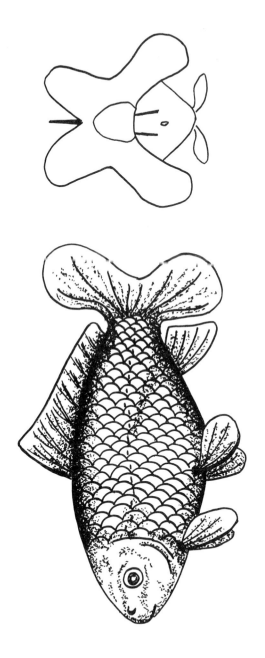

Figure 6.3 *Jikin*

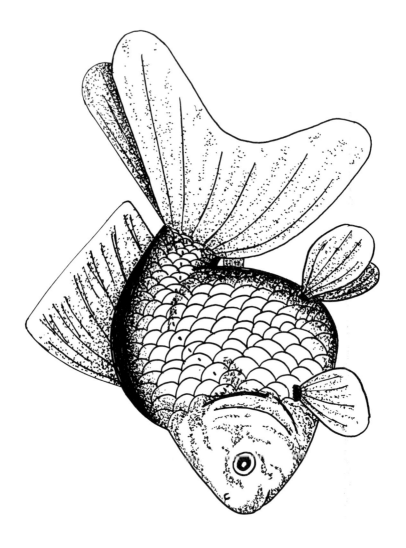

Figure 6.4 *Ryukin*

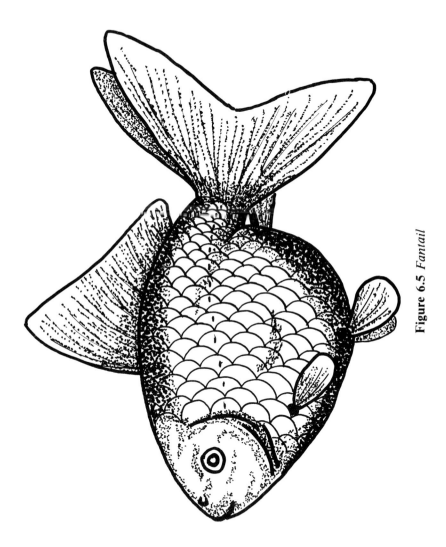

Figure 6.5 *Fantail*

Tosakin (Metallic group). Probably a sport from the Ryukin, which it resembles. The main differences are a slightly shallower body and shorter fins together with a peculiarity of the caudal fin. The lower lobes of the caudal fin are greatly extended with up-turned outer edges, the fin has the appearance of being reversed and spread out in the direction of the head.

This variety is raised in Kochi City and its environs, where they are kept in very shallow water. Due to the difficulty these fish have in swimming they are unable to spawn naturally, and must therefore be stripped by hand. Suitable for the aquarium only.

Comet (Metallic group). A slimmer fish than the Bristol Shubunkin, it has similar finnage except that the caudal fin is as long as the body, and very deeply forked. Yellow is the most usual colour; however, a deep reddish-orange is preferred. Suitable for aquarium or pond, but probably happiest in the latter environment where it can exercise its occasional turn of speed.

Veiltail (Metallic and Nacreous groups). There are both normal and telescope-eyed forms of this variety. The ideal fish has a deep round body, the depth being greater than half the body length. The height of the dorsal fin should be equal to the body depth and commence on the highest point of the back. The caudal fin is long and broad, falling in graceful folds, with a square cut lower edge. The fin is fully divided to form two matching fins. The anal fins are also long and paired. The remaining fins are equally well developed. As the flowing length of the fins makes them susceptible to damage, this fish is best kept in an aquarium to lessen the chance of the fins being torn — and where its grace can be fully appreciated.

Moor (Metallic group). A telescope-eyed variety, the colour is a velvety black extending to the tips of the fins. The body and finnage is identical to the Veiltail in all respects.

These Veiltail varieties have been cultivated to a high state of development by British aquarists, who consider them the height of goldfish perfection.

Oranda (Metallic group). In all respects similar to the red metallic Veiltail, except for the distinguishing feature of the head growth. In Japan this growth is known as the 'wen', Western aquarists refer to it as the 'hood'. The head is broad and short and covered by a warty growth of small, round blister-like excrescenses giving a raspberry-like appearance to the head. This abnormal cuticular growth develops

114

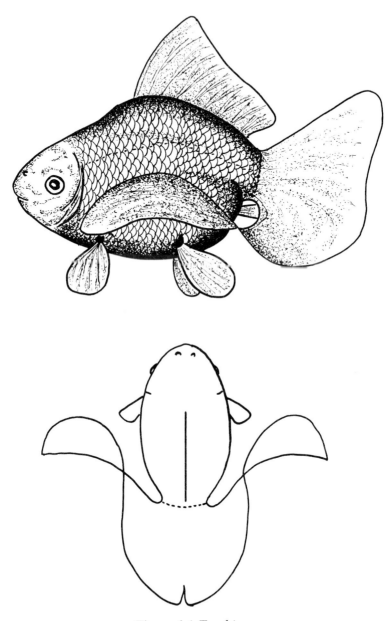

Figure 6.6 *Tosakin*

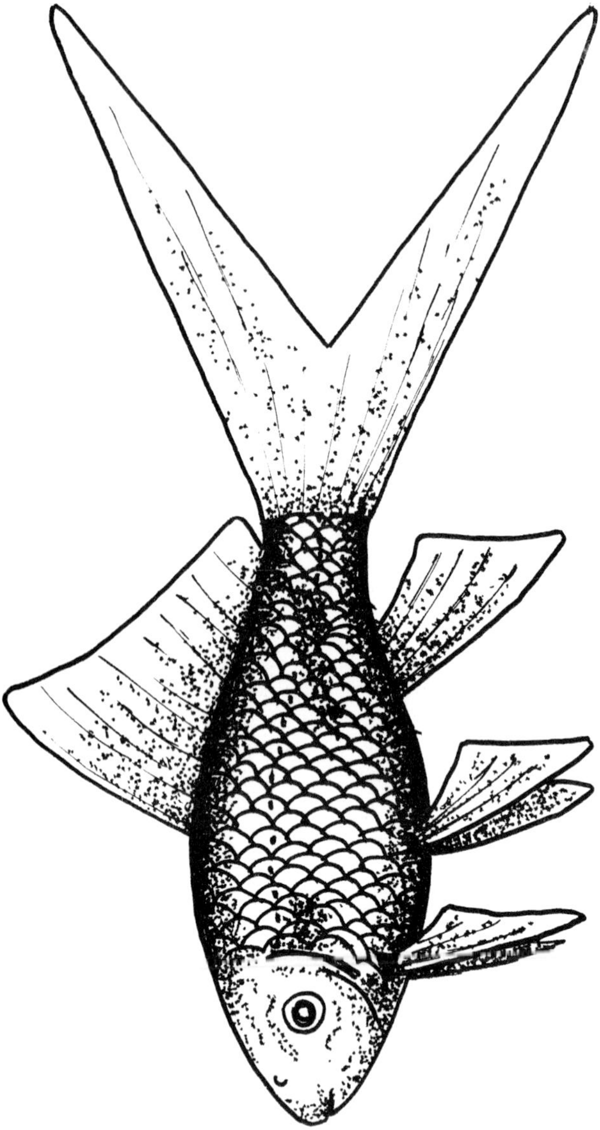

Figure 6.7 *Comet*

Figure 6.8 *Veiltail (Nacreous)*

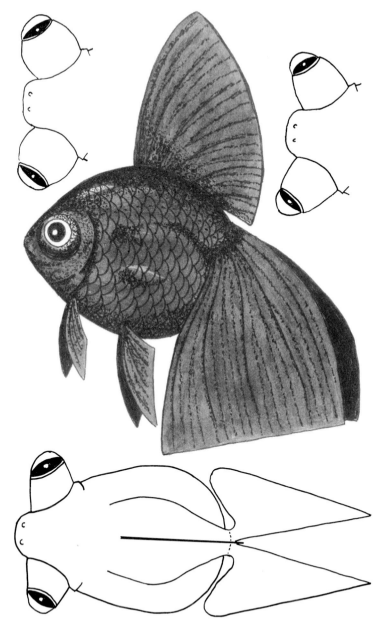

Figure 6.9 *Moor*

in three areas: the cranial, infraorbital and operculate. The hood should ideally grow equally in all sections, leaving only the eyes and mouth exposed, however, in this variety the greatest hood development is usually in the cranial region.

Azumanishiki (Nacreous group). Identical to the Oranda except for its colours. This, and the previous variety, are best kept in the aquarium, although they could spend a warm summer in the pond.

Redcap Oranda and Redcap Lionhead. (Metallic group). These are simply colour variations of their particular variety. The body is silver and the hood, which is restricted to the top of the head, is red — hence the name. Suitable for pond or aquarium.

Lionhead (Metallic group). The Japanese know this variety as the Ranchu, and consider it to be the 'King of Goldfish'. They have a number of societies devoted to its cultivation. National shows of Ranchu are held each year, on a rotating basis, in Tokyo, Nagoya, Kyoto and Osaka, each attracting around 3000 entries. The foundation of the modern type of Ranchu began in the 1800s, when Ishikawa, of Ōji Ward, developed a fish with a 'helmet', a pronounced high curve to its back, and a partially divided caudal fin. In 1885 he formed a society of breeders, it was called Kangyo kai and is still in existence. At the present time 80 per cent of Japanese Ranchu have Ishikawa characteristics, although there are four distinct lines, each having distinctive differences. Named after their creators, they are Ishikawa, Takahashi, Uno and Sakuri.

Before considering the type of Lionhead preferred by most Western goldfish keepers, the types that exist in Japan are described:

RANCHU (Metallic group). The type preferred by the modern Japanese enthusiasts. It has a short, rather deep, roundish body that is broad across the back. The dorsal curve is arched quite high, descending to the peduncle — in many specimens the peduncle makes a sudden downward curve (which I term 'cur-backed'). There is no dorsal fin. The fins are short, and the anal fins paired. The caudal is double, but not always fully divided, and carried very high. In the best specimens the upper edge of the caudal fin should form a ninety degree angle to the curve of the peduncle.

The shape of the hood (or wen) varies depending upon the particular line. A fish which has most development in the cranial region is known as 'hooded', if the growth is more pronounced

119

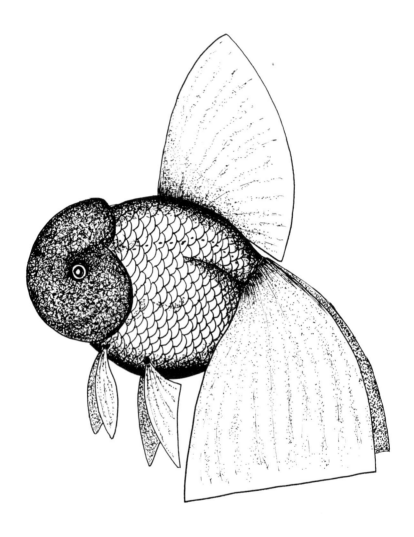

Figure 6.10 *Oranda*

around the sub-orbital area it is called 'Okame' — so named after a comic theatrical mask representing a fat girl. Where there is equal development in all areas it is known as the 'Lionhead'. Suitable for the pond during summer months, it does well in the indoor aquarium.

OSAKA RANCHU. This variety has no head growth, the head being small and pointed. The body is very rotund and broad. The caudal fin is short, double and joined along the upper margin. Spread well out, it gives a fan-like appearance from above. It has lost its popularity and, although a few are still raised, it is slowly dying out. Suitable for aquariums and ponds.

NANKIN RANCHU. Very similar to the progenitors of the Ranchu lines, it is raised mainly in the Shimane district of Japan. The body is a little long, the head is pointed without any head growth. It has a distinctive colour pattern — silver body and head, the tip of the mouth is red, and the gill covers and fins are also red.

LIONHEAD (Metallic group). Although the Western type of Lionhead is similar to the Japanese Ranchu, there are some definite differences. The hood must be well formed in all regions. The back is only moderately curved, with no sign of 'cur-back' to the peduncle, the dorsal curve should follow a smooth line from the hood to the start of the caudal fin. The body should be deepish and broad across the back, leading to a very short strong peduncle. The divided caudal fin is of medium size and moderately forked, carried stiffly; it is not so steeply inclined as that of the Japanese Ranchu. Pelvic and pectoral fins are short and paddle-like. The ventral curve should be very similar to the dorsal curve. Western enthusiasts consider joined anal fins and webbed caudal fins to be signs of regression, and very bad faults. Suitable for aquarium or pond.

EDONISHIKI (Nacreous group). Apart from colours, this fish is identical to the Ranchu, but does not have such a good head growth. Some English aquarists are attempting to improve the hood of this variety. Keep in an aquarium, or a pond in warmer months.

Chinese Lionheads. Usually have very large fully developed hoods, but tend to be longer in both body and finnage than the types raised in Japan and Western countries. Pond or aquarium.

121

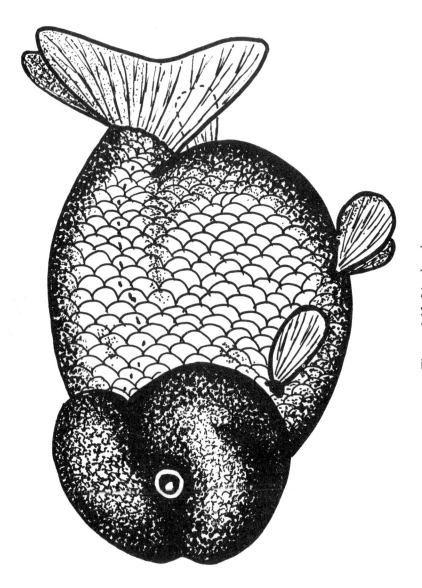

Figure 6.11 *Lionhead*

Phoenix (Nacreous group). This, like the following varieties, originates from China. The body is midway between the Common Goldfish and the Ranchu, it also lacks a dorsal fin. The fins are very long, the anals being paired and the double caudal fin very deeply forked to give a 'Ribbon-tail'. Suitable for the aquarium.

Pearlscale (Metallic group). Usually silver with large patches of red — the nacreous form is not often seen. The body is very fat, almost dropsical in appearance, with a deep belly and flatish back. The head is small and pointed with a small mouth. The fins are very similar to those of the Fantail, however, the divided caudal fin is nowhere near so deeply forked, being somewhat shallow. The main feature of this variety are the scales, which are 'domed'. With raised centres, the outer margin of the scales are slightly darker than the inner part. The scales lie in even rows along the body and give a distinct 'pearl-like' effect as they reflect the light. A hardy fish, but best seen in the aquarium where their bright colouration and unusual scale formation can be easily seen.

Pompon (Metallic and Nacreous groups). In body and finnage this fish resembles the Lionhead somewhat, however, the head is normal. There appears to be two types of this variety: one form has the full complement of fins, whereas the other lacks a dorsal fin — British aquarists prefer the latter type. The fish derives its name from the fact that the narial septa — the tissue which divides each of the two nostrils — are abnormally enlarged into bundles of fleshy lobes, known as narial bouquets. These float in front of the eyes and may be so grotesquely developed that they are continuously sucked into and expelled from the mouth of the fish — a most bizzare sight. Probably best suited to the aquarium although hardly enough for the pond.

Celestial (Metallic and Nacreous groups). A longish bodied fish with similar finnage to the Ryukin. In this variety the telescope-eyes turn upwards, so that they gaze heavenwards — hence the name. Various stories exist about how this variety originated, but it is a matter of opinion whether any of them are to be believed. Due to the position of the eyes the fish does suffer from a handicap when competing for food, and is at a distinct disadvantage when trying to catch live food. Should only be kept in an aquarium with fish of its own kind.

Toadhead (Metallic group). A very similar fish to the Celestial. The eyes are normal, but below them is a small bladder-like growth which gives the face a somewhat toad-like aspect.

Bubble-eye (Metallic group). Again a fish that is similar to the

Figure 6.12 *Phoenix (nacreous)*

124

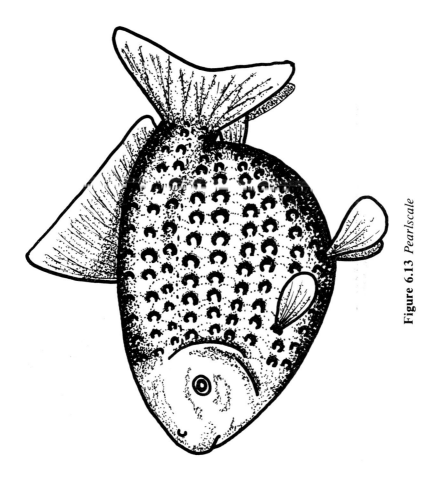

Figure 6.13 *Pearlscale*

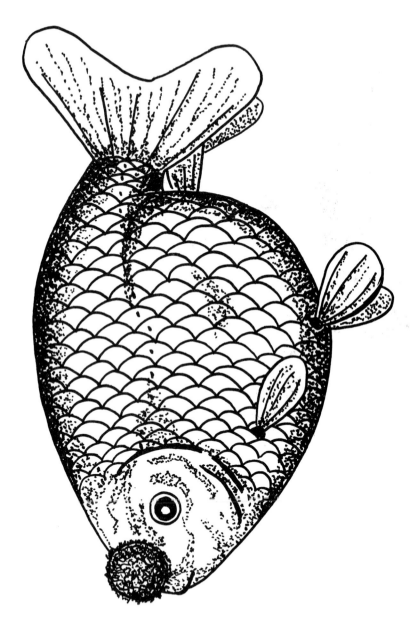

Figure 6.14 *Pompon*

Celestial. Below the normal eyes are very large fluid-filled bladders, so that it appears vaguely 'telescope-eyed'. However, whereas the telescope-eye is firm, the bladders on the Bubble-eye are soft like water-filled balloons. As the fish swims the bladders move in a most grotesque fashion.

Like the Celestial, this variety is best kept in an aquarium with its own kind. The bladders are liable to damage, therefore there should be no sharp object that could possibly cause a puncture.

Meteor (Metallic group). A strange egg-shaped fish which has no caudal fin. The lack of a caudal fin is compensated by the over-development of the other fins — especially the pectoral and anal fins.

Other varieties. It has been estimated that there are more than one hundred different varieties of fancy goldfish — those which I have described being but a few. Many may never be seen outside their homeland, others may be too grotesque to find acceptance by Western aquarists.

Many of the best varieties have been, are, and no doubt will continue to be, produced by amateur goldfish breeders. This applies in Japan, and also in England. Both have recognised centres of enthusiasts who cultivate the goldfish, and both have produced goldfish breeders whose names have become linked with certain varieties.

As in Japan, England has recognised centres of goldfish cultivation. Fancy varieties are produced in the Birmingham area, London, Bristol and Lancashire; and in each area there are strong societies devoted to the goldfish.

It should perhaps be mentioned that the nacreous group of goldfish are often referred to as 'calico'. Whereas the term 'nacreous' refers to the mother-of-pearl shine. 'calico' refers to the multitude of colours that can be exhibited by the fish.

Although many of the foregoing varieties of goldfish have been described as suitable for keeping in a pond, discretion should be used. The further a fish diverges from the original form the greater the protection it needs. Obviously the prevailing conditions and temperatures must be taken into consideration when deciding whether it is safe to keep a particular type of goldfish in an open garden pond. The single-tail varieties are usually hardy enough to withstand quite a wide range of water temperature; however, the twintail varieties may well suffer in low water temperatures — it is all a matter of common-sense and consideration for the well being of the fish. There is little point in keeping

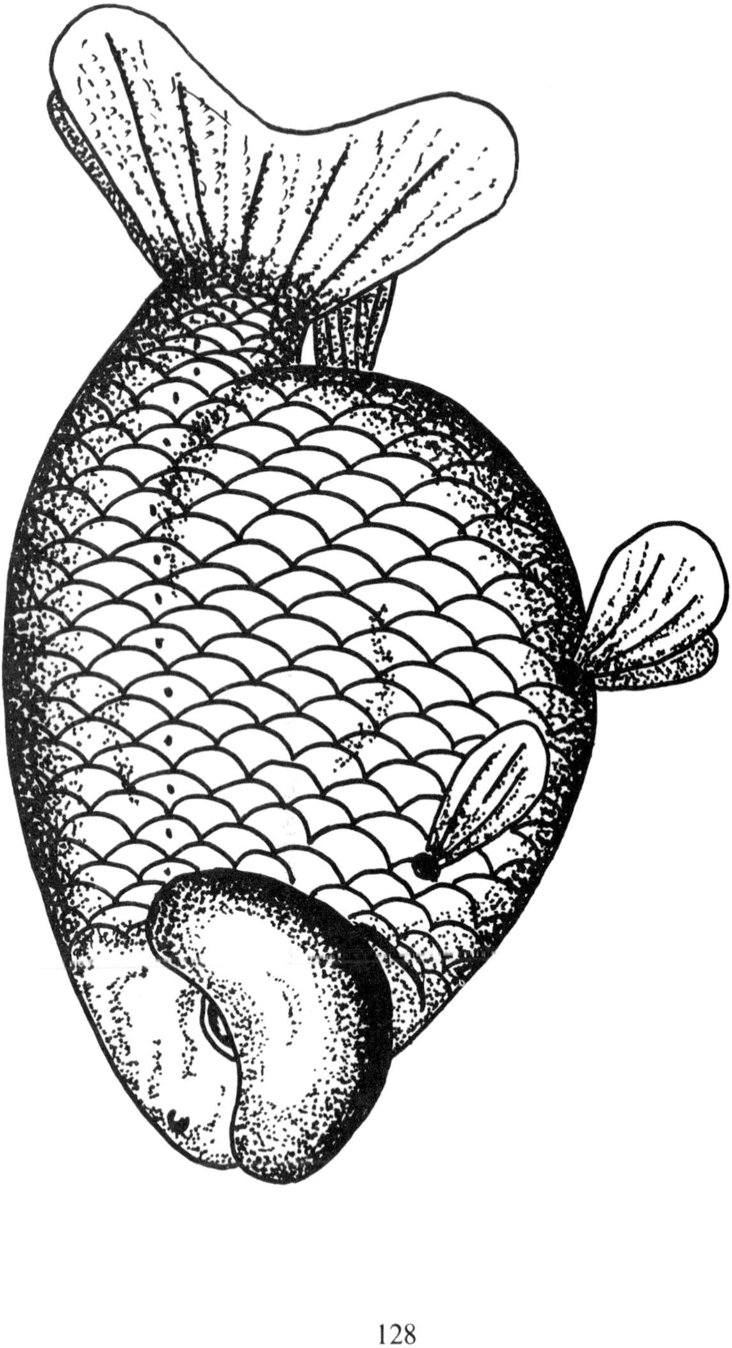

Figure 6.15 *Bubble-Eye*

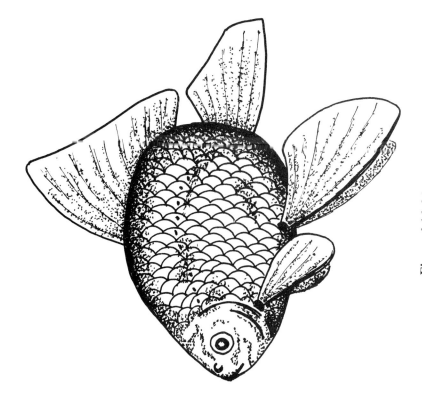

Figure 6.16 *Meteor*

the more exotic goldfish in anything other than an aquarium. To do otherwise would prevent its true beauty being seen to the best advantage — and why else would they be kept if not to admire them?

CHAPTER 7

Selection and Transport

In the chapter dealing with the various types of goldfish many fancy varieties were described, but not all are yet available to the Western aquarist. Of the number that are available it will be found, in practice, that there are normally only a limited number of varieties from which to choose. Although the Common Goldfish is plentiful and comparatively inexpensive, the more fancy types are not so numerous. The more exotic varieties are not, as a general rule, available from the usual pet dealers, and must be obtained from an amateur specialist breeder of the variety. Prices are not cheap, in fact the more fancy varieties can be very expensive indeed. It has been said that the exotic goldfish is 'worth its weight in gold'.

Almost invariably the newcomer to the hobby will obtain fish from a local pet-shop or the larger departmental store and these sources will, almost without exception, offer imported stock. Many of the fish are raised in America, Italy, Hong Kong, Japan and Singapore by professional fish-farmers and tend to be of the less fancy types.

FROM EXPORTER TO IMPORTER

At one time exporting fish was a very complicated business, involving many weeks of travel as ship's cargo. Constant care and attention were necessary, involving water changes and occasional feeding, even so the losses were considerable. Obviously the importers had to charge high prices for the surviving fish in order to cover the losses and still show a profit. Nowadays fish can be sent by fast jet-plane to most parts of the world and will arrive at their destination within a comparatively short time.

Although the advent of air transport has reduced the time the fish spend in transit, it is still a very expensive business, with high freight charges and various taxes. In an effort to keep shipping costs as low as possible, the fish are placed into plastic bags with a bare minimum of water, just sufficient to enable the fish to survive. The number of fish packed in this way is greatly increased by the use of tranquilizers, which reduce the rate of breathing and also help to prevent them fouling the water too quickly. In order to lessen still further the possibility of the fish polluting the small amount of water in which they are transported they are starved for several days prior to their journey. The bags are then filled to capacity with oxygen before being sealed, and packed into lightweight corrugated cardboard or polystyrene containers.

Improved methods of transport have not, however, simplified the problems involved in exporting fish. The high density in which the fish are packed means that transit times must be carefully calculated, because a few hours' delay anywhere along the route could result in the whole consignment being killed. In addition, the importer must be informed of the exact time of arrival at the destination, so that prompt collection can be arranged. Even after arrival the fish must be handled with great care, for they will be in a 'shocked' state and suffering from stress. Lack of food, changes in temperature and air-pressure, plus handling and other factors, will all have served to weaken the fish. Inexperienced people can easily injure or even kill the fish by wrong treatment in untrained hands after reaching the importer. It will be realised, therefore, that the exportation and importation of fancy goldfish is still a fairly difficult and risky undertaking.

Although some importers quarantine the new arrivals for a short time, most do not. The importer is in the business to make a profit, therefore, within a few hours of arrival the fish are again in transit to the retailer. At that stage the fish has reached a very debilitated state and is in need of rest and food to aid its recovery. Unfortunately few receive such treatment, thus many die within a short time of being sold to the private individual.

OTHER SOURCES

A council of perfection is to advise the would-be buyer to purchase home-bred fish from an amateur goldfish breeder. Of course the novice may not even be aware that such people exist; nevertheless, it would be very worthwhile to make some enquiries — perhaps from a local aquarists society — in an effort to trace one. Once contact is made you will be able to ascertain from the breeder the names and locations of other goldfish breeders. There is no doubt that fish purchased from such a source stand a much better chance of surviving. The fish will suffer far less transit stress, will be well fed and usually healthy — no amateur goldfish breeder would risk disease infecting his or her stock and most subject their fish to periodic disinfectant baths as a precaution. The fish, whether young or adult, will be expensive because they will more than likely be from an established strain of far superior quality to anything that could be purchased from a trader — and raising decent fancy goldfish is an expensive hobby.

At times advertisements are seen offering goldfish for sale. **Beware, unless they can be seen before buying.** To say the very least, the vendor is unable to know exactly what you want, and yet the very fish may be there. At the worst, you could receive very inferior, stunted, mongrel, diseased fish doomed to an early death. If the fish must be purchased unseen, from some distance away, be sure to give the vendor a very good description of the type of fish you hope to acquire, stress the times that you could arrange to collect the fish from the nearest delivery point, and state where it is. Remember that you will be expected to pay all carriage charges, and that the vendor will not accept any responsibility for the safe or live arrival of the fish. Often the advertiser is genuine and will supply healthy fish as near to your requirements as possible, nevertheless there is always a risk involved.

IN GENERAL

Although most pet dealers, nowadays, put the fish into a plastic bag in which the buyer can carry it home, there is always the possibility of an accident. From whatever source the fish are to be obtained, be it pet-shop, departmental store, or amateur breeder, it pays to take your own container. Probably the safest container is a bucket with a lid — such plastic buckets are available from a number of sources — the lid will prevent any water splashing out during the journey home. It is not necessary to have holes in the lid, as these can be a nuisance, and the bucket should only be filled to between half and three-quarters of its capacity. By this method I have carried fish many miles, safely, to various competitive fish shows in England and Wales, and carried them back again, without harming the fish.

The beginner should not be tempted into buying the very fancy types of goldfish, until experience has been gained by keeping some of the hardier varieties. The loss of a few Common Goldfish is to be regretted, but would not cause any great financial loss. However, to lose, say, half-a-dozen Veiltails would prove a most expensive lesson. Many an inexperienced fishkeeper has spent large sums of money upon fish, which demanded the care of the knowledgeable, only to suffer the disaster of seeing the fish die. The sensible novice will commence fishkeeping with the more easily managed varieties of goldfish. From these the instincts and skills will be learned that are necessary for the successful maintenance of the more delicate and fancy varieties.

Need the reader be reminded that no fish should be acquired unless the aquarium, or pond, has first been made ready for them? Nor should any fish be added to existing stock until it has been proved healthy; no matter how healthy a fish may appear, it could be carrying a latent disease which could break out and infect the healthy stock. Many are the fishkeepers who have had cause to regret their failure to isolate new fish in quarantine for a precautionary period. Although it should be obvious, disease can be transmitted from a sick fish to healthy fish and by nets and other equipment. Common sense dictates that all equipment reserved for the quarantine fish should be kept well away from the healthy stock. Disinfecting everything, and washing the hands after dealing with sick or suspect fish, before attending to the healthy fish, is a simple and sensible precaution — but one that is often overlooked by the novice.

SELECTING HEALTHY FISH

Care and attention should be given to the selection of any fish that is to be purchased. Careful observation and a sharp eye can help to reduce, to a degree, the risk of buying a sick or ailing fish. If there is the slightest doubt, it is much the safest policy to resist any temptation, and seek another vendor who has healthy stock for sale. Patience and discretion will pay dividends by lessening the risk of buying a 'pig-in-the-poke' and wasting your money. Much can be learned from the first impressions when entering a dealer's premises. The attitude of the vendor, and the cleanliness of the premises and tanks, will clearly indicate whether to consider the fish — or beat a hasty retreat.

A close inspection of the tanks will reveal whether the dealer is concerned for the welfare of the stock. The tanks should be spacious and clean, without undue overcrowding of the fish. The fish should appear active, not sulking, with no dead fish in evidence. If all seems well, greater attention can be paid to the condition of the fish. They should be swimming actively without any difficulty or jerkiness. The eyes should be clear and bright with no trace of a cloudy, whiteish film. The fins held erect and well spread should be free of any milkiness or blood streaks. The body must appear to be well nourished and have no sign of injury or disease.

A wasted body that makes the head appear too large; dull cloudy eyes, or eyes covered by a whiteish film; split or torn raggedy fins; blood spots or streaks upon the body or fins; a greyish-white bloom or film that partially obscures the colour on any part of the body or head; scales that seem to be raised instead of lying flat. Any traces of small white 'cotton-wool' tufts of fungus, any minute white spot, pimples, ulcers, or holes, and apparent pieces of 'thread' anywhere on the fish. These are all positive signs of future trouble and such fish must be avoided — together with any seemingly healthy fish that occupy the same tank. Be cautious at all times, especially when considering imported stock; be safe rather than sorry — far better to swallow your eagerness and go away empty-handed to try elsewhere.

Before setting out to purchase the chosen type of goldfish, firmly set into your mind the main features and shape of the particular variety. If purchasing fish in the nacreous group always remember that the pinky-white and red coloured fish is not considered of any value; often as the fish ages its colours will tend to get lighter — for this reason many fish-keepers prefer the darker coloured types of nacreous fish. The old tale that recommends crossing a red metallic fish with a blue nacreous is bad advice: in practice the majority of the progeny will exhibit large areas of red or yellow, the desired blue is unlikely to be obtained in any of the young. This should be borne in mind if selecting fish with the idea of a future spawning from them. Two nacreous fish bred together are more likely to give a better result in the colours of the offspring.

AMATEUR GOLDFISH BREEDERS

As already mentioned, quality fish are best bought from an amateur goldfish breeder, especially one who specialises in a particular variety

135

and has built up a good reputation amongst fellow fishkeepers. Prices will, almost invariably, be higher than those asked by a commercial dealer — but the quality usually surpasses the imported types and, of course, they are acclimatised to conditions similar to those which the purchaser will provide, both in quality of water and temperature. Prices will also vary according to the variety, age, size and standard of the fish. Quite obviously a full grown adult of 'show standard' quality will cost considerably more than a young fish of the same variety. Do not make the mistake of expecting to be able to buy the best specimens — the breeder will not part with them, for they are required for continued improvement of the strain. However, if the strain is well established, the fish which are offered can produce young fish that are as good as the breeder's best. It must be remembered that, in buying stock from a recognised breeder of fancy goldfish, many years will have been spent in creating the strain by continuous selective breeding, and the potential to produce first class progeny will be carried in the fish, even if not up to standard themselves. On the other hand, imported fish will be of unknown parentage and may produce only worthless rubbish. To establish a good line of fish from such stock will take many years of hard and dedicated work — not to be lightly undertaken by the novice. When the benefit of another's hard work can be reaped by buying fish of known parentage, it hardly seems worth the effort of trying to breed quality fish from unknown imported stock. Therefore the higher cost of home-bred fish can be well warranted, and there are obvious advantages in seeking out an amateur goldfish breeder.

Having located a breeder of goldfish, contact should be made, by letter or telephone, to ascertain what varieties, if any, are available, the ages and size of the fish and, of course, the prices required. It is then advisable, before paying a visit, to confirm a convenient date and time to view the available stock. Most amateur goldfish keepers are interested in the welfare of the goldfish, and will readily answer any questions that the novice may have. A visit to any amateur goldfish breeding establishment can prove most interesting and informative. The newcomer to the hobby may well be surprised at the warm welcome, for the average enthusiast always hopes that the beginner will take up the hobby seriously and help to swell the tanks of the goldfish keeping fraternity.

Having memorised the requirements for adult fish it should not be too difficult to assess any fully grown fish that may be offered. However, the selection of young stock is not so simple. The characteristics take some time to develop — possibly two or three years for some varieties — therefore a young, small, longfinned Veiltail, for instance, may look very attractive but is more likely a runt that is doomed to an early death. Even if it survives, it will be a grossly over-finnaged, under-sized fish of little, if any, value. When choosing young fish it should be borne in mind that the fins of many of the longer finned varieties will continue to grow long after the body has reached maturity. However, there are points to look for in the immature fish, and the following will give the novice some guidance.

Metallic Group Fish should, ideally, have changed colour from the wild olive by the age of twelve months, preferably they should have changed much earlier.

Nacreous Group Fish should be showing their colours, avoid the pinky-whites, although it can be up to three years before the final colours show.

Bristol Shubunkin should have a well-formed caudal fin in keeping with the body length but not over-large.

Fantail types. The anal and caudal fins should be divided. None of the fins should be too greatly developed for the age of the fish.

Veiltail types. Both the anal and caudal fins should be divided. The caudal fin in the young fish is short; however, the trailing edge should be as 'square-cut' as possible. The pelvic and anal fins longer than for the Fantail and somewhat pointed, whereas the fins of the Fantail are rounder and 'paddle-shaped'. A young Veiltail should have a deep, short, chunky body.

Dorsal fin-less types. A nice clean dorsal contour is required. The back must have no sign of hollows, bumps or spikes to mar its smooth appearance, nor should there be any 'cur-back' fall to the tail.

Hooded types. It normally takes some time for the hoods to develop on these varieties; however, the head of a young fish should be short, broad and blunt. A close inspection may well reveal a slight roughness on the top of the head as evidence that the hood is starting to form.

Telescope-eyed types should have developed this feature by the time they are ready for sale.

Moors, which belong to the metallic group, should have assumed the black coloration — if they appear to be 'brassy' they are better left alone.

In general, no matter what variety of fancy goldfish is being purchased, the immature fish should have evidence that it has the required potential to develop the necessary characteristics. Pay careful attention to the fins of the young Fantail types: if they appear pointed and slightly over-developed the likelihood is that they are 'throw-out' Veiltails and not true Fantail stock. The eyes of the normal-eyed varieties should be normal. If they seem large and slightly bulbous the chances are that they are inferior telescope-eyed young, or the result of crossing a normal-eyed fish to one with telescope-eyes. The serious goldfish hobbyist considers such crossbred fish to be 'mongrels' and of little value. They are worthless for future breeding purposes and will do no good on the show bench; an experienced judge will immediately recognise them for what they are.

The quality of the breeder's stock can be assessed by a close study of the adult fish. This will also serve as a rough guide to the future potential of the young, although the fact that the adults are excellent fish of their type is no guarantee that their offspring will be of equal quality. The final decision must always be based upon the quality of the young which are being considered, but nevertheless, the adults should be proof of the likely potential of their progeny.

It is exceedingly difficult, if not impossible, to tell the sex of immature goldfish and, while the experienced breeder may be able to make an educated guess, no guarantee would be given that a particular young fish was either male or female. If buying young fish of unsexable age, and fish of both sexes are required, a minimum of six fish should, by the 'law of averages', ensure the presence of each sex. The better method, although very much more expensive, would be to obtain an adult breeding pair of the desired variety.

Always remember that once fish have been purchased and taken from the seller's premises, whether amateur or commercial, the responsibility for the fish, and their well-being, is that of the purchaser. The vendor should not be asked, or even expected, to replace any fish that may be lost. The purchaser should, for this reason, make sure, as far as possible, that the fish are healthy and have no obvious physical disability. If, for instance, a fish seems to have difficulty in maintaining its balance, or has any trouble in rising from the bottom of the tank, it is reasonable to assume that it is suffering from a problem of the air-bladder. If the fish is seen to make sudden wild dashes through the water, and rub itself against the inside of the tank or any other firm object, the chances are that it has an infestation of flukes — or some other parasite — and may have become very weakened. Such fish are better left unpurchased. The sensible fishkeeper will not allow the attraction of a fish to over-ride good judgement and discretion. Note the temperature of the water in which the fish are kept. Adult fancy goldfish should not require any form of artificial warmth. Too often the mistake is made of treating them like tropical fish; they should be quite capable of surviving in the normal temperatures of unheated water. Young fish, on the other hand, are usually kept warm for the first few months of their lives to promote growth.

TREATMENT OF NEWLY-ACQUIRED FISH

Before setting out to obtain any fish, a small aquarium, or some other container, can be partially filled with water and set on one side to await the newly-acquired fish.

Having chosen the fish, fill the carrying bucket about half full with some of the water from the tank in which it has been living, and gently place the fish into it. Having made payment and said your 'goodbyes', transport the fish home as quickly as possible to avoid it depleting the oxygen in the water, although it may well take a considerable time before the fish suffers any ill-effects. It is possible to buy small battery-operated air-pumps, which would be very useful if the journey was likely to be excessively long. Aeration could be supplied to the water for a short spell every hour or so, allowing safe carriage of the fish for many hours — possibly days — without the fish suffering from lack of oxygen. Food is not necessary; a healthy goldfish can go without food for a number of days if need be, and feeding would only cause possible fouling of the water.

Upon arriving home the bucket should have the lid removed, and then be placed near the previously prepared container for an hour or two, to allow the temperatures to equalise. After sufficient time has elapsed, some of the water from the bucket can be poured into the container. Ideally, the mixture of the waters should be very approximately fifty per cent of each. This is to give the fish as little shock as possible if the characters of the waters are very different. The fish can then be very gently placed into the receiving tank, where it should be left for around twenty-eight days. During this period partial changes of water should be made to help the fish adjust to the new water conditions, always making sure that there is no great variation in the water temperatures. Throughout this period of acclimatisation a careful watch must be kept for any sign of disease, or other malady, and appropriate action taken should any symptoms appear. Two weeks is usually long enough for any dormant disease to break out, if the fish has the misfortune to be carrying any. While the fish is in the holding tank, it is a wise precaution to give it one or two disinfectant baths against flukes, with a final bath prior to being placed into its permanent home.

During the isolation period, the fish should be fed sparingly, commencing with very small feeds and gradually increasing the amounts offered. Normally fish purchased from a commercial source have been fed very frugally and are somewhat starved. Heavy feeding after a prolonged fast is exceedingly bad for the fish — as it is for most creatures. The strength and appetite of the fish must be built up slowly by offering good nourishing types of foods, a little at a time. There may be times when a newly acquired fish is so starved, or perhaps suffering from severe stress, that it may show no inclination to accept dried foods. In that case gently aerate the water and offer a little live food, such as daphnia. This may well revive the fish's interest — for most fish are attracted to moving food. Additionally, such a fish should be kept quiet and interfered with as little as possible until it has recovered and commenced to feed normally.

If, at the end of the fourteen days quarantine period, the fish has proved itself healthy, it may be placed into its new quarters, be it aquarium or pond. The same admonishment with regard to water temperatures must be observed, and the risk of chilling the fish avoided. The easiest method of making the transfer is to place the fish and its water into a bucket which can then be floated in the water of the new home until the temperatures have equalised. If the container is then gently tipped onto its side the fish will swim out. On no account should fish ever be tipped or thrown into the water; such action is uncaring and will shock the fish. It could result in the loss of the fish, or at least cause the fish to develop air-bladder trouble, so that the poor fish can

140

Plate 5
Top: Nacreous Veiltail
Bottom: Celestial

no longer swim properly. Always treat the fish with care and consideration, because only the foolish invite trouble.

Although not given to bullying, the goldfish is an extremely inquisitive creature, and a new fish introduced into an aquarium or pond which already has a population of fish is, for a time, likely to be chevied around. There is very little that can be done to prevent this, although many fishkeepers believe that, if a new fish is introduced during the hours of darkness, the newcomer will be ignored. Others prefer to make the transfer shortly after feeding the fish: possibly a full stomach may make the fish lazy and so have no interest in any new resident. It is, of course, preferable to try to ensure that any new acqustion is of a similar size to any other fish with which it may have to live.

There can be little doubt about the best time of the year to buy fish. Spring means that the warmer weather lies ahead, and the warm months encourage fish to develop a greater appetite and thus put on growth. Knowing the advantages of the warmer conditions, the sensible aquarist will arrange to acquire any new stock during the time. As a rule young fish are not available until the late spring and early summer, at the earliest, and this is another factor to be considered. Autumn is not a good time: the cold months of winter lie ahead. During the time of low temperatures live food will virtually disappear and the fish in the pond will become dormant and cease to feed. It is therefore quite evident that autumn will not provide the ideal conditions for a newly-acquired fish to settle down and become acclimatized. Fish which are purchased at the latter end of the year are not so likely to succeed, or make the same progress, as fish bought during the spring. Whereas a weakened fish will have every chance of recovery, if looked after, during the warmer months of the year, the same fish may well succumb during the rigours of the colder months.

Little more can be said, nor further advice or caution offered. At the end of the day it is the common-sense, discretion, care and observation by the purchaser that will decide the health and quality of any newly acquired stock.

CHAPTER 8

Foods and Feeding

The goldfish is omnivorous, and there is little in the way of food that will not be eaten. Live foods, fresh, frozen or dried animal and vegetable matter will be readily accepted: indeed, the diet should be as varied as possible. No matter how good a food may be, it is a mistake not to offer alternatives (even we humans would find that a surfeit of prime steak would quickly dull the appetite, and the goldfish is no exception). In the spring and summer there is never any shortage of live foods. During autumn and early winter, the household pantry can, with a little experimentation, supply a variety of foods suitable for the goldfish. It may well involve the fishkeeper in a little extra effort to find and supply a varied diet for the fish; but it is well worth going to a little trouble if it results in healthy, alert fish in the peak of condition. Goldfish have lived for years on a diet of commercially prepared dried foods, but their growth and development does not compare with a fish that has had its diet supplemented with live foods of one sort or another.

The goldfish, as do most creatures, requires protein, fat, carbohydrates, minerals and vitamins in its food, combined in the correct proportions, if it is to grow strong and healthy. These essential components are briefly summarised as follows:

Proteins are composed of amino acids, and are the compounds from which the essential tissues are formed. Approximately twenty-one amino acids have been isolated, although not all may be necessary to life. However, those which are, are termed 'essential amino acids'. In the digestive system of the goldfish protein is broken down into amino acids to aid its growth. A good food should contain at least twelve per cent protein*.

---

* This is a simplified version of amino-acid requirements: Readers wishing to study the subject in depth should consult a specialised book.

Carbohydrates. These are the starches and sugars found in the food, and serves as a source of energy, while aiding the utilization of fats. Many of the plants upon which the goldfish browse consist largely of carbohydrates, and have a nutritive value. In the intestine the carbohydrates are converted into simple sugars, and may be absorbed or stored in the liver and other organs. Too much sugar can cause the liver to become enlarged, and this may result in the death of the fish. The minimum carbohydrate content of a good food should not be less than 45 per cent.

Vitamins are just as essential to the goldfish as they are to humans: without them they will suffer from vitamin deficiency. The vitamin requirements will be found in fresh uncooked vegetable matter; however, prepared food must be vitamin enriched. A good food will contain vitamins A, D, E, K, B_1, B_2, B_6, and C. One in particular, carotene or pro-vitamin A, is necessary to the good colouring of the goldfish. It is found in salt-water algae, dark green freshwater algae, egg yolk, and the shell of the pink shrimp. Carrots also contain carotene.

Minerals, such as cobalt, iodine, copper, iron, manganese and zinc, are also essential for the well-being of the goldfish. Some, though necessary, are only required in minute quantities, but, if missing, the organic balance of the fish will be upset. The best commercially prepared foods will contain minerals in the correct amounts. A varied diet, including live foods, will ensure that the fish receives an adequate supply of the necessary minerals.

Fats are another source of energy. In the intestine the fats are converted into fatty acids and glycerides, in which form they are absorbed into the body, any excess being stored by the body as tissues. These fatty tissues are also made up of carbohydrates and protein. The tissues serve as a store for the fat-soluble vitamins A, D, E and K. An excess of fat-producing foods can seriously harm the goldfish, by causing malfunction of the kidneys, and give rise to fatty degeneration of the liver. Foods containing an excessive amount of fat should, therefore, be avoided — 4 per cent is about the right amount.

Foods may be commercially prepared dried foods, home-made foods, frozen foods, various live foods and foods from the household. To list every item of food suitable for the goldfish would make this section unduly long, for, as I have said, there is little that the goldfish will not eat — within reason. A more useful approach will be to confine myself to the better known and more easily obtained foods. The feeding of goldfish fry will be dealt with in Chapter 10.

143

LIVE FOODS

Live foods are regarded by most aquarists as the best form of food, because they are the natural foods that would be eaten in the wild. There is no doubt that fish which are allowed a regular feed of live food, as part of their diet, appear to be more lively than those fed solely upon dried foods.

Earthworm, the beef steak of the fish world, is well recognised as one of the best foods for bringing goldfish into breeding condition. Easily obtained during most seasons of the year, it is readily accepted and acts as a mild laxative.

The red and pink worms, up to about two inches (51 mm) long, are best; larger worms tend to be tough and not so easily digested. The collected worms should first be swilled to remove any soil or slimy mud which may adhere to them. The very small worms can be fed straight to the fish; however, those more than half-an-inch (13 mm) long should be chopped into suitable lengths. Although not a job for the squeamish, this is best done by placing the worms on a piece of glass and then, with two razor blades, cutting them into small segments. It is not necessary to give a further wash, this would only swill away the digested vegetable matter which forms part of this excellent food. It will be seen that the fish will spit out any unwanted matter.

Worms can be brought to the surface by watering an area with two gallons (9 litres) of water in which ½ ounce (14 g) of potassium permanganate has been dissolved. Alternatively, worms can be encouraged to gather in a collecting place, such as under a piece of black polythene sheet or by placing a piece of sacking upon the ground and keeping it damp with used tea leaves. After a time it will be found that quite a number of worms will be available for collection.

Whiteworms (*Enchytraeus albidus*) is an easily cultivated small creamy-white worm which grows to around three-quarters of an inch. Most pet fish stores can usually supply a starter culture. It is a very popular food amongst goldfish enthusiasts because of its ready availability, ease of cultivation, and acceptability by the fish.

To cultivate these useful worms is simplicity itself. Make a lidless wooden box, about twelve inches (305 mm) square and six inches (152 mm) deep, and half fill with a mixture of sterilized loam and peat. The peat should be thoroughly soaked and then squeezed, to remove the excess water. Make a fifty/fifty mixture of the loam and peat and lightly

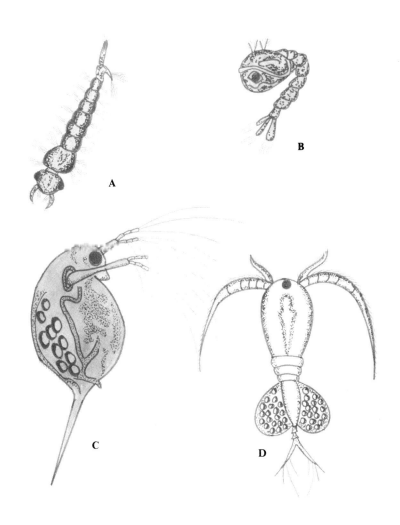

A. Mosquito Larva   B. Mosquito Pupa

C. Daphnia   D. Cyclops

(Greatly Enlarged)

Figure 8.1 *Live Foods*

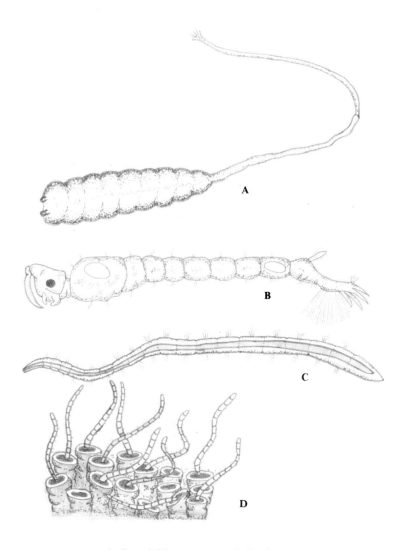

A
B
C
D

A. Rat-tail Maggot   **C. Tubifex**

B. Glassworm   **D. Tubifex in mud tubes**

(Greatly Enlarged)

Figure 8.2 *Further Live Foods*

firm into the box. Take care that no ants or other life are introduced. In fact, some people bake the two ingredients in the oven before damping and mixing together. A shallow hollow is then made in the soil and filled with food, the worms being placed on top. The soil is covered with a loose fitting piece of glass to conserve the moisture, and the box covered with a board to exclude the light. The food for the worms may consist of soaked brown bread, saltless mashed potatoes, or oatmeal — in fact almost any household scraps that can be made into a soft pulp will serve. Place the box in an airy place, with a temperature of about 55° Fahrenheit (12.8° Centigrade). Replenish the food supply as it is consumed, or after removing any uneaten spoilt food, until the worms have established a thriving colony. It will be found that they will gather in thick clusters around the food, and it is a simple matter to roll them into a ball to be picked up and fed to the fish. Further boxes may be cultured in the same manner by transferring a few of the worms. It usually takes around a month before the worms have increased sufficiently to start feeding them to the fish.

Grindal worms. These are slightly smaller worms which are also cultivated in boxes. The box need be no more than two inches (51 mm) deep and fine granulated peat laid to a depth of one inch (25 mm). The peat should be kept distinctly moist, but not soaking wet. Place the starter culture into a shallow depression in the compost. Add the food, and cover with a loose fitting glass lying directly upon the peat. Cover to exclude the light. The culture must be kept warm, about 70°F (21°C); this is most important for success. Food should consist of a pre-cooked baby cereal mixed with warm water to a thin paste. When cool the food can be spread thinly over the worms. Feed as often as the food is consumed.

Aerate by turning the peat over with a fork before each feeding, to help prevent the medium becoming sour. These worms are voracious feeders and with ample feeding and warmth will multiply quite quickly.

Micro worms are an ideal food for small goldfish because of their small size — less than ⅛ inch (3 mm). To avoid any unpleasant smell, and to keep the worms thriving, a new culture should be started every five to six days. Shallow plastic dishes make good containers and these should have a little pre-cooked cereal, made into a stiff paste, spread thinly over the bottom of the dish. Add the starter culture by smearing over the surface of the cooled food. Cover with a sheet of glass and

147

keep at room temperature. After a few days the surface of the culture will be found to be seething with the tiny worms. If a knife-blade is scraped around the inner edge of the dish the worms will be collected; clean, and ready to swill into the fish tank. After about five days the culture will start to 'go off'. Fresh cultures will need to be started, preferably arranging a slight overlap in time between each culture.

Micro eels are minute. Suitable for fry after they are about a week old. Micro eels have the advantage that no 'culture medium' is required that can go bad or need renewing. All that is needed is a pint of water, to which two level teaspoons of sugar have been added and a small pinch of dried yeast. The additives should be thoroughly dissolved and mixed into the water. Add the starter culture and keep at room temperature. After a week or two, if held against a strong light, the water may be seen to be alive with the very tiny eels. Pour through a very fine material such as a handkerchief and swill into the tank of fry. Return the water to its container and the remaining eels should again begin to multiply. If necessary, a number of cultures can be started together. This food will last for very long periods without any attention, until required.

Daphnia, the well known Water Flea, is, of course, a small crustacean, totally unrelated to the parasite. An attractive food to goldfish, it should be remembered that they breathe through gills and deprive fish of essential oxygen, so do not feed too many at a time. Daphnia have a transparent chitinous carapace, and vary in size according to age and genera — up to 1/5 inch (5 mm). The colour can also vary being red, green or almost black, depending upon their food source. Food may be algae, bacteria or infusoria. The bright red colour of some Daphnia is due to haemoglobin, as the oxygen content of the water becomes lower so the haemoglobin increases and thereby causes the blood to become a deeper red.

Daphnia can be found in many aquatic habitats, but mainly where heavy decomposition is taking place. Stagnant pools, ponds, farmyard pools and ponds in city parks are some of the likely places in which Daphnia may be found. In the spring large numbers of females hatch from eggs that have rested over the winter period. These females will produce further young every ten days or so. With a reduction in food or temperature the female Daphnia will begin producing eggs that hatch into males. Following this the Daphnia mate and the fertilized eggs (ephippia) rest over the unsuitable period, hatching as females when conditions improve and start the cycle all over again. To collect this food a fine-mesh net should be used. A figure-of-eight movement will quickly collect a quantity of Daphnia if the water contains a fair population. Place the collected Daphnia in a bucket of water and carry home with as little delay as possible. Arriving home, tip the catch into a white bowl, so that it can be inspected, and remove all beatles, leeches or other suspicious creatures. A surprising number of undesirables are invariably caught. Daphnia can, of course, be purchased from most pet fish dealers if desired.

Cyclops. Another small crustacean so named because of its single eye. They feed upon similar foods to the Daphnia and are generally most abundant during the warmer months of the year. Cyclops are found in the same waters as Daphnia and will often be found as part of the Daphnia haul. They are good food, especially for the smaller fish.

Tubifex. Considered by many aquarists to be one of the finest live foods for goldfish. It is a thread-like worm, slightly over an inch (25 mm) in length, and reddish in colour. They live, often in large colonies, in areas of high pollution and organic decomposition, where they bury their heads in the mud and ooze. The larger part of the body waves in an undulating motion in the water to breathe in the dissolved oxygen — if disturbed the tails are withdrawn into the black silt at lightning speed. Areas near the outfalls of raw sewage are often densely colonised by these tubificids, where they appear as a red mass of waving tails, transforming human waste products into the characteristic black homogenous substance that marks sludge banks.

Occupying such grossly degraded habitats the worms must be treated with great suspicion, until cleaned, as likely carriers of disease. It is not a matter of human disease being transmitted, but sludge beds often contain dead creatures of many species, together with protozoa and bacteria which grow in abundance. Thorough cleaning will do much to avoid the introduction of unwanted organisms into healthy aquariums or ponds.

Collecting tubifex from such sites is a filthy and smelly business, and the collector should dress accordingly. A strong, fine-meshed net should be thrust quickly into the ooze and withdrawn. If the mud is then tipped into a sieve made of 2 inch-high (51 mm) frame and a bottom pierced by ⅛ inch (3 mm) holes, the muck can be swilled. This will separate much of the filth from the worms. The balls of worms can then be carried home in plastic bags for further cleaning.

149

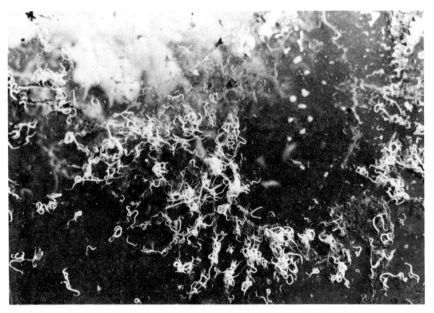

Figure 8.3 *White-worms*
Easily cultured and make a good form of live food for goldfish. The worm reaches a length of around three-quarters of an inch

To clean the worms, first swill in a number of water changes, breaking up the mass of worms each time. They are then placed into shallow containers into which a continuous slow stream of water is run. The period of cleaning should last for around seven days, the balls of worms being broken up frequently to remove any that have died, until the internal matter has been flushed out of the tubifex. Only when the worms are thoroughly clean should they be offered to the fish. Preferably use a perforated worm-feeder, this will prevent too many worms escaping and burying themselves in the bottom compost of the aquarium or pond.

Rat-tailed maggots are the larvae of a drone-fly, sometimes called 'hover-flies', and are often found in the soft bottom mud of polluted waters, usually just a few inches below water. The body of the larva is about ½ inch (13 mm) long and a dirty white to yellow colour, slightly transparent; the skin is thick and tough. From the rear of the wrinkled body a prehensile segmented tail acts as a telescopic breathing device.

150

This snorkel-type appendage can be extended to several times the length of the body, to reach the water surface, and can be very quickly retracted if disturbed. Colonies of the larvae may sometimes be found in quite a small area. Collection is the same as employed for gathering tubifex; however, cleaning is not so tedious. Swill to remove the filth, then keep for twenty four hours in clean water under a drip of water. The larvae can be fed to the larger goldfish.

Bloodworms. The larvae of the *Chironomidae* — the midges — easily recognised by its blood-red colour and figure-of-eight swimming motion. The larva, which is not a worm at all, grows to around ½ inch (13 mm) in length and is available throughout the year. Highly satisfactory food for the goldfish, it can be found in almost all fresh waters, but they are usually found to be most abundant in or on the bottom debris of lakes, ponds, pools and slow moving streams, and even rainwater barrels. Collection and cleaning is exactly as described for the rat-tailed maggot.

Glassworms. By no means a worm, it is a predacious larva of the phantom midge. Although an excellent food for adult goldfish, it can be a danger to small fry. Roughly ½ inch (13 mm) in length, the body of the larva is glass-like in its near transparency through which the four air-sacs are clearly visible. The sacs act as floats, and can be adjusted to suit the specific gravity of the surrounding water. In this way the sacs aid in the daily migration of the larva from the water surface to the bottom. The larva is able to float motionless at any desired depth, but can move at lightning speed to seize its prey.

Some factors characteristic of waters inhabited by the larva are a low intensity of light; a low dissolved oxygen content; a high carbon dioxide content; usually an absence of green submerged water plants; and very often an accumulation of rotting tree leaves with the accompanying protozoa, rotifers, bacteria and fungi. Autumn is possibly the best time of the year to look for the glassworms, in woodland pools. A large fine-mesh daphnia net is most suitable for collecting this food, swept in a figure-of-eight motion through the water, the larvae will collect in a wriggling jelly-like mass in the net. As these larvae are nocturnal feeders the best time to net them is during late evening and night-time. The food is normally quite clean when caught and only needs a quick swill in clean water before being fed to the fish.

Mosquito larvae. Sometimes referred to as wrigglers. Almost black in colour, they are up to ¼ inch (16 mm) long and hang head down from the water surface. When disturbed they leave the surface with a whipping movement but, due to their dependence upon atmospheric air, will quickly return. They feed upon microscopic food. Mosquito larvae will be found in most still waters, even in such unlikely places as a small amount of water at the bottom of an old tin can.

The female mosquito lays her eggs in black canoe-shaped rafts during warm summer evenings. These may be collected and floated on the water surface of aquariums containing fry; as the eggs hatch the fry will eat the tiny larvae. The larger larvae are best caught with a daphnia net. Even a shadow will cause the larvae to head for the depths, therefore approach carefully, make a quick sweep deep enough to trap those at the surface and those which have started to flee. Normally no cleaning is necessary before being given to the fish. Remember, however, not to feed too many at once because any that are not eaten can turn into adult mosquitoes.

Gammarus. The freshwater shrimp ranges in colour from almost white to almost black, through reddish brown, greys, and green. Beware of any which are spotted with red: they are infected with a parasite worm that will do harm in the pond or aquarium. Their bodies are flattened laterally and curved into an arc.

Frequenting slow moving waters that are shallow and contain large beds of aquatic vegetation, they are often abundant in beds of Elodea and watercress. This creature is active throughout the whole year and can be collected from mid-winter to the height of summer. The shrimp has a tendency to avoid bright light and normally hides from intense sunlight within the clumps of plants.

The shrimps can often be found with the males carrying the females on their backs. For a time the pairs will separate while the female sheds her old exoskeleton (shell). Afterwards they again join together for copulation, at which point the eggs are transferred and fertilized — the eggs being carried in an egg pouch until they hatch. The young are exact miniatures of their parents and will often hang onto their mother while she is being carried by the male.

Collection of this food is simply a matter of raking out a quantity of the plant life, and shaking over a sheet of plastic. The shrimps will tumble on to the sheet in a fairly clean state and can be transferred into a bucket of water for transporting home. The hard shell of the shrimp makes them suitable for only the larger goldfish.

Asellus is related to the well known woodlouse, and is not an exceptionally good food because of the very hard shell — although very small Asellus may be accepted by some fish. They are excellent scavengers, frequenting areas of water where there is an accumulation of aquatic plants, leaves and decaying vegetation. Newly hatched young are about the size of Daphnia and can grow to almost an inch (25 mm) in length. Collection is similar to that of the Gammarus.

Tadpoles. Only those of the frog will be accepted as food by the goldfish, those of the toad and newt being refused. If collecting frog spawn always be sure to leave some behind so that it may develop naturally into mature frogs, and so help to maintain the rapidly decreasing population of this amphibian. Frogs lay their eggs in large masses amongst the water plants, whereas the toad, for instance, lays its eggs in strings. The collected spawn can be placed into large shallow pans of water to hatch, and the resulting tadpoles fed on such substances as boiled oatmeal, algae and chopped spinach. The tadpoles are good food for those fish that are large enough to eat them.

Maggots, such as sold by stores dealing in anglers' supplies, are readily accepted by most goldfish. Use the smaller types that have not been artificially coloured. The fish will eat the soft inside of the maggot and spit out the leathery skin. To avoid pollution of the water the empty skins should be removed when possible.

Ant pupae. The old fashioned packets of ants eggs were, and are, of no nutritional value whatsoever, but the fresh soft pupae from an ant nest are excellent food for goldfish.

Aphids, such as the greenfly, are sometimes suggested as a food. The smaller fish may eat them occasionally, but it is tedious to collect them in any quantity and hardly worth the effort.

HOME MADE FOODS

There are a number of recipes for preparing goldfish foods in the kitchen — some being better than others. A food which I devised for feeding to my fish is made up as follows:

1 can of cat or dog food
1 packet of wheat-germ food, such as Bemax
2 tablespoons calcium carbonate
2 teaspoons honey

153

1 packet of pure gelatine crystals
cheese, roughly equal in bulk to the canned meat
½ cup approx. of green soft vegetable, such as spinach
2 eggs

Strain any liquid from the canned meat and, if possible, reduce it to a fine mush. Grind the cheese and simmer in water until the cheese has melted, then add the meat. Stir to prevent the mixture sticking or burning. Remove from heat and stir in two teaspoons of honey, two tablespoons of calcium carbonate and thoroughly blend together. Add the two eggs and continue to mix whilst slowly adding the wheat-germ until the mixture becomes very thick and doughy. Finally melt the gelatine crystals into a half cup of hot water, stir until fully dissolved then beat into the dough thoroughly. The food can then be placed into suitable containers and set aside to cool and set into a rubbery texture. It can be stored indefinitely in a deep-freezer.

The late Dr. Myton Gordon, Fish Geneticist for many years with the New York Zoological Society, devised a formula which is now known as 'Gordon's Formula', and is made as follows:

Remove the blood vessels, connective tissue and other fibrous material from 1 lb (0.45 kg) of beef liver, and chop into ½ inch (13 mm) cubes.
Taking small quantities of liver at a time, add equal amounts of cold water and blend them in a high-speed blender. The resulting liquid should be strained into a large bowl. Add 2 teaspoons of non-iodized salt.
To this add 20 tablespoons of a pre-cooked baby cereal such as porridge oats, and stir thoroughly.
Fill small glass containers, such as baby food jars, but do not seal them. Place them in a pan of water and bring the water to the boil. Allow the jars to remain in the water for half an hour after the heat has been turned off. When they have cooled, seal and keep refrigerated or frozen.

Small portions (the size depending on the number and size of the fishes) may be fed as often as desired. The advantage of this formula is that the blood will not leach out into the water, and a lump placed on the bottom of the aquarium will be picked at by the fish all day long. Any uneaten portion should be removed during the evening.

Other recipes are:

1. A liver-based dried food used at the American Museum of Natural History and the New York Aquarium is composed of 5 lb (2.3 kg) of beef liver; 14 lb (6.4 kg) of wheat germ; 6 lb (2.7 kg) of shrimp shell meal; 6 lb (2.7 kg) of shredded shrimp meat; 3 lb (1.4 kg) of lettuce; and 3 lb (1.4 kg) of spinach.

The liver is cut into two-inch pieces, placed in a pan, covered with water, and boiled for 15 minutes. Then it is finely ground and put back into the pan with the remaining ingredients, and the entire combination is boiled for an additional 15 minutes. The resulting warm paste is then spread thinly to dry, finely broken and ground to size.

2. Use two tumblers of powdered puppy biscuit, one tumbler of powdered dry shrimp, and 3 pinches of salt. Mix together and moisten with water which has had an egg beaten into it. Add enough water and egg to make the mass into a stiff but workable consistency. Spread in pans to dry in quarter-inch (6 mm) thick sheets. When dry break into pieces and grade into sizes.

3. Use a quarter tumbler powdered cod, three tumblers flour, three quarters of a tumbler of powdered shrimp, three teaspoons baking powder, one teaspoon of Epsom salt and three teaspoons of powdered chalk. Make into the consistency of bread dough with two raw eggs and water. Place in a pan and bake, like bread, in an oven. After baking, allow to cool and cut into thin slices. Allow slices to dry, break into crumbs and sift to size.

4. This formula requires a pound of beef liver with all sinewy material cut away, twenty tablespoons of wheat germ and one tablespoon of salt. The liver should first be cut into one-half inch pieces with an equivalent weight of water added. It should then be ground into a mash with the water, by using a blender if possible. Wheat germ and salt should then be added slowly to form a thick lump-free paste. The mixture is then placed in small glass jars and simmered in hot water. When cool the jars should be sealed and stored in a refrigerator.

These foods are ideal for supplementing the live foods.

FREEZE DRIED FOODS

These are various live foods which are quickly frozen at sub-zero temperatures and vacuum-removing the crystallized frozen water. This method of preparing the food ensures that the cellular structure is not destroyed — which is usually the case with normal freezing techniques. It has been found that freeze-drying of foods preserves the essential nutritive values and the food can be stored, in suitable containers, for an indefinite period of time. Within the range of freeze-dried foods will be found Daphnia, Tubifex, Bloodworm and others suitable for feeding to goldfish.

FRESH FROZEN FOODS

Just as the housewife can purchase 'frozen foods and meals' for the kitchen so the fishkeeper can obtain similar products for the goldfish. Available foods include brine shrimp, mussel, prawn, shrimp, lobster, cockle, Daphnia, bloodworms, beef and lobster eggs. These foods are treated with gamma-rays which ensures that they are completely free of any diseases. Often additional vitamins are added such as A, B_1, B_2, B_6, B_{12}, B_{13}, D_2, D_3, E, F, H and K. They are therefore excellent foods, being pure protein and wholly edible.

If a deep-freezer is available the food can be kept safely with the domestic food supplies until required. It is only necessary to break off a suitable portion and return the remainder to cold-storage.

COMMERCIALLY PREPARED DRIED FOODS

Many years ago it was realised that the so-called 'ants-eggs' were not of any nutritional value, and pet-food manufacturers began to research for more sustaining food and better methods of production. Some of the foods were little more than crushed dog biscuit. Others were a more thoughtfully prepared and sophisticated fish food, in the form of granules. As time passed some of the larger companies engaged qualified personnel to investigate the nutritional requirements of fish. From the results of these investigations new and greatly improved foods were devised, some being of much greater value than others.

Nowadays it is possible to obtain a wide range of excellent commercially prepared dried foods. Granular foods are available ready graded to suit various sizes of fish. Pelleted foods are manufactured especially for feeding pond fish; these have the ability to remain buoyant and float upon the water surface for a considerable time. Many pondkeepers prefer this form of food because it brings the fish to the upper water where they can be easily seen. Possibly the greatest innovation has been in the production of 'flake-foods'.

Flake-foods are tissue-thin flakes which, as one leading British manufacturer states, are especially formulated and manufactured directly from whole fresh ingredients based upon eight different basic formulae. The flakes vary in colour according to the individual formula — pink coloured flakes are based upon whitefish; green flakes contain vegetation such as kelp and spinach; light brown is fresh meat and liver plus blood and ground bone; yellow is high in protein of soya and egg; red combines fish, mixed cereals and blood; orange is described as a colour food for enhancing the colours of fish and contains

Figure 8.4 *Commercially Packed Food*
Pellet type goldfish foods are suitable as a basic diet for larger fish

Canthaxanthin; dark brown has meat offals, blood and ground bone; and black has extra vitamins and minerals in its make up.

Goldfish appear to accept these flake foods readily, which float for a short time before slowly sinking through the water. They are therefore a useful form of alternative feeding.

OTHER FOODS

Canned dog and cat foods, fed in small quantities, are very popular with some aquarists and can be stored in the refrigerator. Scrambled eggs are a good fish food. Prepare by allowing one teaspoon of water for each egg, beat thoroughly, then pour into a pan of boiling water while stirring. Strain the resulting flakes before offering to the fish. Cooked heart and liver can be scraped or finely chopped for fish. Boiled fish and shellfish can be suspended in the water for the fish to peck at. Wheat-germ foods, cooked or uncooked oatmeal, soft boiled green peas, and crumbled wholemeal bread are all suitable foods for the goldfish. In fact, by experimentation the fishkeeper will be able to find that many different foods will be accepted by the goldfish family.

FEEDING

The frequency and amount of feeding is dependent upon a number of factors: not least of these is the quality and temperature of the water. The goldfish will have little appetite if the water is becoming polluted or the amount of dissolved oxygen is low. It must also be borne in mind that as the temperature falls so the appetite of the goldfish will diminish until, at around 40° Fahrenheit (4.4° Centigrade), the fish ceases to feed. Therefore gauging the amount and frequency of feeding becomes a matter of practice and experience; however, observation will act as a safety guide in the matter.

The sensible approach is to offer the fish just a small amount and keep watch to ascertain how quickly they consume it. If the food is eaten greedily with no signs of the fish slowing down or losing interest, add just a little more; continue to do this until the fish show that their appetite is being lost. It will not be too long before it becomes possible to gauge the correct amount of food to offer at any given time.

There is a danger in overfeeding, not because the fish will eat too much, but because of the risk of the uneaten food causing the water to become polluted. Of course, certain live foods do not present this problem — although a great many Daphnia can deplete the dissolved oxygen content of the water, and so cause the fish to suffer.

Few fish have died from underfeeding, although the rate of growth may well be stunted and the fish becomes less resistant to minor diseases.

During the warmer months of the year the fish are able to digest their food quite rapidly and, to obtain maximum growth, should be fed three times daily. In fact, if a light is left burning above their quarters they will feed during the night. However, intensive feeding (which forces the growth) is not to be recommended, nor is it necessary.

As the year progresses the water temperatures will become lower, and the speed with which the fish digests its food will begin to slow. The frequency and/or quantity of feeding must be adjusted accordingly — again the appetite of the fish will indicate the corrections needed to the feeding schedule. Fish that are kept in fish-house tanks or outdoor ponds will exhibit these changes much more positively than those kept in the more protected environment of the indoor aquarium.

During the autumn it will be noticed that the appetite of the fish will revive. This is an instinctive desire to put on extra fat in preparation for the winter fast, and should be catered for. During the cold months the goldfish — especially in the pond — will become dormant when the water cools to around 40° F (4.4° C) and below. At these low temperatures the digestive system of the goldfish is unable to assimilate any food, and the fish lives off the accumulated body fats. To attempt to feed at such a time is both wasteful and dangerous. Any food in the digestive tract is likely to decompose and may well result in the death of the fish. It is therefore essential that the fish is encouraged to build up a good reserve of body fat to enable it to survive the hard period. Plenty of good nourishing food, such as earthworms and other meaty morsels, should become a prominent part of the diet. In this way the fish will be assisted to develop the very necessary reserves of fat.

With the welcome return of the spring, temperatures will begin to improve, and as the water slowly warms the fish will again begin to show an interest in food. Due to the winter fast the fish will not be able to digest, nor will it require, large meals. Commence by offering small amounts of Daphnia and similar live foods, gradually increasing the feeds to include prepared foods as the appetite of the fish improves.

In the wild fish have periods of plentiful feeding and periods when food is in very short supply. The wise aquarist will endeavour to follow Nature in the feeding arrangements, and will recognise that there are times to feed and times to withdraw from feeding.

Many novice fishkeepers are worried about feeding their fish during holiday periods. I have known many who refused to leave home in case their fish starved. Such fears are groundless, and it is foolish to forego the annual vacation. A period away from home will not occasion the fish any harm — they may, in fact, benefit from the temporary lack of feeding. Far better to deprive the fish of food for one or two weeks than to ask a well-meaning but inexperienced friend, relative or neighbour to look after the fish.

Placing the care of the fish into the hands of an inexperienced person can quickly undo all the good practices which the aquarist has established. Overfeeding and a lack of understanding can soon lead to pollution of the aquarium, and even the best of friendships may be sorely strained when the owner arrives home to find an aquarium that has become a stinking mess of foul water and dead fish!

Invariably I depart for my annual vacation, after locking the door of the fish-house, and seldom give a thought to the fish until I return. This has been my practice for many years, and not once has a fish been lost. Perhaps it is an illusion but the tanks always appear to have developed a sparkling clarity during my absence, and the fish swim with an extra alertness as they browse off the green algae in their tanks.

At the risk of repeating myself, I would stress that the way to keep the fish healthy, and make sturdy growth, has much to do with a varied diet, the quality of the food, and the correct frequency of feeding. During the Spring and Summer there is an abundance of live foods available to the aquarist. In the autumn and winter it is not so easy to find so great a range of live foods, but there are alternatives — as can be seen from the previously listed foods. The caring fishkeeper will always be willing to go to some trouble to ensure that the fish are provided with a good nourishing and varied diet, to maintain the fish, not only in good health, but in the very best of condition.

Finally, to conclude this chapter, I will illustrate a varied diet by giving a suggested 7-day menu for the spring and summer, and another for the autumn:

Spring and Summer Menu

Sunday	a.m.	Daphnia	p.m.	Tubifex or earthworms
Monday	a.m.	Bloodworms	p.m.	Home-made food
Tuesday	a.m.	Earthworms	p.m.	Pellet food
Wednesday	a.m.	Flake-food	p.m.	Bloodworms
Thursday	a.m.	Daphnia	p.m.	Porridge oats
Friday	a.m.	Whiteworms	p.m.	Flake-food
Saturday	a.m.	Earthworms	p.m.	Home-made food

Autumn Menu

Sunday	a.m.	Porridge oats
Monday	a.m.	Whiteworms
Tuesday	a.m.	Flake-food
Wednesday	a.m.	Boiled fish
Thursday	a.m.	Home-made food
Friday	a.m.	Finely chopped cooked liver
Saturday	a.m.	Daphnia or earthworms

These menus have been based upon the more easily obtained foods and, of course, the cooler temperatures of autumn mean that only one feed each day is required. The novice should use discretion and adapt the suggested feeding schedules according to the available food supplies and prevailing water temperatures.

CHAPTER 9

Pests and Diseases

Although all forms of life can suffer from various maladies, and fish are no exception, the problems usually only arise if circumstances in some way have brought about a lowered resistance. Much can be done to avoid attacks by disease and pest. Of prime importance is the strict observation of quarantine and the disinfection of all new stock — both fish and plant. It is also very necessary that the best of living conditions be provided, and that careful attention is given to the diet of the goldfish. Follow the rules and it is not difficult to keep the fish in a state of good health. Generally, the goldfish has a great resistance to disease so long as it is not weakened by bad treatment, poor food, lack of oxygen, rapid fluctuations of water temperature, or some other adverse condition.

If the tank, plants and fish are perfectly clean and healthy, any parasitic infection must be introduced from an outside source. Parasites may be introduced by insufficiently quarantined and cleaned fish or plants; or live foods obtained from waters containing fish may be responsible. Always exercise care and parasites are not likely to become a difficult problem.

Despite the most careful attention it is a sad fact that there will be times when disease will raise its ugly head. The symptoms of the different fish diseases will vary according to its nature, but there are a number of signs that will indicate whether the fish may be suffering from some complaint. A simple test will quickly establish the health of any that is suspect. If a sick fish is taken in the hand (under water) and turned on its side, the eye will remain in its normal position allowing the pupil to be seen. If, however, the fish is healthy, the eye-ball will roll — remaining upright — so that the pupil cannot be seen. This trick will reveal the state of health of the fish, even though there may be an absence of more definite symptoms.

The cotton-woolly appearance of a fungus infection is easily recognised. Other diseases of the skin are often indicated by a prolonged fading of the colours; there may also be a formation of a grey, slimy excretion, covering small or large areas of the body. Upon dark coloured goldfish these symptoms are easily observed, but may not be so easily seen on the bodies of those with lighter colours. Some skin infections are evidenced by the appearance of white, brown or blackish spots. Irritation of the skin, by disease or parasite, causes the fish to rub itself against various objects — it may also make wild dashes through the water.

Bacterial diseases are generally characterised by the presence of red spots on the skin. Eye infections often result in either a greyish cataract or an enlargement of the eye.

Many diseases will result in the fish lingering near the water surface, or hiding in a corner, with fins tightly folded. Gill infections cause the fish breathing problems. The suffering fish will open the gill coverings much wider than is normal, and the frequency of breathing will be greatly increased. The gill sheets will become pale, and may have small red inflamed spots. Very pale gills are a sure sign of disease in a living fish; the gills of a healthy fish will always have a bright reddish colour.

Internal disorders may cause abnormal swellings or, conversely, result in a thin hollow-bellied appearance. Constipation can cause the fish to go off its food. The deep bodied varieties of goldfish, such as the Veiltail, can be particularly prone to this problem. Air-bladder (or swim-bladder) problems result in the victim having difficulty in maintaining its equilibrium, it may make tumbling movements, or have difficulty in rising from the bottom; in other instances it may continuously float, like a cork, to the water surface.

It should not be thought that, because of the daunting list of symptoms, the fish will be plagued by illness, for I have already said that, with proper care and attention, the goldfish is a hardy creature and resists disease remarkably well. Most problems are generally the result of some action or mistreatment by the aquarist. However, observation and awareness of symptoms will assist the fishkeeper to recognise a possible problem before it can get out of hand. Early recognition and treatment of a disease gives the fish an excellent chance of recovery; whereas neglect can lead to its death.

RULES TO OBSERVE

Before considering specific complaints the aquarist should learn to observe the following rules:

1. Do not rush into treating a suspect fish unless it is proved to be afflicted by a definite complaint. Fish, like humans, have their 'off-days' and a listless fish may only be feeling a 'little under the weather'. If there is real cause to suspect that the fish is ailing, separate it in an isolation tank for observation.

2. Always ensure that, when moving fish to an isolation tank or medicinal bath, the water temperature has been adjusted to that of the water from which the fish has been removed.

3. Handle the fish as little as possible. There is no fear of the aquarist being infected, because no fish disease can be passed to the human, but, like all sick creatures, the fish should be disturbed only when absolutely necessary.

4. If the fish is proved to be suffering from an ailment, keep an eye on any other fish which have been in contact with it, in case they have also been infected.

5. Medicinal baths should be freshly prepared as required, long term baths being renewed daily.

6. Should a fish show signs of distress after being placed in a medicinal bath, remove it immediately, and weaken the solution before replacing it. A close watch should always be kept when immersing the fish in treatment baths, for individual fish can vary in their level of tolerance.

7. If the fish fails to respond to treatment after a reasonable period, it should be destroyed without further ado.

8. Do not over-dose in the belief that it will bring about a speedier cure, it could well have the opposite effect and result in the death of the fish.

9. Encourage the invalid to eat by offering good nourishing food. If the fish eats its food it stands a better chance of recovery.

10. Always wash the hands, and disinfect nets and other equipment, after being in contact with a sick fish. Failure to observe this elementary precaution may lead to the infection of the healthy stock.

THE MEDICINE CHEST

The following list of chemicals will be found useful for the treatment of the various diseases and parasites of fish. All chemicals must, of course, be kept safely beyond the reach of children, and are best kept in a locked cabinet. Many of the medicaments will be available from the retail drug store; others may have to be obtained through a veterinary surgeon.

Ammonia. A stock solution is made by adding 10 parts by volume to 90 parts of water. The medicinal bath is made by adding 45 cc of stock solution to each gallon of water, mixing thoroughly. This treatment must not be used in planted tanks or ponds. Infected fish are bathed in the solution for no longer than 20 minutes.

Aureomycin. Use 60 milligrams to each gallon of water for four days, or 600 milligrams per gallon for 24 hours. Treatment should not be extended beyond the stated periods.

Chloromycetin. To be used at the same rates and with the same caution as the above antibiotic.

Friar's Balsam. To be used as a protective dressing for wounds. Wrap cotton wool around a match stick, dip it in the balsam and quickly paint over the open wound. Treatment can be repeated until the wound has healed.

Iodine. Dilute by the addition of an equal amount of water, to produce a half-strength medicament. Apply with a soft watercolour brush. Take care that the solution does not come in contact with the eyes or gills of the fish.

Malachite Green. This must be of the zinc-free medical grade only. Prepare a stock solution by adding 1 gram to 500 cc of distilled water. The medicinal bath is made by mixing 9 cc of the stock solution into one gallon of water. Do not use in zinc or galvanised iron containers. Immerse the fish for up to 1 hour.

Methylene Blue. A stock solution is made by adding 1 gram of medical grade methylene blue to 100 cc of hot water. Use 4 cc of the stock solution to each gallon of water. Can be used for a prolonged period. This chemical increases the respiratory capacity of the fish, therefore no aeration of the water need be employed.

Phenoxethol. Stock solution: 1 cc mixed well into 9 cc of water. The medicinal bath consists of 90 cc of stock solution stirred into each gallon of water. Infected fish can remain in the bath until cured.

Potassium Permanganate (Permanganate of Potash). A stock solution is made by thoroughly dissolving 1 gram of the crystals in 99 cc of warm distilled water. In ponds and planted tanks the stock solution should be mixed in at the rate of 2 cc per gallon. A bath of half an hour duration is prepared by adding 4.5 cc to each gallon of water. It is not necessary to change the water, which will clear after a time. The chemical is sensitive to light and should be stored in a dark bottle. Never add the crystals directly to the water without first dissolving them.

Salt (Sodium Chloride). Table salt should not be used because it contains other chemicals. Use marine salt, cooking salt, or rock salt. A 30 minute bath is made by dissolving 5 ounces of salt in each gallon of water. A three phase treatment consists of adding 1 ounce of salt per gallon for the first day. On the second day fifty per cent of the bath is removed, being replaced with a fresh saline solution of 2 ounces per gallon. A further half of the treatment water is removed on the third day, and this is replaced with water containing salt at the same rate as the second day's change. Fish may be kept in the final bath until cured. After completion of the treatment, the saline bath must have one-third of its total removed and replaced with fresh water, on each of three days. After the fourth day in the weakened solution the fish may be returned to the aquarium or pond.

Terramycin. Usually packed in a drum together with a scoop for measuring. Use by adding one level scoop of the powder to each gallon of water and stir in. A fresh bath must be made each day, but consecutive treatments should not exceed 48 hours.

Commercially prepared medicines. There are a number of medicaments specially prepared for use by aquarists, available from pet stores. Some are very good and contain precise instructions for treating sick fish. They are useful to the person who feels unsure about preparing treatments from 'raw' chemicals.

USEFUL IMPLEMENTS

The careful fishkeeper will keep a number of implements specifically for the treatment of sick fish, so that, while being always ready for use, they do not come in contact with the healthy stock. The following will be found useful:

One or two soft fine-meshed nets
Two small tanks of 3 or 4 gallons (9-13.6 litres) capacity (the plastic type is ideal)
Aeration equipment
Combined aquarium heater and thermostat

166

Thermometer
A square block of hardwood, about 6 inches (152 mm) square
A safety razor blade or surgical knife
Forceps — one pair with flat ends and another with pointed ends
One or two eye-droppers (or fountain pen fillers)
A set of dry measures
A graduated liquid measure
One or two camel-hair water colour brushes
A small amount of cotton wool

These items of equipment will not be over-expensive to acquire, especially if purchased as required.

SYMPTOMS

By carefully checking the symptoms of the afflicted fish against the following list, the aquarist will be able to diagnose the most probable cause of the malady. By referring to the specified complaint in the following pages, the fishkeeper will find both the cause of the problem, together with the treatment. It should hardly need saying that, not only must action be taken to cure the complaint, but steps must also be taken to remedy the original cause of the problem. The list is:

White cotton woolly tufts on the body or fins — Fungus.

White film on the eye — Cataract.

Fish knocks against firm object and has a flat transparent green creature, about the size of a ladybird, attached to it — Argulus.

Fish rubs and scratches itself, fins twitch, and the fish makes sudden wild dashes. Breathing rate accelerated — Flukes.

Gills inflamed and swollen, skin dull with milky-white patches on the body. Loss of appetite — Branchiitis.

Scales stand out, bloated body — Dropsy.

White pin-head spots on body and fins — Ichthyophthiriasis.

Thread-like worm attached to fish — Lernaea.

Difficulty in swimming. Fish cannot rise from bottom. Floats like a cork at water surface. Turns on back. Floats head down — Derangement of air-bladder.

Air bubbles in faeces. The fish is sluggish with swollen belly — Indigestion.

Slow clumsy movements. Fish remains stationary and waddles

167

body from side to side — Shimmies.

Fish hollow-eyed with sunken chest. Loss of appetite and sluggish — Tuberculosis.

Air-bubbles in fins. Air Embolism.

Blood-streaked veins in caudal and other fins. Later the fins split and rot — Fin-rot.

Eyes protrude on normal-eyed fish — Exophthalmis.

Dark grey patches on body which later turn black and peel leaving raw spots — Melanosis.

Small worm-like creatures attached to fish — Leeches.

Slimy, greyish-white mucous covering body. Fins folded, loss of appetite. Fish may lie on its side. Most obviously noticeable on dark coloured fish — Chilodonelliasis.

Pale gills with signs of rotting. Breathing rate much increased. Loss of appetite — Gill rot.

Cotton wool tufts at mouth and on gills. Swollen lips. Loss of appetite. Sluggish — Mouth Fungus.

Lies near surface without movement. Fish lies on its side. Gills inflamed. Skin of the belly dark red. Anal fin and lower lobe of caudal inflamed — Red Pest.

Open sores on the body — Ulcers.

Large open wounds on body — Hole-in-the-body.

Lack of appetite and swollen belly — Constipation.

COMPLAINTS

Fungus (Saprolegnia). This cotton woolly fungus attacks only fish which have been wounded, weakened by parasites, or kept in bad conditions. The fungus spores are present in most waters, but cannot infect healthy fish. The individual threads of the fungus grow into the skin like roots. Remedy the conditions which have caused the infection. If only small areas are affected by fungus, touch the infection with iodine solution. If large areas are covered treat with salt or Phenoxethol.

Cataract. There are two forms. **Cataracta Traumatica** — this disease is characterised by a whitish film covering the lens of the eye. Generally only one eye is affected. Cause of disease not yet known. The iodine treatment, to which nine parts of glycerine has been added, will often bring about a cure. **Cataracta Parisitica.** At first glance resembles the first mentioned form. Closer inspection through a magnifying glass will reveal the film to be composed of white spots. In reality the dots are little worms, which feed upon the lens and destroy it. Worm cataracts are due to the larvae of sucking worms. The adult parasite lives in water-birds, eggs are discharged with the droppings into the water. The eggs hatch in the water, the resulting miracidiae being taken into the body of a snail, where they change shape and become sporocysts. After about six weeks the larvae leave the liver of the snail and move into the water. Upon meeting a fish the larvae enter the body and migrate to the eye. If the larvae fail to penetrate the fish within two days they die. Treat the affected fish with Phenoxethol, also soak food in the solution prior to feeding. If the eye is too badly affected it may not be possible to cure it — destroy the fish.

Argulus (The fish louse). One of the better known fish parasites. A round, flatish creature armed with two large suckers and eight legs. In addition it has a large hollow 'sting'. The 'sting' is pushed under the scale of the fish to feed upon the blood of its hosts. The louse can be introduced to the aquarium or pond with Daphnia, so care should therefore be taken when screening this food. Being a large creature, the louse can be removed with forceps or, alternatively, they can be rubbed off. Hold the fish in a wet net when carrying out these operations. Allow the tank or pond to dry out for 7 days, to kill both eggs and adults. If preferred the potassium permanganate treatment may be tried.

Flukes. Gill Fluke (Dactylogyrus). Infests the gills of the fish and are egg-laying. Fish affected by these parasites have increased breathing freqency, the gills are stretched wide open and pale in colour. The eggs are very resistant to chemical treatment, and for this reason it is necessary to make repeat treatments to kill the newly hatched flukes. Treatment may be given by first applying the 15 minute ammonia bath, afterwards placing the fish in a long-term bath of Methylene Blue. **Skin Fluke** (Gyrodactylus): Closely related to the former fluke, it is live-bearing. Fish affected by this fluke will tend to lose some colour, the fins droop and may become torn, the skin becomes very slimy and may show small blood spots. In strong light it may be possible to see these tiny parasites, especially if the fish has a dark colour. The fluke is an unsegmented flat worm, with an elliptical-shaped body that is flattened on the ventral side. At the front there are two conical projections, through which glands pass a thick, sticky

169

liquid with which it clings to the fish. The other end carries a strong disc-shaped attachment of small hooks in the shape of a ring in the middle of which are two larger hooks. The parasite first grips the skin of the fish with the small hooks and then drives in the large ones.

Flukes can be introduced by anything that has been in fluke infested waters. Disinfection and quarantine techniques will do much to avoid the problem. Treatment of affected fish is as mentioned for the elimination of the Gill Fluke. 'Sterazin', a commercial preparation, is possibly the best of all treatments.

Branchiitis (inflamation of the gills). Caused by polluted water or over-crowding reducing the oxygen content of the water. Remedy the cause and give the fish treatment in Methylene Blue.

Dropsy is an accumulation of fluid within the tissues of one or other of the internal organs. The belly of the fish swells so greatly that it appears likely to burst. However, the fish dies long before the pressure becomes great enough for this to happen. The belly is filled with an almost watery liquid. The disease can be infectious, and is caused by a bacterium which can always be found in water and milk. Investigations seem to indicate that the disease mainly attacks fish that are poorly fed and have lowered resistance. Treat the fish with chloromycetin, keep the water cool and do not feed. Difficult to cure.

Lernaea (Anchor worm). Only the female of this parasite attacks fish. She has a long body with an anchor-like appendage on the head. The creature is not, in fact, a worm but is related to the Cyclops. It grows to a length of around ¾ inch (19 mm). By means of the anchor-like appendages, which are buried deep into the muscles of the fish, the creature becomes very firmly attached to her unwilling host. After shedding her fertilized eggs the female dies, leaving deep wounds in the fish which heal very slowly. The young which hatch from the eggs can re-infest the fish. To rid fish of this parasite it must be held in a wet net, and the parasite touched with a brush dipped in very strong potassium permanganate. This should kill the parasite so that it can be removed with forceps. Touch the wound with iodine solution and cover with Friar's Balsam. The treated fish must be placed in clean water, while their infected quarters are kept free of fish for a period of about two months, during which time the pests, young and adult, should have died through lack of a host.

White Spot (Ichthyopthiriasis). This parasite is a protozoan which penetrates the upper layer of the epidermis and causes a small whiteish

170

blister to appear. The parasite feeds upon the red blood corpuscles of the fish. When mature, the parasite leaves its host and sinks to the bottom, where is encysts in a jelly-like covering. Rapid division takes place within the cyst to produce between 500 and 1000 young parasites. At a temperature of 68° F (20° C), the process takes about 18 hours. The rate at which the parasite infection increases can so weaken the fish that it will die unless treated. If the young parasite does not find a host within a few days it dies. White spot is introduced by infected fish and/or plants and material that has been in contact with infected fish. A strict routine of disinfection and quarantine will prevent the parasites infecting healthy stock. To be quite sure that newly acquired goldfish are free of the parasite, they should be kept in isolation for at least four weeks. Treat in a permanent bath of Malachite Green or Methylene Blue, raising the water temperature to 68° F (20° C). The infested fish can be treated in their tank. If the fish lives in a pond, the parasites will die after two months if every fish is removed There are some excellent commercial remedies for the eradication of this dangerous parasite.

Disorders of the air-bladder. These problems are very often the result of mismanagement. Incorrect feeding, i.e. too much dried food; rapid temperature fluctuations; chilling or prolonged low temperatures. The deep, round bodied varieties of fancy goldfish can be prone to air-bladder problems unless care is taken. There is little that can be done to cure the afflicted fish — raising the temperature slightly may give some temporary relief — and it is probably kinder to destroy the fish. Do not use any afflicted fish for breeding purposes because the weakness can be inherited.

Indigestion is the result of too much dried food over too long a period. Although not serious it can lead to the above complaint unless treated. Starve the fish for 7 days, then feed live Daphnia or chopped earthworms, to act as a laxative. Vary the future diet by including more soft food and live foods.

Constipation. The above remarks apply to this complaint.

Shimmies. Is the result of chilling or prolonged low temperature. Raise the water temperature slightly until the symptoms disappear, then gradually reduce the artificial warmth to normal water temperature. Feed for a time on live foods if possible.

Tuberculosis. This disease cannot be passed to humans. Fish tuberculosis is caused by bacteria that only attack cold-blooded animals.

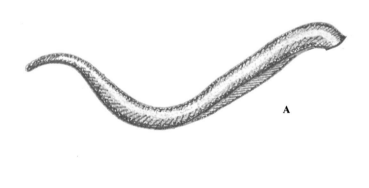

A

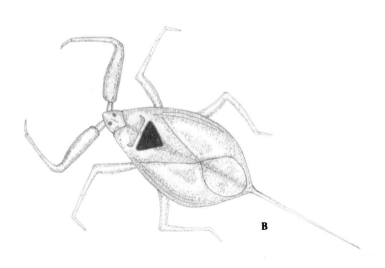

B

A. Leech

B. Water Scorpion

(Greatly Enlarged)

Figure 9.1 *Predators*

172

Plate 6
Top: Bristol Shubunkin
Bottom: Bubble-eye

Symptoms are loss of appetite, progressive thinness, sluggish movements, loss of colour and tightly folded fins. However, these symptoms also occur in other diseases and a definite diagnosis can only be made after a post-mortem examination. Because this disease is very contagious, any fish which is suspect should be isolated without delay to avoid infection of the healthy fish stock. Place the infected fish in a permanent bath of Methylene Blue and tempt it to eat with live Daphnia. There is no certain cure, therefore if the fish has not started to recover after two or three weeks it should be destroyed.

Air Embolism. The complaint is due to an excessive amount of dissolved oxygen in the water. In a well planted tank or pond, with a strong growth of algae, in direct sunlight on a hot day, the vegetation may produce an over-abundance of oxygen. The oxygen-saturated water can cause over-saturation in the blood of the fish. The symptoms are air-bubbles in the fins. The cure is to either gradually change 50 per cent of the water, or place the affected fish in fresh water. To prevent the problems arising again, provide shade on the brightest and warmest days.

Fin Rot (Bacterioses pinnarium). The common name of this disease aptly describes the symptoms — putrefaction of the caudal and other fins. The fins become torn and ragged and are gradually consumed by the action of the bacteria. Often Fungus occurs as a secondary infection. It is a most serious complaint. If the infection spreads to the body of the fish it will be too late to cure, and the fish will die. Chilling, dirty conditions, wrong feeding and (some think) excessive illumination, can all be causative agents of the disease. If the tail is badly affected, hold the fish with its tail on a block of wood and cut back to healthy tissue with a razor blade. Treat with Chloromycetin or Phenoxethol until cured.

Exophthalmia (pop-eye). In this disease the eye swells and, becoming too large for the orbit, protrudes. Sometimes the swelling is so great that the eye is forced out of its socket completely. It is seldom contagious, and the fish may live quite happily despite the disease. No known remedy.

Melanosis. A rare complaint, thought to be a disorder of the pigmentation cells. The cause is unknown. Treat by painting the infected areas with iodine solution, and give Aureomycin treatment. No certain cure known.

Leech. If care is not taken this creature can be introduced with

173

plants, and other material collected from the wild. It is a worm-like creature with a membered body which has a large sucking disc at each end. One of the suckers surrounds the mouth. Eggs are laid in cocoons on water plants and stones. Place the affected fish in a 15 minute salt bath; this will paralyse the leeches and most will fall off. Any that remain can be removed with forceps. Be sure to kill the leeches in boiling water. There is no cure for a leech-infested pond, apart from stripping it down and leaving it dry for a longish period.

Chilodonelliasia (Slime disease). A disease sometime attacks goldfish which is characterised by a slimy secretion of the skin. The colours of the fish appear pale under the thin, grey film of the thickened mucus. The disease can remain latent as long as the fish is healthy, but strike when the resistance is lowered. It is more likely to attack fish kept in an aquarium than fish living in the more natural conditions of a pond. Affected fish can be cured by either of the salt treatments, repeating the treatment after a two day interval.

Gill Rot. This is a highly dangerous disease, most prevalent during the summer months. The occurrence of the malady is furthered by high temperatures and decaying organic matter in the water. The disease is caused by some of the lower fungi which produce branched hyphae that grow into the veins of the gill sheets. This results in a complete stoppage of the blood circulation in the affected areas. Being deprived of a blood supply, sections of the gill sheets start to die, decay and fall off. The fish usually dies from suffocation. By the time the symptoms are noticeable it is already too late to save the fish. If this disease is suspected, treat the ailing fish without delay to the long salt bath.

Mouth Fungus (Chondrococcus columnaris). This is not a fungus infection, but is caused by a slime bacterium. It is both contagious and dangerous. Infected fish lose their appetite. Movements are sluggish. If treatment is delayed the whole frontal part of the head may be eaten away, and the fish will die. Treat with phenoxethol, aureomycin, or chloromycetin. If treated at an early stage the disease can be cured within a short time.

Red Pest (Purpura cyprinorum). Seldom found in the aquarium, this is more a disease of the pond with too high a population of fish. The skin of the belly becomes a dark red colour. The lower part of the caudal fin and the pelvic and anal fins may also be inflamed. The reddening is due partly to an abnormal widening of the blood vessels and

174

also haemorrhages of the skin. The gills may appear blood-shot and have areas of dying tissue. The disease can be very contagious; however, if given good conditions and prompt treatment the chances of recovery are good. Provide ample aeration and run a strong stream of water through the pond or aquarium. Chloromycetin can be used to treat affected fish. Avoid future over-crowding.

Ulcers. The disease commences with a small lesion which becomes a pimple-like swelling. The swelling then develops into an open sore. Separate the fish and treat with chloromycetin or terramycin; also soak food in the solution before feeding.

'Hole-in-the-Body'. An extremely contagious and dangerous ulcer-like disease. The disease may remain dormant for some time, only to break out in rapid activity. The ulcers quickly become large open sores with rapidly decaying walls. The disease can infect and kill every fish that has been in contact with the original source of infection. This is a disease that has been introduced during recent years, mainly through imports from the East. A great many koi and goldfish have died from this virulent disease. It is a wise policy to treat all imported coldwater fish with the greatest suspicion. Give prolonged quarantine, and thoroughly disinfect all equipment that comes in contact with the fish, or the water in which it is kept.

Separate infected fish immediately and keep very close observation on those which 'appear' healthy. No certain cure has yet been found. However, there have been reports of some cures by using aureomycin, chloromycetin and terramycin. Treat by making a thick paste from the chemical and place in the wound, repeating every day. Isolate the fish in a bath of the same chemical in the proportions given under the drug heading. It may require prolonged treatment before the fish recovers.

Autumn Sickness. At times, but often during the autumn, the novice fishkeeper may suffer a number of deaths amongst the fish. There is no sign of parasite or disease, yet the deaths may seem like an epidemic. Generally the pond or aquarium is fully planted and the population of fish very crowded. The cause of the deaths is, very basically, due to lack of oxygen and a high concentration of toxic nitrites.

Autumn sickness can be avoided by taking a few simple precautions. As the darker days approach, reduce the number of plants if they have become excessive. Ensure that the tank receives adequate illumination. Be sure that the population of fish is not too high. Keep the water clean, syphon over the aquarium gravel frequently, and do not overfeed. Give the pond an autumn clean-out.

If Autumn Sickness does appear, quickly change the water, then remedy any other contributory factors.

PREDATORS

The larger predators such as cats, some birds and other animals can be guarded against by stretching a net over the pond. However, there are some predators that are not so easy to avoid. The aquarium, being more protected, is not as vulnerable as the open pond and not so likely to be troubled. The pond is not so fortunate. A list of the better known predators follows, some being more dangerous than others. The rule for safety is to remove any creatures, large or small, whose habits are not known. Predators should be removed and killed immediately they are seen. To ignore them is courting trouble, for many can damage a fish quite considerably — even if they do not kill it.

Alder-Fly. The common Alder-fly is a familiar sight around ponds, lakes and streams during May and June. The female can lay up to 2000 eggs in clusters on stones and plants near the water's edge. The larvae remain in the water for around 2 years, which they spend crawling in the bottom mud. Brown in colour, the larvae grow to a length of 25 mm. They will attack any smaller creature, seizing their prey in powerful mandibles.

Dytiscus (Great Diving Beetle). This is probably the best known of the predatory water beetles. It reaches a length of 35 mm (1.4 inches) and can be found in most natural ponds. Olive-brown in colour with a yellow margin around the thorax and wing-cases. It is ferociously carnivorous, attacking creatures much larger than itself.

The larvae grow to 50 mm long and carry powerful sickle-shaped mandibles. If anything the larvae are even more vicious than the adult beetle. The victim is seized, and a digestive fluid pumped into its body, the dissolved solid contents are then sucked back, leaving only an empty skin. The larval period lasts for about one year after hatching from the sausage-shaped eggs, which are laid in slits made in submerged plants.

Great Silver Beetle. Frequenting waters that have a plentiful growth of vegetation, this beetle is omnivorous. It reaches a length of 45 mm (1.8 inches) and lays its eggs in silken cocoons which cling to plants at the water surface. Unlike their parents, which eat both plant and

176

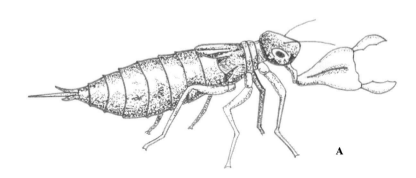

A

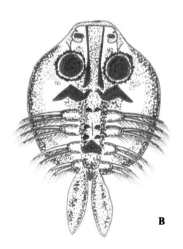

B

A. Water Tiger

B. Argulus

(Greatly Enlarged)

Figure 9.2 *Further Predators*

177

animal foods, the larvae are strictly carnivorous. They grow rapidly and can attain a length of 70 mm (2.8 inches).

Water Boatmen. These grow to approximately 15 mm (0.6 inch) long, and are abundantly widespread. It is a common sight in ponds where it rests upside down at the surface, the tip of the abdomen and the fore and middle legs just touching the surface film. They also swim in an upside down position, with the two long oar-like legs outstretched. This bug will feed upon living creatures, and does not hesitate to attack creatures larger than itself. Eggs are laid in slits made in submerged plants and hatch into white, red-eyed miniatures of the adult. Remove and kill.

Water Scorpion. Looking like a dead leaf, it is flat and dark brown in colour. Attaining a length of 30 mm (1.2 inches) or more, it lurks in the mud of shallow water at the edge of the pond. The front legs are modified to grasp the victim in a vice-like grip, the juice being sucked out of the prey.

Water Tiger. The larval stage of the Dragonfly. They have a so-called 'mask', formed from the third pair of jaws being fused into a

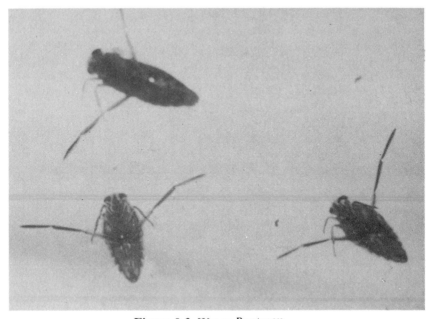

Figure 9.3 *Water Boatmen*

178

moveable structure with strong claws at its end. When at rest the mask is folded back under the head, but as soon as any prey comes within reach, the mask is shot forward to seize the victim in the claws, after which it is slowly eaten. Normally sluggish, this creature lurks in wait for its victim to come within striking distance.

Stick Insect. Related to the Water Scorpion, it has a stick-like body and reaches a length of 65 mm (2.5 inches). Its habits are similar to those of the Water Scorpion.

Hydra. Of danger only to small fry, the Hydra looks a little like a tiny sea-anemone. When extended it is visible to the naked eye, but if disturbed will quickly contract its tentacles and body into a minute blob. Hydra are usually plentiful in weedy waters, and may be introduced into the aquarium or pond with plants or live food gathered from such a source. To eradicate the pest, remove the fish, then stir one teaspoon of ammonia to each four gallons of water into the infected quarters. Leave for 48 hours before emptying Flush to remove all traces of ammonia. Refill and replace the fish. If necessary repeat the treatment until the Hydra are completely wiped out.

Figure 9.4 *Dytiscus Beetle*
A large ferocious beetle that will readily attack fish much larger than itself

ACCIDENTS

Apart from disease, parasite and predator, fish can also suffer from accidents. Most accidents are caused by the aquarist mishandling the fish, but some can arise from other causes. Always remember that any break in the skin offers an invitation to Fungus. Torn fins and missing scales are often the result of spawning activities. Net the fish and paint the wound with Friar's Balsam, unless other treatment is required. Lost scales will regrow and the torn fins will mend with time and care. The eyes of the telescope-eyed varieties are sometimes knocked out or, rarely, sucked out by another fish. The minnow is an offender in that respect. Normally, the loss of an eye does not appear to inconvenience the fish to any great extent and, therefore, it need not be destroyed. Careless handling can result in the goldfish falling from the hands or net. In a more solidly-boned creature bones would break. However, although the goldfish will not break any bones it can be very severely bruised and the fish may die as a direct result. Always exercise extreme care when handling fish out of water. If the fish should have the misfortune to be dropped, treat it to the long term salt bath away from bright light and disturbance. During the breeding season, a male frog will sometimes clasp a fish in its nuptial embrace; this will cause very severe bruising and, probably, loss of scales.

Deep wounds inflicted by birds and cats require painting with iodine solution and then placing the fish into a saline bath. Careful watch must be kept to ensure that the wounds do not become attacked by Fungus. Fish which, for some reason or another, have been out of water for any length of time should be placed into clean, fresh water, and aeration applied until the fish revives. Treat with salt as soon as it has fully recovered. Very often a fish which is floating in a semi-comatose state will recover when placed into fresh water.

PAINLESS DESTRUCTION

If treatment and ministering care fail to cure an ailing fish it should be destroyed. Professional breeders, and many experienced amatuers, kill the fish by hitting it on the head. The fish can also be dropped into boiling water, which kills it instantly. Flushing the fish down a lavatory-pan may get rid of the fish, but it does not kill it — instead the fish will suffocate in the sewerage system. Most definitely sick fish must

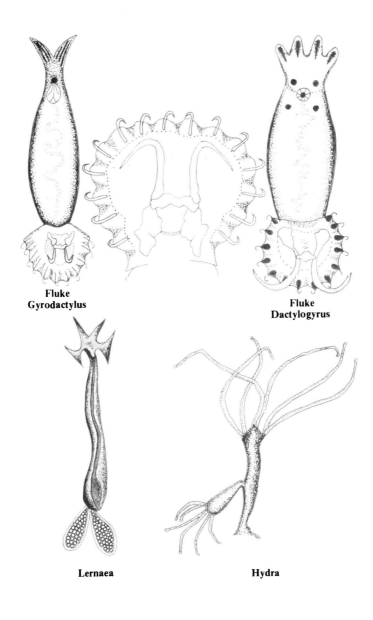

**Fluke
Gyrodactylus**

**Fluke
Dactylogyrus**

Lernaea

Hydra

Figure 9.5 *Parasites*
(Greatly Enlarged)

181

not be thrown into any natural wild water; such unthinking action can have dire consequences. Infecting the wild fish population could result in many deaths of our native species.

DISINFECTING PONDS AND AQUARIUMS

When fish are treated *in situ* the pond or aquarium is automatically treated, because the treating chemical is mixed into the pond or aquarium water. However, there are times when more drastic measures are required.

The aquarium can be disinfected by soaking for 24 hours in very strong potassium permanganate, or by adding 'Dettol' until the water turns milky. In both instances the plants and gravel should be removed and treated separately. The alternative is to remove all fish from the aquarium for about four weeks, in which time the disease or parasite should have been eliminated. Any source of pollution must, of course, be cleared to ensure a perfectly healthy tank.

Ponds may be treated with a strong solution of potassium permanganate, which will also kill the plants. In some cases, for instance, when leeches infect the pond, it is better to allow the pond and the planting medium to dry out thoroughly for a period of four weeks or more. The plants can be treated separately and stored elsewhere ready for replanting.

Having read the formidable list of problems that can afflict the goldfish, many may think that to keep goldfish entails a continuous battle against diseases, parasite and predator. However, the reader should not be alarmed, for if correct and adequate care is taken, the majority of the complaints can be kept at bay.

In almost every instance, problems can only arise — if the fish and water are healthy — through neglect or introduction. The careful fishkeeper will, therefore, exercise care and discrimination when acquiring any new plant or fish. Strict quarantine and disinfection of all new stock, together with regular maintenance of the aquarium and pond, are the primary rules of good fish management, and strict application of the rules will greatly reduce the possibility of many of these problems arising.

To sum up: obtain all stock from reliable sources. Treat imported fish with suspicion. Select only fish that appear healthy and are kept in clean conditions. Do not add any new stock to existing stocks, unless it has first been quarantined and disinfected. Always ensure that the fish are not subjected to sudden changes in water temperatures, especially when transferring fish. Avoid pollution of the water by not over-feeding with dried foods. Keep tanks and ponds clean, do not allow sediment or decomposing matter to reach a dangerous level. Do not try to keep more fish than the aquarium or pond will safely support. Vary the diet. If necessary, shade the water during hot sunny days. Provide adequate illumination to aquariums during dull days. Take care when handling fish. Remove and isolate any ailing fish, if necessary giving them appropriate treatment. And always have patience — remember that Nature will not be rushed. Obey the rules and problems should be few.

CHAPTER 10

Breeding

Although a great deal of pleasure can be derived from keeping the different varieties of fancy goldfish, it cannot compare with the pleasure and interest that is to be enjoyed from breeding the fish. Indeed, only those who raise their own stock can be considered true aquarists. Those who are only interested in keeping fish that have been produced by others will never become anything other than a 'fishkeepers' — which is a pity, for the satisfaction of seeing the first young fry hatch out of the egg will never be known.

Every year, as the warmer days approach, the goldfish breeder becomes filled with a renewed feeling of anticipation. Always there is the feeling that this is the season when that once-in-a-lifetime perfect fish will be produced. The breeding pairs are selected with care, and spawning awaited with mounting excitement. The growth of the young are studied closely and with expectation as they develop. Most enthusiasts will freely admit that their greatest pleasure is the annual production of young fancy goldfish.

Sooner or later many novice goldfish keepers will be filled with the desire to raise their own stock. Some, perhaps, in the mistaken belief that they will be able to make a fortune from the anticipated sales. Such dreams are doomed! It requires a great deal of knowledge and effort to produce even a few quality fancy goldfish and, despite the popularity of the hobby, the market is very restricted. There are easier and safer ways of making money. Even the best known amateur breeders of goldfish do little more than cover their expenses. However, if the skills of raising fancy goldfish are sought purely for the pleasure they will bring, then the novice can succeed.

The act of reproduction is the same for all vertebrate animals. It consists of the male fertilizing the ova of the female. Most people associate the act with the pairing of each sex and union between the two, the eggs of the female being fertilized whilst still in her body. In most fish the act is much simpler. During the breeding season the male may fertilize the eggs of a number of females, the eggs of the female being fertilized, in turn, by a number of different males. There is no sexual union between sexes in the accepted sense. The female ejects her eggs which are then fertilized by the spermatozoa of the male; these are shed into the water during the spawning drive in a milky cloud of milt. In order to ensure a good spawning the pair of fish must be brought to the peak of condition. Spawning usually takes place in water that has a temperature of 60° F (15.5° C).

Conditioning the fish. During the autumn the fish should be plentifully fed, as described in Chapter 8. This enables the female to produce eggs in readiness for the next breeding season. As spring approaches, the sexes should be fed liberal quantities of chopped earthworms and other live foods. If it is intended to breed the fish in tanks — as experienced fish-breeders do in order to exercise control over the selection of parents — the males and females should be separated. There is little doubt amongst experienced aquarists, that if the adults are allowed to have a semi-dormant period during the preceding winter, and then conditioned in separate tanks the following spring, the spawning is the better and the males more vigorous.

When the female appears somewhat more plump in her body than usual, and the male has developed the small white pinhead-sized pimples (tubercles) on his pectoral fins and gill plates — both swimming in an alert manner with erect fins — it can be assumed that they have reached that peak of good health which is known as 'breeding condition'. At this stage an attempt can be made to obtain a spawning from the selected pair.

Spawning tank. Ideally a specially prepared tank should be set up for the adults to spawn in. For this purpose employ a tank of around 36 inches x 15 inches (915 mm x 381 mm) and 12 inches (305 mm) deep. Disinfect and clean thoroughly to avoid any possible inclusion of un-suspected parasites or snails — although, if my earlier advice has been heeded, snails will have been eliminated from both pond and aquariums.

Place the tank where the rays of the morning sun can reach it; early morning sunlight often encourages a spawning. It should then be filled to a depth of about ten inches (254 mm), and the water left to mature for a few days to rid itself of any chlorine or excess oxygen. It is not necessary to include any gravel or plants, the tank need contain nothing other than clean fresh water. Visit any goldfish breeder, and it will be seen that most keep even the adult fish in bare tanks. This allows the aquarist to maintain scrupulous cleanliness, which would not be possible in the less utilitarian decorative aquarium.

Spawning mops, being artificial, are easier to clean than natural plants and are quite easy to make. Unravel one or two woven plastic pot-scourers, and cut into crinkled strands of around 12 inches (305 mm) long. Bind the strands into bunches of a dozen. Alternatively, lengths of nylon wool can be bound into bundles of similar length. For safety they should then be boiled and washed; this precaution is necessary to remove any water soluble dye that might prove dangerous to the eggs or fry. Having made the mops, suspend a number at both ends of the tank. They should not be so thickly placed that they hinder the passage of the fish, nor so sparse that the fish can avoid them. The slight friction as the fish swim through the mops appears to encourage the female to shed her eggs.

When all is ready the male can be placed into the spawning tank. It is usual to do this during the evening in order to allow the male to settle down in the strange surroundings. At this stage some people insert a square of glass to divide the tank into two compartments. The following evening the female is also placed into the tank (if the separation method is being used, she should be placed in the opposite compartment to the male). I prefer to allow the fish to swim together. If within a short time the male commences to lazily chase the female there is a likelihood that they will spawn the following day. If the pair are separated the glass must, of course, be removed. Should the fish show no immediate interest and the male ignores the female, have patience and continue to feed earthworm. Allow two weeks to elapse before interfering with the pair. If, at the end of the period, they have not spawned they should be placed back in the original tanks and conditioned further. The spawning tank will need to be cleaned and reset.

Spawning and fertilization of the eggs. When spawning the fish show great exuberance, even the most sluggish fish becoming active. The males pursue the females wildly to and fro. As they do so, the males bump the female in the region of her vent. This action stimulates the female who, when ready, will allow the males to chase her into the spawning area. At this time the fish become oblivious to all else — the instinct to chase dominating the fish — and in the unguarded pond many fall easy prey to fish-eating birds and other animals. The action of the spawning fish cannot be mistaken. The drive normally commences quite early in the morning and may last for some hours, depending upon the size and vigour of the fish. It is not uncommon for the longer finned type of goldfish to receive badly torn fins, and sometimes some of the scales are knocked off, but, with good treatment, the injuries will heal.

The male will chase the female into the spawning area, with much bumping, and there he will manoeuvre himself close to her side. Pressing against her, the pair will make a shivering movement as eggs and milt are released. Immediately the pair will separate, to continue the drive until the female is stripped of ova. Remove the pair when the spawning ceases, otherwise they will start to eat the eggs.

The eggs are flatish when expelled by the female, but quickly assume a round shape. As they expand by an osmotic uptake of water any nearby sperm is drawn into the micropyle. This tiny hole is only large enough to admit entry to a single sperm, and closes immediately. The eggs, which are approximately 1/16 inch (1.5 mm) in diameter, are a pale amber colour. As they sink through the water they will adhere to anything with which they come into contact. The rate of development is governed by the water temperature. Most western aquarists find that a water temperature of 70°F (21°C) gives the best results and a hatching in about four days. Infertile eggs will become opaque and white. Within a short time they will be attacked by fungus. Some writers suggest that the furred, infertile eggs should be removed. I have never found such a tedious task necessary, nor have I found that the fungus affects the fertile eggs.

DEVELOPMENT OF THE EGG

Development of the fertile egg follows a set pattern. Upon penetration by the spermatozoon, oily droplets contained with the egg fall to the bottom of the egg, leaving the yolk clear. The yolk granules drift to the top of the egg, forming a bump on the surface. In the meantime, the egg shell becomes slightly larger, hardens and lifts away from the egg. The surface bump quickly divides into two cells, these two cells divide and double in number again. Each cell so produced continues

Centrosomes

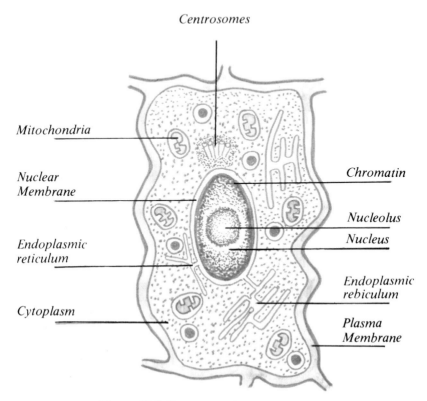

Mitochondria

Nuclear
Membrane

Endoplasmic
reticulum

Cytoplasm

Chromatin

Nucleolus

Nucleus

Endoplasmic
rebiculum

Plasma
Membrane

Figure 10.1 *Structure of Typical Animal Cell*

to divide and double itself, eventually forming two distinct layers of cells. The size of the multiplying cells get smaller and the number greater, until a rounded cap is produced in the area of the animal pole. This stage is known as the blastula, and becomes flatter as tiny cells continue to increase and move down over the yolk. As they progress towards the vegetal pole, the cells lift slightly to form a gap (the blastocoele) between themselves and the yolk.

Before long about one-third of the egg surface becomes covered by the blastoderm, and they begin to build up at the advancing margin. This 'piling-up' at the lateral margins of the blastoderm forms the 'germ-ring', and is the start of gastrulation. Gastrulation involves the

188

cells in the thickened germ ring moving underneath the blastoderm. The cells form a band which progressively elongates at the end nearest the vegetal pole, to produce the embryonic shield. The gastrula expands to almost cover the surface of the yolk, and a band of cells forms the embryonic keel in the centre of the shield.

As development continues optic vesicles form, which eventually become the eyes, and the main divisions of the brain appear as bulges on the dorsal surface of the keel. The head of the embryo lifts away from the yolk and soon slight contractions of the embryonic heart begin. The embryo grows substantially to cover about half the circumference of the egg, and the tail lifts off the yolk. The notochord, which will become the backbone vertebrae, becomes visible, as do the pigmented eyes.

The pectoral fins form completely, but the only other fin is a combined dorsal/caudal/anal fin. This latter fin will split into the separate fins after hatching. The pelvic fins form after the pectorals.

Shortly before hatching the embryo makes violent movements inside the egg shell. These movements, aided by an enzyme which softens the shell, enables the fry to break free. The tail first emerges from the egg shell, followed by the head.

On emergence from the egg shell the fry is approximately $\frac{1}{5}$ inch (5 mm) long, and appears as a tiny glass-like splinter. The dorsal region is slightly greenish and has irregular dark spots of pigment. The most prominent feature to the casual observer is the yolk-sac, carried abdominally.

At this stage the fry hang by a sticky secretion to any firm surface, occasionally labouring towards the water surface. On no account should they be disturbed. Any that fall may have difficulty rising due to the water pressure. During this period the yolk is consumed. After a time the fry will manage to struggle to the surface of the water, and the tiny air-bladder will become inflated. From that stage on the fry become free-swimming, and will commence to search for very fine food. At this point many will die unless sufficient food is made available.

FEEDING THE FRY

Conditioning the goldfish and encouraging them to breed is a fairly simple matter, and many beginners are successful in obtaining spawnings. However, many novices fail in the following weeks to keep the fry alive and growing. During the first few weeks of its life the tiny fish will eat almost continuously, and ample food of the correct size must be available to satisfy the need. One of the 'secrets' of raising fish is to keep the bellies of the young filled — for a young goldfish is capable of eating more than its own bulk in a day. Suitable cultures of live food should be started as soon as the embryo can be seen inside the egg; it should then be ready for feeding to the fry when they become free-swimming.

Infusoria. In the old days, before the advent of Brine Shrimp eggs (see below), this was the live food most commonly cultured — some goldfish breeders still use it. Infusoria was a collective name given to microscopic unicellular organisms. There are many ways of cultivating infusoria, some giving better results than others. Six or so large glass jars (the type used by confectioners are ideal) are filled with water from an established pond or aquarium. The water is strained through some very fine material to exclude any small insects or other creatures. Into these jars is placed some form of vegetation, which may be any of the following: chopped dry hay, dried leaves from aquatic plants, rotting lettuce leaves, bruised banana skins, and so forth. The jars are then placed in a warm dark place for about one week. At the end of this period a good culture of microscopic food should be visible. Water containing infusoria almost always has a bad smell and looks as though a greyish-white cloud of dust is suspended in it. The culture must be kept fresh by gentle aeration. It must also be fed, and this is best done by adding a small amount of decomposing lettuce leaf from time to time. Fresh cultures are set up exactly as before, having a small amount of an existing culture added to speed up the cultivation.

The method of feeding to the goldfish fry is quite simple. A jar of infusoria is stood slightly above the tank, and a short length of air-line tubing is used to syphon the water from the jar into the fry-tank. Normally an air-line clip is used to regulate the flow to a slow drip. Thus the food could be left to 'drip-feed' the fry continuously, the supply jar being topped-up from the other cultures as needed. Every effort must be made to see that the temperature of the infusoria water is near to that of the tank water, otherwise the infusoria could be killed, and so pollute the water in which the fry were swimming.

Although countless numbers of fry have been raised by this method, it is a smelly business. Nowadays most goldfish breeders prefer to cul-

190

ture the cleaner, but expensive, brine shrimp nauplii.

Brine Shrimp (Artemia salina). Since the introduction of this food it has become exceedingly popular, especially the newly hatched nauplii which are used to feed fry during the early weeks of their life.

This small shrimp is found throughout many parts of the world, but strangely never in the oceans. It is common in bodies of water, natural or artificial, where there is a very high salt concentration. Most of the eggs which are offered commercially come from the United States of America, especially the Great Salt Lakes in the State of Utah. The eggs are a brownish colour and only about $\frac{1}{5}$ mm in size — like small grains of dark coloured sand. They are very hard-shelled, and will remain viable for many years if kept dry. The naupilii are pale pink to red in colour, depending upon the concentration of the salt; in strong saline water the newly hatched shrimp is deeply coloured.

Although a very expensive food, it is convenient to use, readily accepted by the young fish, and cannot introduce any freshwater disease or parasite into the fry-tank. For obvious reasons it is only fed until the fry become large enough to eat less expensive foods such as small Daphnia.

To cultivate this food is reasonably easy. Using glass jars, as described for infusoria, fill them to just below the neck with a saline solution of two teaspoons of salt — preferably marine salt, obtainable from aquatic dealers — to each pint of water, stir thoroughly until the salt has completely dissolved, then add a teaspoon of eggs. The jar should then be stood in a tank of water which has been warmed to 80° F (26.7° C), and strong aeration applied to bubble the eggs around. The eggs should begin to hatch in about 24 hours. To collect the newly hatched brine shrimp, pour the water through a square of finely woven material; the food can then be swilled into the tank of fry. Return the strained water to the jar and add another teaspoonful of eggs. The quantity of eggs depends entirely upon the number of fry to be fed, but a level teaspoonful should be sufficient.

It will be noticed that as the fry consume this food their bellies will turn red. Although the food will contain a certain amount of brine, it is not necessary to swill it before feeding; the small amount of salt is unlikely to reach a concentration high enough to harm the fry.

Other Foods. As the fish grow, they should be offered larger foods graded to suit their size. Small sifted Daphnia and well mashed whiteworms can follow the brine shrimp; in turn larger Daphnia, chopped

191

whiteworm and dried foods can follow.

SPACE AND CULLING THE FRY

The fry must be allowed ample swimming space if they are to grow and develop in a satisfactory manner. Failure to observe this fundamental requirement will result in stunted fish, or the death of a great many through being over-crowded. To attempt to grow every one of the fry into adult fish would be impossible. The amount of space alone could hardly be provided by the majority of fishkeepers. The answer is to reduce the number, by keeping only the better specimens.

To sort the fry it is necessary to have certain items of equipment. A large white wash-bowl, two smaller bowls, a magnifying glass, a large flour sieve with a handle, and a smaller sieve. The large sieve is used to catch the fry. A net would kill many by crushing them as they were lifted from the water, whereas the sieve keeps its shape and supports the baby fish. The smaller sieve is for picking out the selected fish. An alternative, which I use, is to make a small round wire frame of about 2 inches (51 mm) in diameter, attached to a handle — rather like that of a small net — and across this stitch a tightly stretched piece of nylon stocking.

Fill the bowls with clean water of the same temperature as the water in which the fry are swimming. With the large sieve catch a few of the fry and gently swill into the larger white bowl. The fish must then be carefully inspected through the magnifying glass. Remove any weak or malformed fry and place into one of the smaller bowls. It will be seen that some will have bent or twisted backs and are badly deformed. If one of the twintail varieties has been bred, the young fry should have little spear-shaped tails. These must be gently removed and placed into the other bowl. Continue in this fashion until the tank is empty of fry, and each has been sorted according to its quality. The poor specimens can then be discarded — they can be fed to the adult fish.

Before replacing the selected young, clean their tank and refill with clean water which is at the correct temperature. As I have already said, space is important. If possible spread the sorted fish throughout a number of tanks, allowing approximately twenty-five fry to each 24 inch x 12 inch (610 mm x 305 mm) surface area tank. As the fish grow, the number will need to be reduced accordingly. It is quite possible to exceed the number which I have suggested, but the more space and food each individual fish is allowed the better will be the rate of growth. The greatest mistake of the novice is trying to raise too many fish, a hopeless task unless the large tanks of a public aquarium are available. The successful breeder of goldfish will never attempt to raise more fish than available space allows; therefore, severe culling is practised from a very early stage and continued at frequent intervals, to ensure that only the best specimens are left.

In an emergency, foods other than those mentioned can be used. Fine oatmeal, cooked to a stiff paste, can be squeezed through fine muslin to form a cloud in the water. The hard-boiled yolk of an egg can be fed in a similar manner, or there is a commercially prepared liquid food that is specially manufactured for fry. However, a substitute is always a substitute and cannot supply the same nourishment and various essential elements that are found in live foods. It is a fact that the best growth is produced when the fry are fed upon a diet of live foods, and, of course, they do not present the same risk of water pollution.

SORTING FOR QUALITY

By the time the young fish have reached a length of ½ inch (13 mm), the Nacreous types of goldfish should be exhibiting their colours. This makes it an easy task to recognise the Metallic and Matt types. These latter fish can be removed, allowing the remainder to benefit from the additional swimming space.

Regular sorting of the developing fish must be carried out, the frequency depending upon the rate of growth. I should mention that the larger, fastest growing fish do not always make the best. In many instances it will be found that the medium sized fish often turn out to be the better specimens; whilst the very small fish are quite likely to be 'runts' — small undersized fish, often with greatly over developed finnage. Many of the less desirable types can be netted out, if a close inspection is made of the young in the tank. A poor fish will never improve and is better removed as soon as it is noticed.

At a size of around 1 inch (25 mm) it is possible to sort the young fish for their finer points.

Singletailed varieties. These types are without doubt the easiest for the novice to sort. Select those young which have good body contours

193

and sturdy finnage. Any fish that has the slightest sign of a droop to the caudal fin should be rejected. As the fin develops the fault will become progressively worse. Fish that have a single caudal fin must carry the fin stiffly.

Fantailed varieties. The bodies of these fish are egg-shaped; there should be no trace of 'snoutiness' nor any sign of a hump back. The anal fins must be fully divided and well separated. The caudal fin is also divided into two matching tails. They must be carried firmly and not droop into a 'draggletail'. Preferably the two halves of the twin-tails should be fully separated from each other. There should be evidence that the particular feature of the fish will develop as it matures.

Veiltailed varieties. These fish have deep, short, roundish bodies. Like the previous types, there must be no 'snoutiness' and the anal and caudal fins should be evenly matched and separated. However, the caudal fins must have as near to a square cut trailing edge as possible, and will have a slight downward angle. The anal and pelvic fans will appear pointed and rather longer than those of the Fantail. Any young fish of this type which has a forked caudal tail and short anal fins, together with rounded pelvic and pectoral fins must be rejected — when adult it will look like an over-long finned Fantail.

The fins of the Fantail and Veiltail types should not be too long. They will continue to grow as the fish develops and, if too well developed at this stage, will be grossly over-finned by the time that it is fully grown.

Telescope-eyed. The Moor is a black metallic scaled fish, therefore discard any which appear 'brassy'. The eyes should have developed at this stage, and be matched in shape and size. The eyes of the Celestial variety of goldfish will, at first, protrude sideways, but as the fish develops the eyes will slowly turn upwards.

Dorsal-finless varieties. The body shape of these fish is very similar to the Fantail, and so are the fins. The dorsal contour of the back must be broad and smoothly curved. There must be no sign of any dips or bumps, nor must there be any trace of a fin or spine to mar the even contour.

Hooded varieties. This feature will take some time to develop; however, the head should be short, blunt and 'squarish'. This type of head forms a good base for the hood, whereas the more pointed head is unlikely to develop a very good growth. The fish with the greatest potential will exhibit a slight roughness on top of the head — evidence of the future hood.

Nacreous types. Normally the darker coloured fish are the best, because the colours can get lighter with age. It will be two or three years before the final colours of these fish can be fully assessed.

Metallic types. Select those specimens that change colour at an early age. It is better to reject any fish that has not changed from the olive colour within twelve months, for the tendency will be for any off-spring from it to take even longer — and many may never change colour. Select the deeper coloured fish in preference to those of a lighter shade.

It must always be remembered that these young fish are not adults, and should not be replicas of the adult. Therefore, refer to the section which describes the different adult varieties of fancy goldfish. Judge the young fish as it will appear when two or three years old against the particular description, and assess the fish accordingly.

LINE-BREEDING

The ambitious breeder of fancy goldfish will wish to develop a strain, and this will require careful selective breeding techniques, together with line-breeding and in-breeding of the stock. Only in that way will the quality be improved and desired features accentuated. Haphazard crossings may occasionally produce a first-class fish, but it will not bring a consistent long term result. The crossing of different varieties is gross folly and deplorable. It does the breeder no credit, yet many still persist in crossing a Moor to a Veiltail to try to obtain a better blue coloration of the nacreous Veiltail. The number of different variations — mostly of no use — that are found in a goldfish spawning are legion. Even from the best quality strain of fancy goldfish, the adults produce only a small percentage of worthwhile young. Cross breeding the varieties only adds to the problem. The best of the progeny from such a crossing are nothing more than mongrels — despite their outward appearance — as any subsequent breeding will prove.

The goldfish is a 'law unto itself', and refuses to breed true. In fact, it is continuously trying to revert back to its original wild form. Therefore the goldfish breeder must use skill and knowledge to preserve and improve the variety. It is a 'battle' between Man and Nature. How much easier it would be if, like the majority of tropical fish, the young were produced like 'peas-in-a-pod'.

LINE-BREEDING CHART

LINE 'A'

Year	Cross	Select from Young	Remarks
1	Good Female with a good Male	The best Male and Female	The Adults should be from an established strain
2	The first year Male back to its Mother	The best Male and Female	The Female is the foundation fish — be sure that she is the best available
3	The second year Male back to its Grandmother	The best Male and Female	After this spawning the old Female will not be needed
4	The third year Male with the first year Female	The best Male and Female	
5	The fourth year Male with the second year Female	The best Male	
6	Last year's Male with both third and fourth year Females	The best Female from the total produced	Take two separate spawnings, one from each Female
7	This line not bred this year		By now the line should be greatly improved
8	Last year's line 'B' Male with the Year 6 Female	Best Male and Female	
9	This line is not bred this year		
10	Last year's line 'B' Male to Year 8 Female	Best Male	
11	Last year's Male to line 'B' Year 9 Female	Best Male	Next year cross with Mother Continue line from Year 2

LINE-BREEDING CHART

LINE 'B'

Year	Cross	Select from Young	Remarks
1			
2			
3	The first year Female with her Father	The best Male and Female	This will consolidate the Father's features in the line
4	Last year's Male with its Mother	The best Male and Female	
5	Last year's Male with the young Year 3 Female	The best Male	
6	Last year's Male with the Year 4 Female	The best Male	
7	Last year's Male with the Year 4 Female:its Mother	The best Male and Female	
8	This line not bred this year		The line should now carry many improved features
9	Brother with Sister from Year 7	Best Male and Female	Brother and Sister are known as 'Siblings'. This cross is 'inbreeding'
10	This line not bred this year		
11	Year 9 Male with line 'A' Female from Year 8	Best Male	Next year cross with Mother. Continue breeding as chart for line 'B' from year 4

If line weakens, or loses vigour, outcross with fish from related strain.

In order to improve the percentage of good young stock, the goldfish breeder must learn the art of selecting the right adults for breeding, the skills of breeding and growing the young fish, and the ability to pick out the best of the young when they are very small. The successful amateur goldfish breeder invariably specialises in only one or two varieties, keeping no others.

The best age at which to spawn the female goldfish is when she is between two and three years old. Until then she is immature and, although able to breed, will only throw small eggs which tend to produce weak fry. If the males are well grown they can be used at an age of twelve months, and will drive a female hard.

In order to build up a strain of goldfish by 'line-breeding' a really good pair of the desired variety should be acquired from a well-established quality strain of repute. If possible ensure that the female is the best available, and better than the male in desired characteristics. Be prepared to pay a high price for such a fish; the expense is warranted to create a good base from which to build the future breeding programme. The female will be the foundation of the strain and must be chosen accordingly.

Commence by breeding the male and the female together. From their young select the best male and female to start line 'A'. (It will be advisable to create two lines 'A' and 'B'.) In the second year cross the young male and female. The following year the 'old' female is crossed with her grandson who was raised the previous season. Again the best young male and female are selected. In the fourth year, last year's young male is crossed with the three-year old female from the first year's spawning, keeping the best opposite pair. In year five, cross last year's young male with the female produced in the second year, this time keeping only the best young male. During the sixth year cross the previous season's young male first with the female from year three, and then with the female from year four. From the young produced pick out just one fish — the best female. No breeding of this line is carried out during the following year. However, in the eighth year the best male produced the previous year, by line 'B', is crossed with this line's year six female, keeping the best young male and female. Again, the ninth year is missed. For the tenth year, cross this line's year eight female with the line 'B' male produced last year, keeping only the best young male. In the eleventh year cross last year's young male with line 'B' female raised during the ninth year. In the twelfth year cross last year's young male with its mother — as was done in year two of this line. The following year the same type of crossing is made as for year three, and so the breeding continues to follow in sequence.

Line 'B' is not started until the third year, when the young female from the first year of line 'A' is crossed back to the 'old' male — her father. From this spawning the best male and female are chosen. In year four, cross the young male from last year with its mother, keeping the best male and female. In year five cross last year's young male to the female produced in the third year, keeping only the best male. In the sixth year cross last season's male with the female from the third year spawning. During the seventh year use the previous year's young male to cross back to its mother, and keep the best young male and female. The line is not bred during the following year. A sibling cross is made in the ninth year, when the brother and sister produced two years ago are bred together. From this 'in-breeding' the best opposite pair are selected. Again the line is not bred during the tenth year. In the eleventh year the young male from the ninth year is crossed with the

Figure 10.3 *Nacreous Lionheads Spawning*
The male fish pushes and lifts the plump female with his head towards the nylon wool spawning mops

199

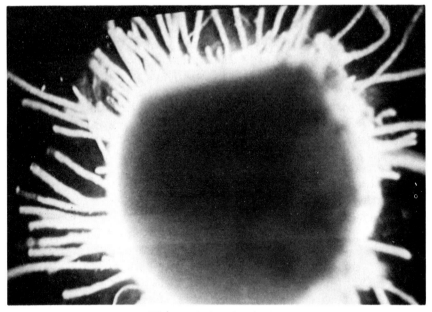

Figure 10.4 *Infertile Egg*
As seen through a low power microscope. Note fungus strands

line 'A' female from the eighth year. During the twelfth year, the only young male chosen in the previous year is crossed with its mother. Keep only the best young male and female. The following year continue as for year four of line 'B', continuing the sequence in the following years.

The illustrated 'Line-breeding Chart' will make the detailed breeding of the two lines easier to understand. If at any time the strain appears to be weakening, or the fish lacking size, breed a fish from the original strain (or a related strain) into the line. This is known as an 'out-cross', and will restore the vigour of the affected line.

There are various methods of line-breeding, some more simple and others more complicated, but whatever system is adopted the goldfish breeder must be prepared for many years of patient and dedicated work. However, the thought of so many years of devotion to the creation of a strain of goldfish will not deter the serious enthusiast. Success is seldom gained without some endeavour. In the early days there will

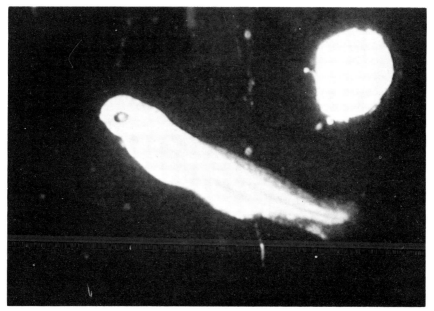

Figure 10.5 *Newly Hatched Goldfish*
A young goldfish immediately after hatching — as seen through a low power microscope

be many disappointments and a seeming lack of progress. With determination and perseverance the quality will improve and, in due time, will bring success.

HAND-STRIPPING

There may be occasions when, for various reasons, the fish cannot be left to finish a natural spawning. Perhaps the aquarist will be away until late in the evening — by which time many of the eggs may have been eaten by the adults. The solution, at such a time, is to hand-strip the fish. The procedure is not quite as difficult as some would have us believe, provided the fish are ready and commencing to spawn. To attempt to strip eggs from a female before she is ready to spawn is a waste of time, and may seriously injure the fish internally.

Make use of the bowls which are used when sorting fry. Fill them with water from the spawning tank, and place the fish separately into the smaller bowls. Line the larger bowl with a square of white material, and fill with water. If the material floats it should be weighted down in some way.

First take the male, hold it gently on its side with the vent facing away from the palm of the hand. If the thumb and forefinger of the free hand is lightly stroked along the body, in the direction of the vent, the sperm will be extracted. The sperms emerge from the vent like a piece of white-grey cotton which then breaks up and disperses into the water. Only a little is required, which should be stirred into the water after replacing the male in its bowl.

The female is treated in a similar fashion. Gently stroke the underside of her belly, whilst moving her through the water in order to spread the eggs over the material. Take only a few eggs before returning her to her bowl. After a few minutes, to allow both fish to recover,

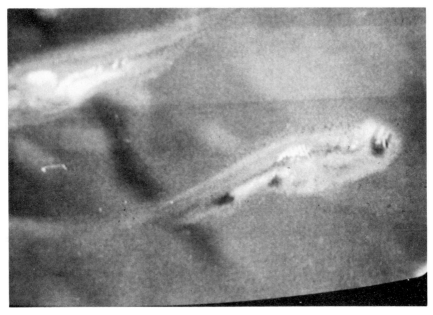

Figure 10.6 *Goldfish fry, shortly after filling the air-bladder*
This is visible as a silvery bubble. At this stage the fish is fractionally over one-quarter inch long

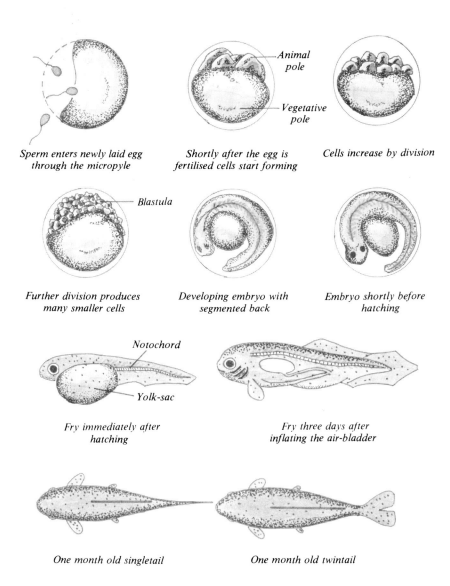

Sperm enters newly laid egg
through the micropyle

Shortly after the egg is
fertilised cells start forming

Animal
pole

Vegetative
pole

Cells increase by division

Blastula

Further division produces
many smaller cells

Developing embryo with
segmented back

Embryo shortly before
hatching

Notochord

Yolk-sac

Fry immediately after
hatching

Fry three days after
inflating the air-bladder

One month old singletail

One month old twintail

Figure 10.7 *Development of Egg
to Month Old Fish*

203

the operation can be repeated.

Do not take too many eggs, nor attempt further stripping when the easy flow of milt from the male or eggs from the female has ceased.

It should, of course, not need saying that the fish must be held below the water whilst they are being stripped. It is also advisable to wet the hands before handling either fish.

Leave the eggs in the bowl for ten minutes to allow the sperm sufficient time to fertilize the eggs. The water can then be poured away. Place the material into the hatching tank, and replace the fish into their aquarium. From this stage on the eggs are treated exactly like a normal spawning.

Whether the fish spawn naturally or are hand-stripped, they must be well fed afterwards with good nourishing foods, to rebuild their stamina.

Throughout this section the spawning of goldfish has been related to controlled breeding in an aquarium. In order to cover the subject fully the breeding of pond goldfish must not be forgotten.

Because the environment of the pond is less protected and temperatures lower, the fish will invariably spawn somewhat later than those in an aquarium. However, when conditions are right, spawn they will. Normally there are a number of goldfish in the pond, often of different varieties, therefore there is no way of knowing the parentage of any young that may survive. Mass spawnings are known as 'flock spawning'.

Although the progeny are unlikely to be of the any real value, the pond-keeper may well wish to raise a few fish. It should be noted where the fish spawn, so that, later, some of the plants with eggs attached can be gathered. These eggs can be hatched, and the young reared, in an aquarium as described earlier.

Unless removed from the pond, the adult fish will consume many of the eggs, small fish will be eaten, and only the lucky few will survive. The pond will also contain various creatures that will attack eggs and fry. It can thus be seen that to raise young fish in the normal ornamental pond is a very risky affair. To succeed special ponds are required, and these will be described in the next chapter.

Plate 7
Top: Japanese-Type Lionhead
Bottom: Two-Year Old Western Type Lionhead

CHAPTER 11

Fish-Houses and Breeding Ponds

There is a limit to the number of aquariums that can be kept in the home — if it is to remain a home. However, the ambitious goldfish keeper will invariably wish to acquire a number of quite large tanks. This makes it possible to breed and raise greater numbers of fish than would be possible within the restrictions of the indoor aquariums. There are undoubted advantages to moving aquariums out of the home environment, so that a better system of fish cultivation and management can be employed. It is a fact that practically all successful goldfish breeders keep and raise their stock in tanks that are housed within a fish-house. It is also true that many professional western fish-breeders cultivate the fancier varieties of goldfish in larger versions of the amateur breeder's installation.

Use of a special structure that allows ample daylight, large tanks, and some form of water exchange system, have much in their favour. Add special outdoor ponds, for growing the young fish, and the aquarist has the ideal set-up for the successful, and controlled, cultivation of fancy goldfish.

Almost without exception, goldfish breeders use glasshouse type buildings, generally of the ridge-roofed form, although some may be of lean-to construction. However, all have one common feature: a large area of glass to admit maximum daylight. The long hours of daylight provide a more natural condition than can be obtained by using artificial light, and the fish benefit accordingly. The fish reach breeding condition more readily, and the young fish have longer hours during which to feed. During a hot summer sunlight can become a problem, but it is a fairly simple matter to provide shading if it should become necessary, possibly by painting the glass roof with one of the commercially prepared greenhouse shading paints — this can be easily washed off at the end of the season. However, if a system of water circulation is employed such shading is not usually required. By circulating, or exchanging, the water in the tanks the free-floating algae are avoided, therefore the water remains clear and, at the same time, any oxygen deficiency is made good. The problems of pollution are greatly reduced; although care should still be exercised when feeding. Another feature of the majority of these establishments is the bare, utilitarian aspect of the tanks. Seldom are there any submerged aquatic plants growing in gravel. The tanks tend to be starkly bare of all internal adornments, and in this environment the fish thrive. Having bare tanks, the task of maintenance is substantially eased. It becomes a simple matter to syphon uneaten food and sediment off the glass base, and, of course, there is nowhere for an ailing fish to hide and be overlooked. Thus when the various factors are considered, it can be seen that there are undoubted advantages when the stock is kept in a fish-house — not least being efficiency of management and, possibly, cleaner conditions for the fish.

THE FISH-HOUSE

The size of the fish-house must largely depend upon personal preferences and the space available, although I would suggest that it be the largest that space and finance will allow. It is all too easy to outgrow a small structure, whereas, if the building is too large, part of it can always be used to grow various plants until further tank expansion begins to ease them out.

Choose a site that benefits from maximum sunlight, but is within easy connection distance of electricity, water supply and drainage.

Although it is possible to build the complete fish-house oneself, it is easier to purchase a solidly framed timber greenhouse of the desired dimensions. The sectional type is easy to erect upon a perpared foundation. It should not have glass right down to the ground level, because it will allow to much heat to escape and is prone to breakage from clumsy feet or excited children. Preferably the side and end walls should be boarded to half height. It could be the type that sits upon a brick walled lower section.

Before erecting the building, dig out foundations and build a low brick wall. The eaves height of manufactured greenhouses is usually too low to accommodate fish-tanks at a comfortable viewing level. By

Figure 11.1 *Amateur goldfish breeding establishment*

means of the brick wall the eaves height of the greenhouse should be raised to 5 feet (1524 mm) from the inside floor level. Having laid the foundations and built the brickwork to this required height (complete with damp-proof course) a concrete floor must be laid.

Drainage will save a lot of labour and, if this is to be incorporated, it should be laid in the early stages while laying the concrete foundations. Arrange for a conveniently placed grid-covered water disposal point and also a connection for the overflows from the tanks — both inside the structure.

Lay the concrete floor over a well-rammed bed of hardcore, and finish with a smooth half-inch skimming of waterproofed concrete. Allow about one week for the concrete to set really hard before erecting the greenhouse and glazing it. Once these tasks are completed the inside work can be carried out, and being safely protected from the outside weather, the labour can continue without hindrance.

Around the sides and across the end can be built a 6 inch (152 mm) deep trough, which should be rendered as described in the chapter deal-

Figure 11.2 *A semi-professional goldfish breeding establishment Owned by Messrs. T.G. (Tommy) Sutton and his son T.J. Sutton, near Birmingham, England*

ing with ornamental pond construction. To facilitate emptying, a base drainage point can be built in; this will need to be about 1¼ inch (32 mm) plastic pipe with a connector to allow a standpipe to be fitted. The standpipe will allow the trough to be flushed through without overflowing, maintaining a constant water level. (The trough could receive the overflow from the tanks, which would ensure a continuous through-flow of water.) To drain, the standpipe is withdrawn from the connector which is embedded in the concrete base. Before use the concrete must be cured to remove all free lime and make it safe for any fish. Curing raw concrete is described in the chapter dealing with pond construction.

It has already been mentioned that the tanks should be as large as is reasonably possible, the depths can be between 6 and 12 inches (152 and 305 mm) — there is no need for a greater depth. Large tanks will require substantial support. Using strong timbers, construct tiered

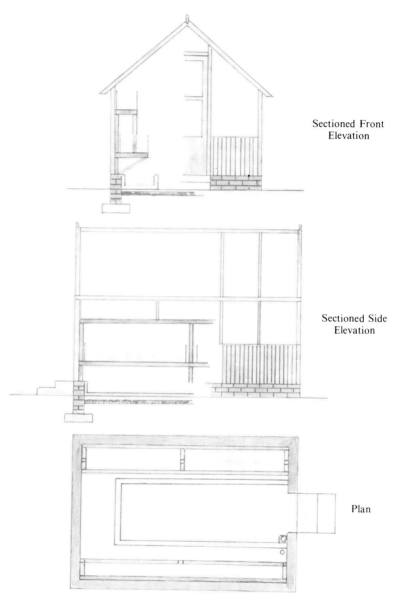

Sectioned Front
Elevation

Sectioned Side
Elevation

Plan

Figure 11.3 *Typical Amateur Fish-House Design*
Most amateur fish-houses are based upon a greenhouse type building, which allows maximum penetration of natural daylight **Not Drawn To Scale**

209

staging around the walls of the building, allowing at least 12 inches (305 mm) between the top of each tank and the lower edge of the staging above. If less distance is allowed it may be difficult to attend to the tanks when they require servicing. The rear frame of the staging can be screwed to the framework of the greenhouse, while the front is supported by uprights to prevent any possible bowing. It is often an advantage to have the width of the upper tanks and staging about 6 inches (152 mm) less than the tanks below. This arrangement allows a better penetration of top light to the lower bank of tanks. If only for the sake of appearance, paint the timbers to preserve them from what will be the damp atmosphere.

Next to be installed is the electricity. Exercise great care to ensure that it is, and will remain, safe. If there is the least doubt about how to install the wiring and points, a qualified electrician should be employed to carry out the work. Arrange for a switched point above each tank — if individual heaters and thermostats are to be used — together with a point for an air-pump and, perhaps, a fan-heater (for use during the winter). An electric light point will also be needed; this can be set mid-way along the ridge to give a good spread of illumination.

Finally, a water supply should be brought to a control valve above each tank. This must be plumbed in with plastic piping. On no account should copper be used, because it is toxic to fish. If possible, install the valve at the opposite end to the tank overflow, as this will allow water to flow through the tank from one end to the other.

Depending upon the size of the fish-house, it may be necessary to obtain planning permission from the local authority before the work is commenced. Certainly most water authorities will require payment for the water supply if it is drawn from the mains. To avoid any future difficulties they should be consulted before and after completion of the plumbing.

WATER EXCHANGE SYSTEM

Prior to placing the tanks into position they will require holes drilled into them, to accommodate the overflow pipes. The necessary plastic fittings can normally be obtained from a plumbers' merchant. These fittings comprise a threaded and flanged connector (such as are used to fit overflow pipes into domestic water cisterns), ¾ inch (19 mm) piping, elbow joints and 'T' pieces. Also required will be suffi-cient 1¼ inch (32 mm) plastic pipe together with elbow joints and 'T' pieces as necessary, to run below the tanks and connect to the drainage point previously installed. Suitably sized brackets will be needed to hold the drainage pipes in place. While at the merchants,' purchase a short length of 1 inch (25 mm) external diameter copper tube, a ¼ inch (6 mm) hexagon-headed bolt, and a small amount of plumber's lead. A tube of silicone rubber aquarium adhesive will also be needed from the local pet store. The only other requirements are a tube of coarse grade carborundum paste from a garage or engineers' supplier, and a hand-brace, plus a square of hardwood.

First a grinding bit must be made. Cut about 3 inches (76 mm) from the copper tube, stand on end and half fill with dry sand. The bolt is then carefully positioned, centrally and upright, inside the tube. Place the bolt head down to rest upon the sand. Melt the plumber's lead and slowly pour into the tube until filled. It must then be left to go cold. For additional security, the cold lead-filled bit can have a small hole drilled right through the tube to pierce the bolt, and a nail pushed through, the ends being bent over. This will prevent the bolt moving when the bit is used. Having emptied the sand from the tube, cut two ¾ inch (19 mm) saw slots on opposite sides of the hollow end — the bit is then ready for use.

Drill a 1 inch (25 mm) hole through the centre of the square of hard-wood to act as a drilling guide. This drill-guide should be large enough to allow free movement of the brace without the knuckles of the hand catching the glass sides of the tank. Place the tank on a level, firm sur-face after laying several sheets of newspaper as padding. The wooden drilling guide is then placed into either a front or back corner, accord-ing to where the drainage hole is required. Insert the shank of the cop-per drilling bit firmly into the brace, fill the open end with carborundum paste, place the bit into the guide, and with a gentle but steady pressure, commence drilling. This is a slow job which requires patience. If preferred a slow speed electric drill may be used instead of the hand-brace; however, take care not to let any heat build up which could crack the glass. Continue until each tank has been drilled. The holes and surrounding areas should then be cleaned with a solvent such as carbon tetrachloride, to leave both faces of the glass clean and free of grease.

The tanks can then be placed into position in the fish-house, being

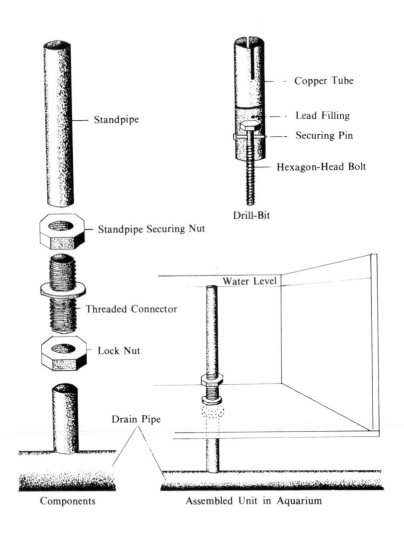

Standpipe

Standpipe Securing Nut

Threaded Connector

Lock Nut

Drain Pipe

Components

Copper Tube

Lead Filling

Securing Pin

Hexagon-Head Bolt

Drill-Bit

Water Level

Assembled Unit in Aquarium

Figure 11.4 *Aquarium Overflow and Base Drain*

sure that they are quite level. If the tanks are frameless they should be seated upon expanded polystyrene, as described in Chapter 2.

Check the correct position for the screwed connectors, normally the threaded section is inserted from above. A ring of silicone adhesive should then be placed around the upper edge of the drainage hole, and another ring to the underside. Insert the connector and tighten the retaining nut sufficiently to hold firm. Any rubber which is squeezed out can be smoothed with a moistened finger. The tanks must now be left for twenty-four hours to allow the adhesive to set and make a water-tight joint.

Lengths of the ¾ inch (19 mm) piping are then cut, of sufficient length to reach to the larger diameter drainage pipe. Another piece of the pipe is cut to form a stand-pipe, this is pushed into the screwed bottom connector and the lock nut made finger tight. The first cut piece of pipe is firmly pushed into the underside of the connector. These fittings are all tight push-fits and form water-tight joints.

Position the drainage piping, and cut ¾ inch (19 mm) holes into which the overflow pipes should be fitted. It is advisable to seal these points of entry, either with silicone adhesive or a more permanent plastic solvent adhesive. Having made all the connections, the water can be turned on and a check made for any leaks. The level of the water in the tanks is governed by the height of the standpipe. Be sure that all pipes that may need support are fastened with brackets to nearby timbers before testing. The illustration will make the various details mentioned in respect of this water exchange system quite clear.

A continuous water exchange system is the method employed by most goldfish breeders nowadays. In operation the water is adjusted to enter the tank at little more than a fast drip, thus avoiding a strong current against which the fish would have to swim. The slow rate of the water exchange is, nevertheless, sufficient to keep the water clear. There is also the advantage that after a tank has been cleaned and emptied, the rate of water flow can be adjusted to refill the tank with no fear that it might overflow. Emptying the tank only requires the removal of the standpipe to allow the water to drain away through the bottom drainage.

OTHER WATER CIRCULATION METHODS

Another method, not often used, is to recirculate the water through a biological filter. In this case, the overflow water is led to a container that has a 1 foot (305 mm) depth of coarse broken clinker. The water passes over and through the clinker to discharge to a lower container, from where the water is pumped into the supply pipe for delivery to the individual tanks.

A much simpler method is to feed the overflow from the tanks through outdoor goldfish raising ponds, and thence to the drainage. This has the benefit of keeping the pond water clear during even the sunniest weather, and allows the young fish to be easily seen. For reasons of safety, the outlets from the ponds should be screened to prevent the loss of young fish. During periods of water shortage, a water pump can be installed in the pond and connected to the water supply pipe to convert the water exchange system to one of recirculation.

REARING PONDS

Outdoor ponds for raising young goldfish add to the facilities provided by the fish-house. They may be merely timber frames lined with a plastic sheet, children's framed paddling pools or specially constructed concrete ponds. In all cases, only a shallow depth of water is required with a surface area of about 6 ft x 4 ft (1829 mm x 1219 mm). These, like the tanks, are kept free of plants for ease of maintenance.

The design and construction of the concrete pond is very similar to that of the 'above-ground' type described earlier in this book. If possible, at least three should be built side by side. First lay a concrete base of, say, 14 feet x 8 feet (4.26 m x 2.4 m), upon which to build the three units. If standpipes are to be incorporated the pipes should be laid in this foundation. Build up the outer wall to a height of 12 inches (305 mm), then erect the two partition walls to form three sections. Lay concrete floors sloping to the drainage points, giving a deep end of 10 inches (254 mm) and a shallow end of 6 inches (152 mm) from the water level of the completed ponds. Finally render with a smooth finish. When hardened, connect the standpipe and run in the water. The concrete must, of course, be made safe; however, the bottom drainage will make it a simple task to empty the ponds after each scrubbing.

MANAGING THE 'SET-UP'

The breeding procedure is exactly as described in the previous chapter. However, when the young fish reach a size of around an inch

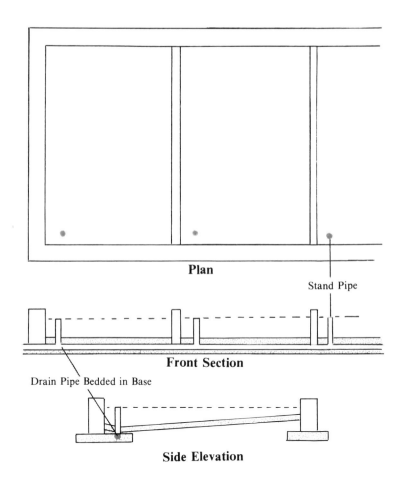

Plan

Stand Pipe

Front Section

Drain Pipe Bedded in Base

Side Elevation

Figure 11.5 *Sections Through Rearing Ponds*
It is an advantage to incorporate a base drain in to which a standpipe is fitted.
This allows easy emptying and also avoids any possibility of the water level
overflowing, which means that it is possible to flush the ponds when
necessary

215

(25 mm) in length they can be placed into the rearing ponds. Be sure, when transferring the fish, to exercise care over the equalization of water temperatures. There will, quite possibly, be a great difference between the temperature of the water in the fish-house tanks and that of the ponds.

Feeding must not be neglected. Although a number of flies and other insects will fall into the ponds they will not provide more than the odd tit-bit. At a size of 1 inch (25 mm) the young fish will accept a varied diet similar to the adults'. Culling must also be continued by the regular removal of any weak or faulty fish that are noticed.

The Japanese goldfish breeder endeavours to cultivate a thriving colony of Daphnia in the rearing ponds, before the young are introduced. After placing the fish into the pond, a watch is kept and as they exhaust the supply of Daphnia in one pond, they are moved to another in which the food is flourishing. Under these conditions the fish grow so fast that they soon outstrip the supply of Daphnia, and the fish then have their diet supplemented with other foods to maintain the rate of growth.

With the approach of the autumn, the best of the young should be brought into the fish-house — all surplus and unwanted fish being disposed of. If preferred, fish that have reached a body length of 2 inches (51 mm) or more can be over-wintered in a specially designed pond. This is of very similar design to the rearing ponds but with a depth of at least 2 feet (610 mm). At least 18 inches (457 mm) of the water depth should be below ground level. No plants are needed in the water. This pond can, of course, be used to house some of the adult fish during the summer months. There is a magic about the outdoors which invariably benefits the fish. It is advisable to bring the fancier varieties into the protected environment of the fish-house for the winter, placing the adults into the trough.

The over-wintering pond must be cleaned before use to provide clean, pest-free quarters. During the autumn the rearing ponds are cleaned out and left dry until required the following season — this again ensures hygienic conditions for the young fish.

During a very hard winter it may become necessary to provide some form of space heating in the fish-house. The object should be to prevent a build up of ice in the tanks which could result in breakages. The heat should not be high enough to prevent the fish becoming dormant. In my own fish-house I have, on many occasions, had

216

¼ inch (6 mm) of ice form upon the water surface of the tanks. Possibly the easiest method of providing heat is to use a fan-heater coupled to a heavy duty thermostat. The thermostat can be set to regulate the heater to switch on and off at freezing point, or thereabouts, and this will usually supply all the warmth that is needed to keep heavy freezing out of the tanks. It is the air temperature that is measured by the thermostat, not the water temperature.

During the breeding season, the top tier of tanks receives most light, therefore it is these which are used both to condition the adults and for spawning. After the first culling, the young are transferred to the lower bank of larger tanks, making the upper tanks available for further spawnings. As the season progresses, and the required spawnings are obtained, the adult fish are moved to outside pounds — perhaps into the ornamental pond, where they spend the warmer months — while the fish-house is devoted to the task of raising the young fish. As the young grow they are continually sorted and spread throughout the available space. The better fish can remain in the tanks, where they can be studied very closely, others can be raised in the trough to a saleable size. Normally goldfish breeders commence to sell the young fish from a body size of roughly 1 inch (25 mm) onwards.

COMMERCIAL VERSUS AMATEUR FISH PRODUCTION

The type of 'set-up' that has been described in this chapter will be found upon a much larger scale at a commercial establishment. In Britain, however, with a very few exceptions, the professional has found it uneconomical to breed goldfish commercially. There have been several attempts to set up fish farms, but most have failed. Trout hatcheries have at times been tempted to cultivate the goldfish, but with little success.

The low cost of the imported Common Goldfish could not be undercut by British producers and still leave a margin of profit. The only alternative is to produce the more exotic varieties of goldfish. The high cost of producing these fish, against the small percentage of worthwhile young obtained, has not proved a viable undertaking. It can be said, with little fear of contradiction, that there are few, if any, large scale professional goldfish breeders in the United Kingdom They have found it easier, and more profitable, to import fish which have already developed their special characteristics and, if necessary, grow them on. Many combine this activity with the production of water lilies and other aquatic plants.

The amateur breeder, having a full time occupation in some other sphere, is not so concerned with the profit motive. It is a hobby first and foremost. For this reason the amateur can specialise and produce good quality fancy goldfish. Quality not quantity is the aim of the true amateur. It is these people who supply the British market with the various varieties of exotic fancy goldfish. Indeed many dealers willingly buy the unwanted surplus fish from amateur breeders, knowing the fish to be home produced, healthy and mostly superior to the imported fish which they normally handle.

There are one or two semi-professionals who produce large numbers of young from various varieties of goldfish — but even then it is a sideline. Few last for a great many years. Sooner or later, the long hours involved in the running of the establishment, coupled to doing a full day's work elsewhere, begin to wear out the enthusiasm of the early years. Added to this is the cost of running the set-up, plus the worry of disposing of all the fish produced during the season at an economical price, and finding an adequate supply of food in sufficient quantity. I cannot help feeling that there can be little pleasure to be gained from such a venture.

218

CHAPTER 12

Competitive Showing

Although many aquarists strongly disapprove of exhibiting their fish, the vast majority of goldfish enthusiasts derive a great deal of pleasure from visiting fish shows. The competitive fish show is an important event in the annual calendar for most goldfish breeders. It provides a means of having an independent assessment made by a judge of fish of the quality of the exhibited fish. The fish can be compared against others of the same variety and personal conclusions drawn as to how much progress is being made in the improvement of the exhibitor's stock. Competition provides the spur to greater endeavour, and, when an exhibitor's fish begin to gain awards, the incentive to do better in the future.

There are many advantages to the open show, apart from the element of competition. It enables the experienced breeders to display their pedigree fish, and thus find a market for their stock; it enables the novice to see top quality varieties of fancy goldfish, to meet experienced breeders, and to learn from them much about the art of breeding and raising good-sized goldfish to maturity. It brings together hobbyists from various parts of the country, and so permits new friendships to be formed, ideas exchanged and knowledge imparted. It provides publicity for the hobby by attracting the general public, teaches the novice to distinguish a good fish from an inferior one, and provides a meeting place for all who are interested in the goldfish.

THE FIRST SHOWS

The first competitive show held in Britain, I believe, was arranged by the now defunct British Aquarists' Association. It was staged at the British Sea Anglers' Society Rooms, Fetter Lane, London and was held from 24-27 September 1926. The success of the venture prompted the B.A.A to arrange two further annual open shows which were five-day events, the first at Chelsea Polytechnic Hall, the other at Trinity Hall, Great Portland Street, London. As a point of interest, the B.A.A. drew up the first British standards for fancy goldfish.

Those early open shows inspired other societies in other areas to arrange similar events, and so the trend grew. The outbreak of the 1939-45 war meant that such activities had to cease, and many fishkeepers had to give up their hobby. However, the post-war years saw a great increase in fishkeeping — mostly tropical — with many goldfish enthusiasts returning to their former interest. With time, import restrictions were relaxed and fish from overseas began to arrive; amongst these were various types of fancy goldfish. The ranks of aquarists, both tropical and coldwater, grew ever larger, resulting in societies being formed, where a common interest could be shared. In turn, many of the societies began to hold shows at which other fishkeepers were invited to compete.

PRESENT DAY SHOWS

Nowadays there is hardly a town or city that does not have at least one fishkeeping society. (Most are dominated by the interests of the tropical fish enthusiast, but there are some specialist goldfish societies which will be mentioned in the next chapter.) As a direct result the number of shows has proliferated, until the stage has been reached when there are very few months of the year that a show is not being held somewhere.

The majority of these events are one-day affairs (usually held in a church hall or some similar venue) and cater, in the main for the exhibitor of tropical fish with a few classes for goldfish and other coldwater fish. Some, however, are larger, longer-lasting events such as the National Shows. In Scotland, the Scottish Aquarium Society holds a three-day show in Glasgow. The British Aquarists' Festival is organised by the Federation of Northern Aquarium Societies and held in Manchester for two days during October. During the latter part of the same month the Federation of British Aquatic Societies stages a three-day open show in London.

Of premier importance to the goldfish hobbyist are the specialist coldwater shows. These attract the country's best-known exhibitors, many travelling a considerable distance to enter their fish, and so allow the visitor to see some excellent specimens of fancy goldfish. A typical schedule of show classes is that provided by the Bristol Aquarists' Society:

Class 1	Goldfish (red)
Class 2	Goldfish (yellow or variegated)
Class 3	Bristol Shubunkins (3 inch body limit)
Class 4	Bristol Shubunkins (3-5 inch bodies)
Class 5	Veiltails
Class 6	Moors
Class 7	Telescopes (other than Moors), Celestials, Bubble-eyes, etc.
Class 8	Lionheads
Class 9	Orandas
Class 10	London Shubunkins
Class 11	Comets
Class 12	Metallic Fantails
Class 13	Nacreous Fantails
Class 14	Any other variety of fancy goldfish
Class 15a	Koi
Class 15b	Bitterling, Sunfish, Bass
Class 15c	Pond fish (Golden Orfe, Tench, Rudd, Carp)
Class 15d	River fish (Minnows, Sticklebacks, Eels, Gudgeon, Loach, Roach, Dace, etc.)
Class 16	Bristol Shubunkins bred during the year
Class 17	Moors bred during the year
Class 18	Orandas and Veiltails bred during the year
Class 19	Lionheads bred during the year
Class 20	Any other variety of goldfish bred during the year
Class 21	Team of 4 Bristol Shubunkins bred during the year
Class 22	Team of 4 Veiltails, Orandas, Moors bred during the year
Class 23	Team of 4 any other variety of goldfish bred during the year
Class 24	Team of 4 Koi or other pond or river fish bred during the year
Class 25	Matched pairs of Bristol Shubunkins
Class 26	Novice class for Bristol Shubunkins

Class 27   Novice class for any other goldfish variety
Class 28   Furnished aquaria

The judges at this type of competitive show are invariably experienced goldfish keepers with a sound knowledge of the finer points of a
good fancy goldfish. They need a sharp eye, for the quality of the fish
can make judging very difficult — the difference between a first and
second place may be little more than a half-point in the marking of the
judge.

Apart from the Bristol Aquarists' Society, which staged its first
show in 1928, other specialist goldfish shows are staged by the Northern Goldfish and Pondkeepers Society in Lancashire and the Goldfish
Society of Great Britain in London. At one time a show of renown was
held each year in Birmingham, at Bingley Hall. Unfortunately it has
now passed into history, but its high reputation will remain in the
memory of goldfish exhibitors for many years. The organising society
was the Midland Aquarium and Pool Society which had put on the
event for around 32 years, without a missed year, until the costs
involved proved too much and so the show had to stop.

The organisation of these shows differs in some respect. The specialist shows require that an entry form be completed, and the
entrance fee sent, some time before the opening date of their exhibitions. This enables the show committee to arrange for the correct number of show tanks to be available. These are filled with water and
labelled with the class and number of the particular fish which is to be
benched. Upon arrival at the show, the exhibitor presents a copy of the
entry form to one of the official stewards and is then shown which
tanks to place the fish in.

The smaller, mixed shows will generally accept entries on the day of
the show. The difference is that, unlike the specialist shows, the
exhibitor must supply a show tank in which to exhibit the fish. The
stipulated size of a show tank is usually 10″ long x 8″ deep x 6″ wide
(254 mm x 203 mm x 152 mm), for single goldfish, and must be clean.
All panels must be clear, and no plants or other adornments are
allowed. It is the task of the exhibitor to fill the tanks with water, place
the fish therein, and affix the official identification label to the top left
corner of the front panel. They are then handed to a steward to be
placed on the show bench. At the close of the show, the exhibitor
removes the fish and empties the tanks.

At no time, after benching, is the exhibitor allowed to touch the fish without official sanction first being obtained, nor may they be removed from any of the shows unless supervised by a steward.

The reader should be prepared to accept the judge's decision as final, for, although some exhibitors will be aggrieved by the placings, only the petty-minded would be churlish enough to dispute the decision. The fact that a fish has been lucky enough to obtain an award at a previous show does not mean that it will receive a placing on its next outing. A different judge may spot a fault that was missed on the previous occasion, the competition may be keener, or the fish may be off-colour. Without doubt the judges are impartial, conscientious, and do their utmost to allot the awards fairly to what they consider are the better fish.

Despite the many forms of fancy goldfish that exist, only thirteen are recognised by British judges and exhibitors. These varieties are the Common, Comet, Bristol and London Shubunkins, Fantail, Oranda, Veiltail, Moor, Pearlscale, Lionhead, Celestial, Bubble-eye and Pompon. Unless there is a specific class for any other type, those varieties not covered by standards must be exhibited in the class for 'Any other Variety' (usually abbreviated to A.O.V. goldfish).

The would-be exhibitor should make a point of obtaining copies of the show standards, to which the fish will be judged, before entering any show, and carefully study the outlines and requirements of the individual varieties of goldfish. The fish should then be chosen with care. The shape of the body and finnage must conform closely to the standard. The colours of both the metallic and nacreous types should be near to those specified. This is very important, for it is usually a waste of time and effort to exhibit a fish that fails to comply with the required standard, whether for body-shape, colour or finnage. No matter how beautiful the owner may consider a fish to be it will fail if it does not meet the 'type test'. If the caudal of a twintail variety is not divided, the judges will pass it by without a second look. In the same way, a fish with telescope-eyes should have both eyes equally developed in shape and protruberance. It goes without saying that the fish must be in perfect health, with no sign of torn fins, missing scales or other defects. The fish should hold its fins erect, and have a symmetry of body and finnage that gives a good balanced appearance. As pale coloured fish are not held in very high esteem, the colours of the fish should be deep and evenly patterned, if of the nacreous form. Metallics should be as deeply coloured as possible — for this reason a silver fish is not worth showing.

SHOWING

Decide which show is to be entered and obtain a copy of the show schedule. Study the rules and classes carefully. Decide which classes the fish can be entered in. See whether show tanks will be provided or not; it is foolish to carry fish to a show and then find that there is no tank to put them in. Fill in the entry form and return it in good time (unless entries are accepted on the day of the show) together with the correct entry fee. Note the times allowed for benching the fish, and arrive well within the stated hours — late entries may be refused admission. Remember that the show rules are binding upon the exhibitor who should be aware of the conditions governing the show. Take care that the fish are entered and benched in the correct class. A fish entered in the wrong class will usually be disqualified.

Where fish are to be shown as a team exhibit, they should be matched as near as possible in size, shape and colour. It is no good showing a mixture of large and small fish as a team. A well matched team of small fish may gain more points than a team of larger badly matched fish. However, the smaller team should be well grown for their age, and have finnage in keeping with their size.

The secret of showing fish lies in the art of training them to deport themselves well in a show tank. Some fish will naturally show off on the show bench; others will sulk. A quality fish that has not been prepared for public showing may well refuse to swim or spread its fins; again it may be so nervous that it constantly dashes to and fro. In both cases the judge will find it extremely difficult to inspect the fish properly, and, in any event, points will be deducted for poor deportment. A lesser quality specimen, whose owner has taken the time to accustom the fish, by careful preparation, to the unwelcome attentions of the public, will swim in a steady, calm manner, with fins erect, and show no nervous reactions. A fish which is accustomed to being shown will quickly settle down in the show tank, and take the inconvenience of people tapping the tank in its stride. This lack of reaction allows the judge to assess fully its quality and so gain the maximum number of warranted points.

The art of preparation lies in training the fish to accept the abnormal conditions of a show. About fourteen days prior to the event the selected fishes should be caught and placed in separate show tanks. Each tank should be placed in a busy part of the home and screened so that it cannot see any other fish. Members of the household should be asked to stop occasionally, tap the tank and peer at the fish with their faces close to the front glass. This will condition the fish to being alone and, also, to accept the constant attention of humans as they pass by.

The tank must conform to normal show practice and not contain any gravel or plants: it must be absolutely bare. If the fish is not accustomed to artificial light it must be educated. At some shows the tanks are lit by overhead electric lights, and the fish must learn to accept this as normal. Therefore, rig up a small electric light bulb above the tank, and leave it switched on for a few hours each day.

During this period of training the fish should be well fed to bring it into tip-top condition. The finest food for this purpose is chopped earthworm, supplemented with Daphnia and other live foods. The trick, when feeding is to avoid a regular routine: instead, offer the food at irregular intervals. Soon the fish will begin to expect food whenever anyone passes. Condition a reflex action, by tapping the front glass at feeding times, so that the fish will swim to the front of its tank with well spread fins. Thus, when it is on the show bench and the judge approaches, it will swim towards the front of the tank in anticipation of a feed.

The time involved in such conditioning of the fish amounts to this: the preparation of the goldfish can help to gain it valuable points; lack of training may lose it points. Training the goldfish for a show is no different to training any other animal for exhibition and does not involve any cruelty or maltreatment — although the show conditions may not be natural. Conditioning will not guarantee success, but will improve the chances of gaining an award. It is certain that if the fish cannot be accustomed to show conditions there will be hardly any point in entering it. Such a fish will stand little chance of gaining many points, no matter how fine a specimen it may be in other respects.

The majority of goldfish exhibitors carry their fish to and from the shows in buckets as described in Chapter 7. In addition, where tanks have to be supplied by the exhibitor, water is sometimes transported in plastic water carriers. Thus upon arrival, the tanks are partially filled with water from the carriers and buckets, being topped-up with local water. This avoids the fish being subjected to a great change of pH in water quality. It also means that the water temperatures are nearly the same, for care must be taken not to subject the fish to any great difference in water temperature when placing it into the show tank.

Having placed the fish on the show bench, in its correct position within its proper class, wipe away any smears or water tears so that there is nothing to detract from the appearance of the fish or its show tank. It is then a matter of patiently awaiting the outcome of the judging.

If all the careful preparation fails to bring a reward, study the winning fish and note the differences that have put it into first place. Tactfully approach the judge and ask for the good and bad aspects of the unplaced fish to be pointed out — but do not dispute with the judge no matter how harsh the criticism may be. In this way more knowledge will be gained.

A word of warning. Although the great majority of aquarists are trustworthy and stewards do their best to ensure the safety of the exhibits, it is not unknown for a fish to vanish during the busy rush of debenching, but fortunately such incidents are rare. It is, nevertheless, a sensible precaution to remove exhibits as soon as possible after the close of the show.

At the larger national two- and three-day shows stewards are in constant attendance, day and night, throughout the duration of the show. Fish are fed and, where necessary, aeration supplied. In fact the fish on the show bench are very carefully tended; they are certainly better looked after than many fish that are offered for sale by some retailers and importers. Accidents can sometimes happen and a fish may die, but such occurrences are usually unavoidable and are more likely to involve tropical fish than the coldwater entries.

These shows are also of interest because they attract many traders' and manufacturers' stands. A vast range of equipment, foods, fish and plants are usually on offer, with experienced trade representatives to explain the finer points of their products. Invariably large crowds gather around these trade stands.

Whatever the type of show, I would recommend that the novice visit them, and after a little experience is gained, join the ranks of goldfish exhibitors. Certainly a visit should be made to at least one of the specialist coldwater shows — if only to view the fine quality fancy gold fish that will be on display.

Take little notice of the person who claims to have superior fish at home — and it is quite a common remark. It is almost certain to be a lie, for these wondrous fish are never seen! Nor should any attention be paid to the 'know-all' who disputes the age of young fish, shown in the breeders' classes, because of their size. It merely means that they do not know how to grow young goldfish — and the judges are not fooled that easily. Always be prepared to listen to sound advice from experienced exhibitors, and discount the ramblings of fools.

SHOW STANDARDS

As mentioned earlier, the British Aquarists' Association drew up the first British standards for fancy goldfish, but they were superseded many years ago. In fact, during comparatively recent years there has been a proliferation of standards, some lasting only a short time. The Goldfish Society of Great Britain uses standards for what they term Basic and Popular varieties; these standards were produced in the hope that they would receive national acceptance. Unfortunately their concept of certain varieties alienated many experienced goldfish enthusiasts. Possibly the most widely used standards are those of the Federation of British Aquatic Societies — because of the number of societies which are affiliated to this national body. Other groups have also produced standards for fancy goldfish, but few have found wide acceptance.

More recently a number of goldfish societies banded together to form an organisation which they called Associated Goldfish Societies of the United Kingdom, with the intention of producing a set of realistic standards that would have the approval of the majority of goldfish exhibitors and judges, but, due to various clashes of opinion, a golden opportunity was missed and little progress was made. This was a great pity because a number of area bodies had voiced their interest and may well have adopted the new standards for shows held by their member societies.

In my opinion this multiplicity of standards is a ridiculous state of affairs, and must be very confusing to newcomers to the hobby. One cannot help wondering why the hobby finds itself in this position. Other livestock is judged to one single standard, often to an internationally recognised standard, and exhibitors do not have to restrict themselves to specific shows that suit their stock. Why should goldfish be any different? The stupidity becomes obvious when it is realised

227

how similar the various standards are to each other. A little common-sense and goodwill would surely allow the minor differences to be rationalised and agreement reached upon a common outline and description for each of the varieties. The problem seems to lie in a reluctance to admit that there could be room for improvement, coupled to a belief that the different producers have each compiled a standard that cannot be bettered.

This stubborn attitude has existed for many years, although it is not beneficial to the hobby, and recent events indicate that there is not likely to be any change in attitudes in the near future. However, people do change. Perhaps moderation will one day allow the different organisations to agree to forget pride, in favour of a willingness to agree, and put the well-being of the goldfish hobby first. When that day arrives we may see common-sense prevail in the recognition of just one single national judging standard for each variety of fancy goldfish.

Plate 8
Top: Moor
Bottom: Metallic Veiltail

CHAPTER 13

Societies, Books and Magazines

As mentioned in the previous chapter, fishkeeping societies abound. There is hardly anywhere that is not within reach of at least one aquarium society, and there is nothing to prevent goldfish keepers from joining a national society thereby receiving newsletters.

There are, without any doubt, many advantages to be gained from being a member of a well-organised group of fellow enthusiasts. Similar interests provide a common meeting ground for both the absolute novice and the very experienced hobbyist. New friends will be made, and from simply talking to the more knowledgeable aquarist the beginner will widen his, or her, understanding of the goldfish. Problems can be shared and difficulties explained, the experiences of others proving that everyone can suffer misfortunes, but, also, showing that they can be overcome. Sources of good fish are found, goldfish breeders often taking young fish to meetings to be sold to any interested member.

Meetings usually include a talk, a film or slide show, or possibly a table show of members' fish. Demonstrations of various sorts are arranged. Outings are made to places of interest to the fishkeeper. Most meetings are interesting and educational, often leaving the members in animated discussion at their conclusion.

I would thoroughly recommend all goldfish enthusiasts to seek out their nearest society and become members. Invariably they will receive a warm welcome, for, in the main, the fish keeping fraternity are a friendly bunch of people who are ever ready to talk about their favourite subject — fish.

Many of the societies have mixed interests, a combination of cold-water and tropical fish keepers. The majority are affiliated to either a national or area body. By writing to one of these organisations details of local aquarium societies can be obtained. The various addresses can also be obtained from one or other of the hobbyists magazines.

BRITISH GOLDFISH SOCIETIES

Specialist goldfish societies are not so numerous, and people who are within travelling distance of such a group are indeed fortunate. At their meetings there is no divergence of interest; the goldfish reigns supreme. The leading society in the Midlands is the Association of Midland Goldfish Keepers, which attracts members from a wide area and numbers some of this country's best-known hobbyists within its ranks. Bristol is the home of one of England's longest-established groups — the Bristol Aquarists' Society. Lancashire is covered by the Northern Goldfish and Pondkeepers Society — a fast growing band of active enthusiasts. London has two groups, the Goldfish Society of Great Britain, and the Ichiban Ranchu Society. These two latter societies hold their meetings in the London area, but they also have provincial and overseas members who receive regular newsletters.

AMERICAN GOLDFISH SOCIETIES

The Goldfish Society of America is the United States national goldfish society which produces an excellent newsletter for its members. There are also a number of other specialist coldwater societies, amongst which are the Honolula Carp and Goldfish Fanciers; Ikeru Hoski Koi and Goldfish Association; Cahu Koi and Kingyo Club of Hawaii; and the San Diego Koi and Goldfish Society.

Details of these societies should be obtainable from the National Aquarium Club, 11068 Cavell, Livonia, MI 48150, U.S.A. Alternatively one of the area organisations could, no doubt, advise American goldfish hobbyists of a suitable society. Try Northeast Council of Aquarium Societies Inc., 169W Rocks Road, Norwalk, CT; the Canadian Association of Aquarium Societies, c/o 104 Pennels Drive, Rochester, NY 14626., or the San Francisco Aquarium Society, California Academy of Sciences, Golden Gate Park, San Francisco, CA 94118.

FORMING A GOLDFISH SOCIETY

Where there are enough interested people it is very worthwhile considering the possibility of forming a specialist society. Every society originates from the vision of one or two enthusiasts; enthusiasts who are prepared to promote the idea, and work to bring about the creation of a new group. It is often a surprise to discover how many enthusiasts there are in the area who would welcome the opportunity to become founder members.

There are many ways of setting about the task of establishing a new society; it only requires a willingness to 'set the wheels in motion', and a prompt friendly invitation to anyone who shows interest. For the benefit of any reader who may have doubts about their ability to attempt to bring a society into being, I offer the following guidance.

Obviously the first essential is to spread the word around, in order to draw other fishkeepers into the scheme. If contact is to be made with the unknown hobbyists of the locality publicity must be given. Arrange for advertisements to appear in the local press, ask the pet stores to put up notices in their display windows. These notices should explain the proposition in a brief but clear manner, and invite interested persons to make contact. A similar notice inserted in the aquatic press may well bring an unexpected number of enquiries. Be sure to approach any local aquarists and invite their participation. Wherever and whenever there is an opportunity to gain publicity, make full use of it.

It is only necessary to have a few really seriously motivated co-organisers to form the nucleus of the proposed group. Organise a suitable and convenient meeting place, and arrange a mutually acceptable time and day with the potential members.

Prepare a rough agenda for the meeting, keeping it as simple as possible. This need be little more than a few headings as reminders of the essential points to be discussed, such as how often should meetings be held, also when and where; how much should be charged as membership subscription; are juniors below the age of sixteen to be admitted, if so what should they pay; is the number of members to be limited, or is it to be unlimited. A decision must be made as to the composition of the committee and the term for which the appointed officers shall serve.

It will also be necessary to draw up a proposed constitution setting out the aims and principles of the society. Finally, a suggested title for the society which should be simple but descriptive of the group's interests.

Having gathered the interested parties together, they should be warmly welcomed and thanked for their attendance. The outlined proposals are then discussed, and amendments made according to the majority opinion. Careful and accurate notes are made of the decisions, as each is arrived at and agreed. At the conclusion of the meeting, the notes are read out to make sure that the visitors are in full agreement. Before the meeting finally closes arrange the next. This will be the Inaugural Meeting, when the proposals will be finalised and the committee elected. Ask the visitors to do everything possible to promote the next meeting with fellow aquarists to obtain the largest gathering possible. It must be remembered that the decisions taken at the Inaugural Meeting will be binding, unless allowance is made for them to be varied, if need be, at a future Annual General Meeting (or a specially convened Extra-Ordinary Meeting).

The Annual General Meeting is normally the last meeting of the season. At that time the Chairman will address a few remarks to the members, the Secretary will report upon the progress of the society over the past year. The Treasurer will also present the statement of accounts, which should have been previously audited. Each of the reports will be open to question by the membership before they are asked for a vote of approval. This is also the time when subscriptions can be revised if necessary, and a new committee elected.

The ordinary meetings should, of course, be devoted to subjects that are of interest to the members, and which will further their knowledge of the goldfish and its care. Keep the meetings as informal as possible, and restrict the business side to a minimum — a relaxed and friendly atmosphere should be encouraged at all times.

A simple but explicit constitution could be worded along the following lines:

The Society shall be known as the ....
The Committee shall consist of a Chairman, Secretary, Treasurer and such other members as may be deemed necessary.
Meetings shall be held (state day, time and whether each week or month) at a venue accessible to the members. The last meeting of the year to be the Annual General Meeting, at which time a new committee may be elected.
All major decisions shall be decided by a majority vote of the members.
All members, irrespective of experience, shall be treated as equals, information and assistance being freely available to all.
Members shall not be discouraged from belonging to any other

232

Society, but will be expected to work for the good of this Society. The Society will work to promote its own well-being, and to promote friendship and understanding between all goldfish enthusiasts and will encourage the popularity of the goldfish in all varieties.

Members' subscriptions shall be paid at the beginning of each new season, the amount to be decided at the previous Annual General Meeting.

The terms of this constitution may not be varied without the majority consent of the membership.

A newly formed society may only consist of perhaps six or so hobbyists meeting at each other's homes. However, with the present day resurgence of interest in the fancy goldfish, such a group may well attract other enthusiasts who would welcome the opportunity of becoming members. Publicity, both in print and by word of mouth, will do much to recruit others.

While I recommend the benefits to be derived from being a member of an aquarium society, I suggest, most emphatically, that the benefits and pleasure of belonging to a specialist society of goldfish keepers is far greater.

BOOKS

It is a sad fact that, while there are many books about aquarium fish, there are few really good books about the goldfish. Many of the more informative books (such as *Goldfish Varieties and Tropical Aquarium Fishes* and *Goldfish Varieties and Water Gardens,* written and published by the famed late William T. Innes, an American aquarist and publisher) are no longer in print.

Almost without exception modern books are filled with numerous coloured illustrations, but the important reading matter does little to increase the reader's knowledge and barely gets beyond advice to the novice. Price is no guide to the value of the content. Many high-priced volumes are worthless to the goldfish enthusiast who has learnt the rudiments of goldfish management and wishes to learn more.

Of those books which are currently available, I recommend the following as worthy additions to the bookshelf. Not all are directly related to the goldfish, but will serve to increase the reader's knowledge in one way or another. The list has not been arranged in any particular order of merit.

THE GOLDFISH. G.J. Hervey, F.Z.S., and J. Hems. Published originally by the Batchworth Press, later revised and published by Faber & Faber, London. This book is considered by many to be a classic, and covers many aspects of the goldfish in considerable depth. (I am indebted to it for much of the information on the history of the goldfish).

THE BOOK OF THE GARDEN POND. (London: Faber & Faber.) Written by the above two authors, it contains a great deal of information and guidance for the pondkeeper in a clear and concise manner.

GOLDFISH GUIDE. Dr. Yoshiichi Matsui (Professor of Fish Culture, Kinki University, Japan). (USA: Pet Library Limited.) The translation has, I feel, suffered from some inaccuracies, but is nevertheless a most informative book, especially in respect of Japanese fish and methods.

GOLDFISH. Anthony Evans, B.Sc. (London: Muller.)

COLDWATER FISHKEEPING. Arthur Boarder. (Brentford, England: Buckley Press.) The above two books contain sound advice and instruction in the requirements of fishkeeping.

ENCYCLOPEDIA OF LIVE FOODS. Charles O. Masters. (USA: T.F.H. Publications Ltd.) A most interesting book covering many common, and not so common, live foods, their collection and cultivation (in the American climate).

ENCYCLOPEDIA OF WATER PLANTS. Dr. Jiri Stodola. (USA: T.F.H. Publications Ltd.) Written in Czechoslovakia by a trained botanist and published in the U.S.A., this is a comprehensive work that details a vast number of water plants.

FRESHWATER LIFE. John Clegg. (London: Frederick Warne.) This is a standard reference book on the plants, invertebrate animals, and environment of ponds, lakes, streams, and rivers of Britain. Written in an easily understood manner.

Intentionally, I have not mentioned any book dealing with fish ailments. There are one or two excellent books that deal with this subject, but they can be very technical. It is, therefore, advisable for the reader to select a type that can be clearly understood.

The hobbyist who judges a book by its cover, without first assessing the contents, may well be wasting money, for an impressive cover design is no criterion by which to judge a book's worth. Many are the work of writers who have no (or very little) practical experience. Because of their lack of knowledge they tend to repeat the mistakes of others, and the reader, knowing no better, takes it as fact and can thus be led into mistaken beliefs and possibly wrongful actions.

MAGAZINES

AQUARIST AND PONDKEEPER. This is the older of the two given here, first appearing in 1924 as the *Amateur and Reptilian Review*. Over the years its style has changed considerably. Its content is mainly aimed at the tropical fishkeeper, with sections devoted to coldwater queries, tropical queries, koi queries, and marine queries plus 'From a Naturalist's Notebook'. Fuller details can be obtained from the Editor, The Butts, Half Acre, Brentford, Middlesex.

PRACTICAL FISHKEEPING MONTHLY. As its title implies, it is devoted entirely to practical fishkeeping articles, being about equally divided between goldfish (and other coldwater subjects), tropical fish and marines. Sometimes 'chatty', sometimes serious, the articles invariably set out to interest and educate. Details of subscription rates and other information will be supplied upon request by the Managing Editor, Pack House, 117 Pack Road, Peterborough, PE1 2TS.

Both publications contain pages of news from societies, results of various shows, and lists of forthcoming shows, in addition to the usual advertisements. Most hobbyists take one or the other, and very often both, as a means of keeping abreast of events and new developments in the hobby. For the beginner they provide new ideas and broaden the knowledge.

CHAPTER 14

Photography

Nowadays many aquarists combine photography with their fish-keeping activities. The flashing of electronic flash units is especially noticeable at fish shows as cameras record the various fish that are on display. However, the camera also provides an excellent means of recording the progress that the fish-breeder is making in the quality of the fish produced. It is surprising how difficult it can be to recall the early fish — were they really as good, or bad, as we think they were? A photograph with notes would leave no room for doubt.

The approach to fish photography may be as simple or as complicated as one wishes to make it, but certain principles must be followed. The successful photographer develops a method of working that will produce predictable results, for it must be stressed that a fish is not the easiest subject to photograph.

Unless thoroughly clean, smears on the aquarium glass will show on the slide or photograph and spoil the result. The glass and water will act as a mirror so that a reflection of the camera and the photographer may be recorded. Poor quality glass will distort; also the glass and water can bounce back the light of a flash unit and ruin the result by causing a white flare on the picture. Keeping the fish in focus is difficult, unless it can be restricted in some way. But, with care and a little pre-planning, these problems can be overcome.

A photograph of a fish should show the subject sharply in focus and be large enough to see the detail. This latter requirement will mean working in close-up, which adds to the difficulty of obtaining a sharply focussed image. To lessen these two problems is not too difficult.

A small, specially constructed tank is used to keep the fish within the field of focus. The front and back glass panels measure 10 inches x 8 inches (254 mm x 203 mm), the side pieces 8 inches x 4 inches (203 mm x 102 mm), and the base glass is 10 inches x 10 inches (254 mm x 254 mm). Although the back, sides and base may be of cheap glass, the front must be of first class quality and absolutely free of any flaw. Run a thin line of silicone rubber adhesive along one 8 inch (203 mm) edge of each of the side panels, carefully press into position against the inner face of the back glass, and secure with short strips of adhesive tape. Gently stand the assembled glass upright. Next run a line of the adhesive down the other two edges of the side panels, then press the front panel into position — taking care not to cause the glasses to fall apart — and tape securely. Check that the assembly is square. Finally, run adhesive along the top edges and firmly press the base onto it. Allow approximately the same amount of overhang at both back and front, this will help to prevent the finished tank being upset when in

Figure 14.1 *Equipment for photographing fish*
35 m.m. Reflex camera
Extension tube (in sections)
Supplementary close-up lens
135 m.m. Lens

use. Place a light weight on the tank and leave to set for twenty-four hours. As an added precaution against leakage the inside joints can be oversealed with rubber adhesive and left for a further day. After testing and cleaning away any smears or rubber, the tank is ready for use. Obviously, the size of the tank must be suitable for the fish to be photographed, but the dimensions given will be adequate for most of the fancy varieties of goldfish.

Various coloured backgrounds can be placed against the outside of the back glass to add effects to the final picture, and also to keep the picture in the tank.

The modern single lens reflex camera is ideal for fish photography: it allows the subject to be focussed on the special built-in screen, and often indicates the correct aperture setting for the lens. To avoid camera shake, mount the camera upon a tripod and operate the shutter via a flexible shutter release cable.

Most camera lenses will need assistance to focus at very close range, and a simple method of achieving this close focus is to use a close-up lens. These are comparatively simple, one-glass lenses that push on, or screw in, to the camera lens. Close-up (or supplementary) lenses are graded by dioptre strength — the most commonly used being either 1D, 2D or 3D. They are quite inexpensive to buy. Basically, the stronger the supplementary lens the closer the focussing range. The 1D lens, for instance, will allow the camera to focus on an object roughly 3 feet (915 mm) in front of it, whilst the 3D lens will allow focusing at 9 inches (229 mm). There are no problems with exposure when using these lenses; however, they do considerably reduce the depth of field — which, in simple terms, means that anything not sharply focussed will be blurred in the finished picture. This is an advantage in some respects, because it will make the fish stand out.

The factor which limits the ability of the camera lens to focus closely is the separation distance between lens and film. It is, however, a simple matter to increase this distance by placing a tube between the lens and the camera body. An extension tube consists of three or four rings, each ring being threaded at one end to fit the camera body and at the other to accept the lens. Thus, with one or more of the rings in place, the camera is able to focus close to the subject. It is quite feasible to combine both the extension tube and a supplementary lens, in conjunction with the camera lens, for really close work.

Whichever method of close-up is used, it is essential to ensure that

238

Figure 14.2 *35 mm camera mounted on a microscope
for taking photomicrographs*

the camera is held rock steady, and the closer the range the more important this becomes, because it needs only the merest fraction of movement to produce considerable blurring of the image.

Natural daylight is the best source of light for this type of work, although flash can be used. If the latter is used, the flash unit should be held above, and slightly in front of, the tank so that the light points down and away from the camera lens, to avoid any chance of the light bouncing back into the camera lens and spoiling the shot.

To avoid reflections in the front glass of the tank, make a mask from black card. The card should be the same dimensions as the front glass, or slightly larger, and have a hole cut in the centre to allow it to fit around the camera lens. This will effectively eliminate any reflections of the camera or the operator.

The photographic session can now begin. Place the tank in position at a convenient height, and see that the glass is scrupulously clean. Fill with absolutely clean water of the correct temperature. Set up the camera on a solid tripod, and adjust the tank to camera distance to obtain the correct field of view.

Carefully catch the fish and place it in the tank, allowing it a few moments to settle down, then wipe away any water splashes. Place the background in position, so that the camera cannot see right through the back panel.

Look through the camera view-finder, to make sure that the shot is as required (if not, make any necessary adjustments) then screw the shutter release cable into place. Critically adjust the focus so that it is pin-sharp, cock the camera, make a final check that the focus is correct, place the black screen on the camera, then slowly release the shutter.

In the early days it pays to experiment, and make notes, by bracketing the shots. This means taking three pictures, one at the indicated f. stop, another one stop below, and another one stop above. Find which setting gives the best result under different light conditions, then use that setting for future close-up photography.

To photograph fish in the furnished aquarium, it may be that close-up attachments will not be needed; however, steps should be taken to keep the fish near the front of the aquarium where they can be easily seen and focussed upon. This is best accomplished by dividing the tank lengthways with a sheet of glass to hold the fish within an area of sharp focus.

Taking photographs at fish exhibitions has, by its very nature, to be more of a hit or miss operation. Obviously a tripod cannot be used (although possibly a monopod could) because of the hazard to other visitors — not to mention the camera. Lighting is seldom of sufficient intensity, nor is it of the right type for colour film, therefore flash lighting must be used. Here again it would be safest to take more than one shot of each particular fish, hoping that, on the law of averages, at least one will be satisfactory. Under these circumstances use a fast film. Learn to adopt a firm stance, with feet apart and elbows pressed against the sides of the body. Do not jab the shutter release, but slowly and steadily depress the shutter release button, thus avoiding any sudden camera movement.

Always take care not to become a nuisance to others. Too often amateur photographers have impeded visitors who are trying to view the exhibits. Some show committees have received so many complaints that they now forbid photography. Some exhibitors also object to their fish being subject to the brilliant light from electronic flash units. (Personally, I do not think that the fish suffer any harm because the duration of the flash is so extremely short). The thoughtful photographer may well consider it courteous to obtain permission from an official prior to taking any photographs.

PHOTOMICROGRAPHY

This is the art of taking photographs with a combined microscope and camera body (all serious aquarists should own a microscope), and is used to record images of small creatures which are normally viewed through a microscope.

Although this is a specialised branch of photography, the average amateur can, with the right equipment, produce passable photographs or transparencies.

A special microscope attachment is required. In some respects this attachment is similar to the extension tubes described earlier. One end is threaded to enable the attachment to be screwed into the camera body after removing the camera lens. The other end is designed to clamp around the eyepiece drawtube of the microscope.

For the best results a fast film and a strong light source are needed. It is possible to purchase special high intensity microscope lamps, but with a little thought it is possible to devise a suitable light unit. The rays of the sun can be used to good effect.

In practice the specimen is placed upon a glass slide, and this is mounted on the microscope stage. The light is adjusted to give a bright, evenly lit field of illumination. The microscope is then sharply focussed upon the specimen. Next the camera and attachment are clamped to the microscope, and a shutter release cable screwed into the camera. If the camera has a built-in light meter, the indicated exposure will be given, but take a further exposure of one f. stop higher also. It is possible that the indicated exposure is insufficient to produce a good image so the illumination must then be intensified.

If a standard procedure is developed, used with a consistent intensity of illumination, it will be found that the camera settings alter only occasionally.

This form of photography makes possible the filmed development of a fish egg, or the egg of a snail. Various small creatures such as

Daphnia and Cyclops can be photographed, and, as experience is gained, even smaller subjects can be recorded.

Photography can add another dimension to the fishkeeping hobby. However, like fishkeeping, proficiency only comes with experience. Learn the basics thoroughly. Only buy those accessories that are essential. Concentrate on producing clear sharp images that do the subject justice.

Photography mixes well with fishkeeping, and can provide both pleasure and a record of present-day fish, personalities and activities for future reference.

CHAPTER 15

The Goldfish Calendar

The goldfish is a creature whose activity is governed by the change of seasons and water temperature. In the protected environment of the indoor aquarium such changes may have little influence upon the fish. However, in the more rigorous conditions of the outdoor pond the fish will respond to a much greater degree. Whereas fish kept in a fish-house will be affected much more than those in the indoor decorative aquarium, they will react less than those in the pond.

Likewise, because the goldfish responds to the temperature of the water, fish kept in warmer climates will not exhibit the extreme behaviour patterns of those kept in colder areas. These facts should be kept in mind while reading the following notes.

WINTER

During this period of the year the goldfish shows little activity. Indeed, during very cold spells, the fishes will gather together at the bottom of the pond, and remain so quiet that they appear not to be breathing. No attempt should be made to disturb the fish during this dormant period, since this will upset its metabolism and cause the fish to use up its precious food reserves.

During the winter it is seldom necessary to feed the fishes. They will survive by drawing on the food reserves that have been stored in their body tissues during the warmer months. If the fishes are fed, it is possible that their digestive system may not be able to assimilate the food since their body functions are greatly slowed down. Undigested food will begin to putrify inside the fish and may well kill it. The other danger is that they will refuse the food which will then pollute the water.

If the fishes are seen to be seeking food during a mild spell, they can be offered a small amount of Daphnia. Uneaten live Daphnia will continue to swim and will not foul the water. However, it must be remembered that live Daphnia will compete with the goldfish for the available oxygen.

Leave the fish alone, and do not interfere with them. When heavy losses occur during the winter the trouble is often due to interference. Unnecessary attempts to feed the fish, overcrowding, or failure to properly clean the pond earlier in the year can all cause problems.

The only tasks that the fishkeeper need attend to are few. Each day remove any leaves and debris from the water surface. When freezing takes place, ensure that a hole is kept open in the ice to allow noxious gases to escape. It is the gases that harm the fish and not the cold. After a fall of snow it should be swept off the frozen surface in order to permit light to penetrate.

If an electric immersion heater is used, it must be kept just below the surface to preserve an ice-free area. It must not be allowed to warm the water unduly, otherwise the fish will become active and the plants start to make premature growth — neither being desirable.

SPRING

As the temperature of the water slowly begins to warm, the fish will gradually become more active. During their winter fast the fish may have lost between 10 and 20 per cent of their weight. The temptation will be to commence feeding them heavily. The temptation must be resisted — it must be remembered that they are weak and unable to digest large quantities of food. Offer only very small amounts, preferably live food, increasing the quantity very slowly as the water temperature rises. Do not be in a hurry, the activity and appetite of the fish will clearly indicate how much food to offer.

Towards the end of spring the longer hours of daylight and warmer water conditions will have rejuvenated the appetites of the fish and they will be swimming actively. The mature fish may well spawn. Any fish that are required for controlled spawnings should be brought into the conditioning tanks for individual attention, prior to being placed in the spawning tanks.

At this time of the year the pond water may turn green, due to the presence of free-floating algae, but this should clear as the higher plants start into full growth. The shading leaves of the water lily will do much to reduce the problems of 'green-water'.

During early spring, after the fish have become active, the pond can be given a pre-season clean. Surplus frogs and the like can be released into a country pond, but be sure that it is some distance away, otherwise they will find their way back.

Early spring is also the best time of the year for dividing overgrown plants or establishing new plants in the pond.

SUMMER

Water temperatures are now at their highest, and the activity and appetite of the fish greatest. During the heat of the day the fishes will seek shade beneath the water lily pads. Any young fishes that have managed to escape being eaten by larger fish will be growing rapidly.

Blanketweed may become a nuisance. Remove as much as possible by twisting a twiggy stick in its mass and lift it out. Blanketweed, like the free-floating algae, thrives in bright sunlight and water with a high mineral content — such as a new, or newly planted, pond. A good growth of aquatic plants will do much to control both problems — given time.

Feed the fishes in the morning and again during the cool of the evening, making sure that the food is eaten within a few minutes. It is during these warmest months of the year that the fishes will put on maximum growth, and their voracious appetites must be satisfied.

Various beetles may also put in an appearance, some being quite inoccuous while others can be a menace. Keep an eye open for the great diving beetle (*Dytiscus marginalis* — see Chapter 9.) This large brute of a beetle has been known to attack a six-inch (152 mm) long fish, and is a killer. The adult, which flies readily, may turn up in any pond. If its presence is suspected, a quiet watch at the pondside is sure to reveal it, since it must rise to the surface periodically to take in air at the tail end. Both the adult and its larvae are easily netted when they come up for air and should be destroyed without hesitation. Water boatmen should also be netted and destroyed.

Most of the small beetles are safe and may be left to go about their harmless business.

AUTUMN

Days are becoming shorter and temperatures falling. The growth of plants begin to slow. Goldfish react to these pre-winter signs by instinctively eating more in order to build up the essential reserves of body fat that will sustain them during their period of winter dormancy. Assist the fish by reducing the amount of food given at one time. Instead, the frequency of feeding should be increased. The foods should be of good nourishing value and variety.

During mid-autumn the pond should be emptied, and the fishes inspected to ensure that they are fit to survive the coming cold months. Any fish that is less than 2 inches (51 mm) long should be taken indoors for the winter, and returned to the pond the following spring. Give the pond a thorough clean, and remove any dead plants, to provide the best winter conditions for the fish and lessen the danger of water pollution.

Continue the process of tidying-up by weeding the surrounding areas of the pond, such as the rockery and bog garden. Cut down the dying vegetation.

Place a net over the pond to catch falling tree leaves, which might otherwise fall into the water and decompose — thereby undoing the good that was done by cleaning the pond. The net can be left in place throughout the year to prevent hungry herons, gulls or other creatures taking the fish.

Do not attempt to divide plants at this time of the year, this job must be left until spring.

It will not be long before falling temperatures make the water colder, when the fishes will become less active, less willing to take food, and less capable of digesting food. When these signs become apparent reduce the feeding accordingly until it ceases completely.

The care and attention which the fishkeeper gives during the spring, summer and autumn will decide the chances of the fishes safely coming through the winter months. The caring aquarist will willingly give this attention and, consequently, suffer very few losses.

The pleasure of contemplating the grace of the fish during a warm spring evening, relaxing by the pondside after a hot summer day, or enjoying the calm of a quiet autumn afternoon — such simple joys are surely ample reward for the care that has been devoted to the seasonal tasks. They are, after all, less labourious than digging a garden — and far more enjoyable!

CHAPTER 16

Useful Information

GLOSSARY

Acrosome	That part of the head of spermatozoon in the form of a cap over the nucleus.
Air Bladder	Otherwise known as 'swim-bladder'. A sac in the abdominal cavity of the goldfish, filled with a gas and acting as a hydrostatic organ.
Albumen	Material that surrounds the embryo.
Algae	Small, troublesome, single or multi-celled cryptogamous plants.
Alimentary Canal	The digestive tube that begins at the mouth and passes through the length of the body to the vent.
Anus	The lower orifice (vent) of the digestive tube.
Bifurcated	Forked into two branches.
Blastocoele	The cavity formed within the mass of cells within the egg, towards the end of the cleavage period.
Blastomere	A cell formed during cleavage period of the fertilized egg.
Blastula	A hollow ball of cells in the embryonic development of the goldfish at the end of cleavage just before gastrulation.
Carbon Dioxide	Heavy colourless gas used by plants in photosynthesis where carbon is retained and oxygen released.
Centrosome	A minute body, within the cytoplasm, which initiates cell division.
Chitin	Hard shell-like substance containing nitrogen, resistant to acid and alkali.

247

Chromatin	Constituent of a chromosome.
Chromatophore	A cell with pigment in its cytoplasm, changing concentration or dispersion and so altering the coloration of the fish.
Chromosome	A small body of varied shape which occurs in the nucleus of every animal and plant cell.
Cilium	(Plural: Cilia) Delicate, hair-like, protoplasmic process by whose vibrations progress of a body through water is made.
Cleavage	Division of the fertilized egg into many cells which become ever smaller as cleavage progresses.
Crispate	With wavy margins.
Cryptogamous	Not producing seeds or flowers.
Cytoplasm	The protoplasm of a cell excluding the nucleus.
Dentate	Toothed, teeth protruding outward.
Dentoplasm	Yolk.
Detritus	Organic or plant debris which settles on the bottom of pond or aquarium.
Diploid	Having the chromosomes in pairs, the numbers being homologous so that twice the haploid number are present.
Dystrophic	Suffering from faulty nutrition.
Embryo	The offspring of an animal before birth or emergence from the egg.
Emersed	Growing above, or through, the water surface.
Epidermis	The thin outer layer of skin.
Eutrophic	Rich in dissolved nutrients.
Filiform	Threadlike.
Flagellum	(Plural: Flagella) A fine thread which is quickly moved from side to side to impart locomotion to some lower forms of life.
Flukes	Parasitic flatworms of the class *Trematoda*.
Gamete	The germ cell whose nucleus unites with that of another as the first stage of reproduction.

248

Gastrula	The second stage in the development of an embryo following the blastula and cleavage.
Gastrulation	Complex movements of the cells which occur after cleavage.
Gene	The factor in the transmission of an acquired characteristic from parent to offspring.
Glaucous	Covered with bloom.
Haploid	Having a single set of unpaired chromosomes.
Hyaline	Transparent or translucent.
Hybrid	The offspring of two different species or varieties.
Lanceolate	Longer than it is wide. Broad at the base, narrower at the apex.
Larva	(Plural: Larvae) An insect from the time that it emerges from the egg until it transforms into a pupa or grub.
Lateral Lines	A sense organ, marked by a row of perforated scales along both sides of the body of the goldfish.
Naiad	The young of the dragonfly.
Narial Septum	(Plural: N. septa) The fleshy partition between the nostrils.
Nauplius	(Plural: nauplii) The larva of crustaceans.
Notochord	A cartilaginous rod present in young vertebrates, becoming the vertebral column in the adult.
Nucleus	Body present in cells, containing chromosomes.
Oesophagus	The canal between the mouth and the stomach.
Operculum	(Plural: opercula) The gill cover.
Ovary	The female organ which produces ova.
Oviduct	The canal through which the ova pass from the ovary to the exterior.
Ovum	(Plural: ova) The unfertilized egg.
Pectinate	Comblike.

249

Pinnate	Feather-formed.
Protoplasm	A greyish, jelly-like substance, the basis of life.
Pupa	(Plural: pupae) The form taken by an insect between larva and adult.
Sessile	Without a stalk.
Spermatozoon	(Plural: spermatozoa) Microscopic, highly motile, flagellated male gamete.
Trematoda	A class of mainly parasitic worms.
Tubercle	Small tuber. A rounded protruding body.
Variety	An individual within a species, usually fertile, which differs from the normal type in some features that are capable of perpetuation.
Vascular	Containing vessels or ducts that carry fluids.
Vent	The opening from the alimentary canal of the fish to the exterior.
Vitelline Membrane	The membrane which encases the egg.

SCALE COUNTING.

To identify a species of carp the scales may be counted. The method is to count scales from the first ray of the front edge of the dorsal fin, to the lateral line marked 'A' on the illustration, and along the lateral line, marked 'B'.

CALCULATIONS

The U.S. gallon is less than the British 'Imperial' gallon. Whereas the Imperial gallon contains 8 pints or 4.546 litres, the U.S. gallon contains around 6½ British pints or 3.785 litres.

1 pint	= 0.568 litres
1 litre	= 1.7598 pints
A cubic centimetre is expressed as cm³ or 1 cc	= 1,000 cubic centimetres

250

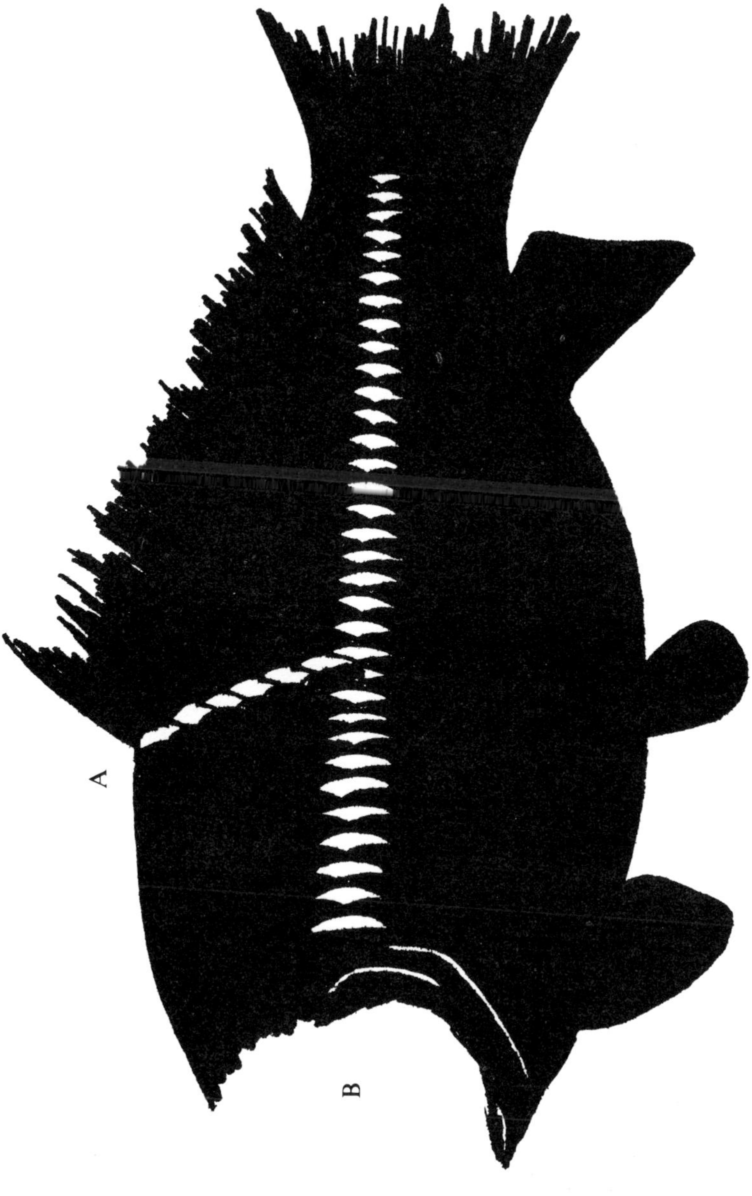

Figure 16.1 *Scale Counting Diagram*

251

1 gram	=	15.432 grains (gr)
1 inch	=	25.40 millimetres (mm)
1 millimetre	=	0.039 inches
1 foot	=	0.305 metres
1 metre (m)	=	3.281 feet
1 yard	=	0.914 metres; 3 feet
1 cubic inch	=	16.387 cubic centimetres
1 cubic centimetre	=	0.06102 inches
1 cubic foot	=	0.02832 cubic metres
1 cubic metre	=	35.315 cubic feet
1 cubic yard	=	0.765 cubic metres
1 square inch	=	0.00775 square metres
1 square metre	=	10.764 square feet
1 square foot	=	0.093 square metres
1 square yard	=	0.836 square metres
1 ounce	=	28.350 grams
1 gram	=	0.035 ounces
1 pound	=	0.454 kilograms
1 kilogram	=	2.205 pounds

A 1 per cent solution contains 700 grams per gallon which is approximately 1½ ounces — this equals 10 grams per litre. The capacity of a circular pond may be estimated by multiplying the depth in feet by the diameter squared by 4.9. This will give the gallonage. The capacity in gallons of a rectangular pond is calculated by the length by the width by the average depth (in feet) and multiplying by 6¼.

Temperature Conversion Chart: Fahrenheit to Centigrade

°F		°C		°F		°C
30	=	1.1		70	=	21.1
35	=	1.7		75	–	23.9
40	=	4.4		80	=	26.7
45	=	7.2		85	=	29.4
50	=	10.0		90	=	32.2
55	=	12.8		95	=	35.0
60	=	15.6		100	=	37.8
65	=	18.2				

INDEX

Numbers in italics refer to illustrations

254